SEARCHING THROUGH
MY PRAYER LIST

A memoir about family, career, and a meaningful retirement

SEARCHING THROUGH
MY PRAYER LIST

SECOND LIEUTENANT AND ARMY AIR CORPS
FIGHTER PILOT RICHARD P. COOLEY.

SEARCHING THROUGH
MY PRAYER LIST

A memoir about family, career, and a meaningful retirement

DICK COOLEY

with

Ann Boreson

Documentary Media

Seattle, Washington

DEDICATION

To Bridget, my wife, without whose support and encouragement this memoir would have never been written.

WITH MY WIFE, BRIDGET,
ON OUR WEDDING DAY IN JULY 2003.

SEARCHING THROUGH MY PRAYER LIST

A memoir about family, career, and a meaningful retirement

Published by Documentary Media
3250 41st Ave SW
Seattle WA 98116
206 935-9292
books@docbooks.com
www.documentarymedia.com

First Edition 2010
Printed in Canada

Author: Richard P. Cooley with Ann Boreson
Editor: Judy Gouldthorpe
Executive Editor: Barry Provorse
Publisher: Petyr Beck

Library of Congress Cataloging-in-Publication Data
Cooley, Dick.
Searching through my prayer list : a memoir about family, career, and
a meaningful retirement / Dick Cooley with Ann Boreson. — 1st ed.
    p. cm.
ISBN 978-1-933245-19-5 (alk. paper)
1. Cooley, Dick. 2. Bankers — United States — Biography. 3. Wells Fargo
Bank — Employees — Biography. 4. Catholics — United States — Biography.
5. Retirees — United States — Biography. I. Boreson, Ann. II. Title.

HG2463.C63A3 2010
332.1'223092 — dc22
[B]
2009047826

CONTENTS

THE PRAYER LIST

This is a story about the interesting events that have formed my life as a person, a husband, a father, a banker, and an educator. Its purpose is to, in some way, describe events and honor people who have been seminal to my life so that my family and friends might better understand my driving forces. It has also provided me with a perspective that I might not have achieved without the soul-searching, gut-wrenching introspection that an honest autobiography demands.

The relationship to my God and my Church has been paramount, and from my earliest years until now this has been a constant, the foundation for my actions, hopes, and fears.

I recite my prayer list daily like a mantra. I do not remember exactly when I started this list, but each name on it represents a time in my life, and it links together those who have given me love, friendship, opportunity, and understanding, as well as those who have asked that I pray for them in their time of need.

I wish to honor all of those people in my thoughts who have stepped forth in my life. They are family, close friends, business associates, and sometimes only casual acquaintances who have become a part of my history. When I pray each day, I ask that God watch over them and protect them as they make their way in this world. They have helped shape the person I am today, and I want to give thanks to God for their appearance in my life. In gratitude, I will always pray for their happiness and safekeeping.

There were many interesting experiences that occurred early on in my life, but I want to start this memoir with descriptions of significant lessons that have stayed with me through my life, from a very religious mother and a shepherding father, to a teacher who taught me the error of my shortcutting ways, a coach who would not settle for anything less than my full commitment to the game I was playing, and most significantly the crash of my P-38 on December 11, 1944, in France. The healing process took slightly more than a year, and it allowed me to graduate from Yale and start my working career in New York City in early 1946.

I married, and in 1949 moved west, where we started a family and a 42-year career in commercial banking. In that period I moved from San Francisco to Los Angeles to Seattle, where I live today. Along the way I worked for two major banks, spending a total of 24 years as a chief executive officer, and I experienced the demands of leadership, suffered losses, and felt the joy of redemption.

Travel has been a part of my life, first between Rye, New York, and California for family visits, and then less luxurious train travel to and from basic training and flight-training bases up and down the West Coast.

I gave back to my country and community when I could. I served on 14 boards over time, and when I retired I created a syllabus and taught MBA and EMBA classes at the Foster School of Business at the University of Washington and the Albers School of Business at Seattle University.

As my journey unfolded I made many discoveries, and I would like to share them with you and describe some of the lessons that have guided my long life.

My parents, Victor E. and Helen Pierce Cooley,
in Yosemite National Park, circa 1950.

INNOCENCE: UPBRINGING, EDUCATION, AND INTERRUPTION

W hen I was very young, my mother and father moved our family to Rye, New York. Rye was a fine suburban community, conveniently located to everything in the New York area, but more importantly in my boyhood, it was bicycle territory. I could go anywhere, it seemed, on my bike. Three or four of us rode back and forth to our various meeting places, never lost steam, and covered a large area daily.

My childhood was idyllic in many ways. I was the oldest and the only boy in the family. Kay and Ann, my twin sisters, were born four years later, and Helen came five years after the twins. We were a close family, but being the only boy and with the difference in our ages, I sometimes felt like an only child. My interaction with my sisters was limited, and like many older brothers, I teased them unmercifully. Today I regret not having been a better brother and not having found ways to help them. Fortunately with the passage of time, we have all become much closer.

My mother was a conventional Catholic, well indoctrinated in her faith. She was extremely concerned about doing the right thing at all times — not only as it related to the church, but socially and in everything else as well. She worried about what other people would think, which was a strong impulse in her and rubbed off on her children, including me.

When she married my father, he agreed that if there were any children they would be raised Catholic. Father was not a Catholic, but he was not opposed to it either. My mother always wanted him to join the church and asked all of her children to pray for his conversion, but it never happened. He would attend Mass with us on Christmas and Easter, and we were told that he prayed on his knees every night before going to bed. We interpreted his absence from the church as a form of self-religion.

Along with teaching us etiquette, manners, and culture, my mother taught me about sex. One day she sat down next to me on the piano bench while I was practicing, and she literally had a book about the birds and the bees. I think I was nine or ten at the time and could not have cared less. She began with a woman's period and how the eggs are fertilized. I will never understand why she picked that particular moment to spring the mechanics of human reproduction on me, but she went through the whole process and in retrospect, she left little to the imagination. The whole thing sounded disgusting to me.

However, I was able to test my knowledge soon afterward with the bicycle gang. All of the boys were convinced they knew all about sex. They were older and thought I was the goody-goody of the group. One day as they were talking about girls, which we innocently did from time to time, I said, "I know how it works." At that moment I felt superior because my mother had taught me, and no one had talked to them. Most of the parents let the guys catch it from each other at school, which means they didn't understand how things really work.

Father, on the other hand, circled around the subject of sex. Off our living room was a den, which is where he liked to sit. It was a wonderful space with a working fireplace and two big easy chairs, and room for a chessboard between the two chairs where we would play. One night Dad broached the subject of women, or specifically the temptations of sex. His talk was not educational like Mother's, but I could tell that he wanted to add a male perspective. He said, "Dick, I never messed around sexually with women for two reasons. First, I did not want to get them pregnant, and second, I didn't want to catch a disease."

With that conversation I got the distinct impression that Father did not want to open up that can of worms because he was afraid of the consequences. I know he liked women and women liked him, but he was never one to play around. In other words, life comes with responsibilities. No one stands alone. Each of us affects someone by our actions. Dad's speech played right into my fear of not doing the right thing and incurring horrible lifelong consequences. I did not want to fail. I never thought about it concretely as if something awful would happen, but I definitely tried to avoid any behavior that would disappoint my family or cause me to turn out poorly.

———————

Not long after we moved to Rye, my family joined the Apawamis Club. It was not far from our home and I could play golf, tennis, and squash there as a junior member. The club's history describes its founders as "a group of God-fearing, rugged and upright individualists who believed there was a need for an institutional meeting place to expand culture and civic consciousness of the community." Their first gathering as a club was in 1890, but as if that weren't already enough, they built a golf course in 1896. The original clubhouse burned to the ground in 1907. The architecture of their main building, constructed after the fire, was set up with a men's locker room situated on the second floor overlooking the golf course and putting green. Down below on the north side of the building were squash courts, which were connected to the main building by a locker room for juniors and guests. The junior locker room was smaller than the senior members' facility, but it had three wonderful old-fashioned showers with huge circular heads that resembled a sunflower and produced a magnificent waterfall-like spray.

One day I was taking a shower in the junior locker room after playing tennis when this enormous man entered with all his natural adornments hanging out. Looking back, this was the first big lesson I ever learned in my life. In those days we did not wear bathrobes. If you were a man, you walked around the locker room as God made you, and no one thought anything of it. As this man came into the shower, I could not help but notice his huge hairy chest and belly. He was solid and strong and there was no denying it. I was in the last shower stall as he took his place in the space beside me. He said, "Hi ya, kid, how are you doing?" I said, "Fine, sir. Thank you. How are you?"

That brief exchange began a conversation. He had just finished a round of golf and was showering before going home. I assumed he was a guest, but it did not dawn on me for a while who he was. Initially he was just a large, likeable man who seemed genuinely interested in who I was, but on the way home I finally got it through my head. The man standing next to me in the shower was Babe Ruth. His career with the Boston Red Sox, Yankees, and Braves was over, and now he was trying to translate his home run ability into a PGA golf swing.

I have never forgotten that meeting with Babe Ruth. His presence and that experience left an indelible impression on me. It was my first indication that all men are the same and they come built the same. Even as a young boy standing next to a great historical figure, I recognized that he had all the same things I had. His were a little more used and developed, but no matter how famous and idolized he was or anyone is, be it a president, a pope, or a movie star in Hollywood, the mold is the same.

That day I changed the way I viewed relationships, or perhaps it formulated a new outlook that has lasted all my life. I learned that people may wear different clothes or have a different color skin, but basically God made us all the same.

He gave us two eyes and ears, two arms (most of us anyway), two legs, and all the other amazing things that compose a human being. No one should ever feel they are put together better or worse than anyone else, because we are all created equal, as it says in our Constitution. There are infinite variations in all of us that make each individual unique. That is why every one of us is our own special work of art. It is a good thing to remember when you worry about meeting someone important. You should not feel intimidated. You can respect someone for what they do or who they are, which I certainly do, but it is important to remember that we all belong to the human race.

Taking that shower next to Babe Ruth, where we used the same soap and the same towels, was my first clue that we all come from the same Maker and have the same basic require-ments. It is how you use your God-given talents that makes the difference in life, and that is what counts. Look what Babe Ruth did with his gifts.

My father ran the public relations division of the New York Bell Telephone Company. He was promoted to this position and had accepted a 10 percent cut in pay before we moved to Rye, but that was the extent of the Great Depression's effect on our family. As the phone company was a utility and a monopoly, the public was the customer and more important than the sharehold-ers. This meant that my father had to get along with absolutely everyone, regardless of religion, political leanings, or what have you. He could never choose sides or show favoritism because everyone had to be considered and listened to. Consensus was his thing, though he never lost sight of his principles or honesty in the process. He was upright and square, and his ethics were impeccable. In retrospect, I do not know how my father's overall job performance was evaluated, but I do know that he was a fine man who was well respected and ran his business and family life with dignity. That was the way I was brought up, and in turn I was always trying to find consensus for courses of action and do the right thing. I could make decisions if I had to, but I always strived to make people comfortable as quickly as possible.

Much later, when I moved to Seattle, I got over my accom-modating way of thinking. What I have learned through the years is that no one can make everyone happy, nor is it a good thing to even try. If your goal is to please the masses, inevitably you do not do some of the things you should. Sometimes you have to respect the fact that you cannot make two opposite sides coalesce. The important thing is to do the right thing, and that can sometimes force a tough decision.

Dad instilled in me a positive attitude. He presented me with many opportunities, but he rarely pushed me into his own bias. Instead, he would listen and remain neutral as I navigated my choices. Inheriting that ability to listen, I was known as "heart-to-heart Cooley" when I was a boy.

I mostly got along well with girls and had lengthy conversations with them when the others would not. Over time it backfired somewhat, as the attractive young women tended to think of me as their friend or brother as opposed to their boyfriend. This, however, was not always the case. I must have been around 11 years old when the Rye bicycle group was in full cycle mode. One day we were hanging out in front of my house with all the bikes scattered on the lawn like a yard sale. It was a larger group than normal, and it included a big-boned girl about my age by the name of Betty Ayer. Somehow Betty and I exchanged some words, and the next thing I knew we were in a fight. To this day I will never understand why she jumped on me and beat me with both her fists. There she was, knocking the stuffing out of me, and I felt too paralyzed to do anything about it. What I remember most about the experience is that I was reluctant to hit a girl because I had been taught that they were off-limits. It seemed unfair that I could not defend myself. Instead, with each blow I felt increasingly mortified that I had lost face and appeared weak in front of my friends.

It was not that she hurt me, although there is no denying that her blows carried a sting. It was the fact that she could do whatever she wanted and I kept my hands at my sides. Betty could haul off and hit me as long as she liked, which she did for quite some time, and I was supposed to take the higher ground because she was a female. Afterward I went upstairs into my room and cried. A short time later a few friends came up the stairs and knocked on my door. "Hey, come on, Dick, it's alright," they said. But I hardly heard them. I was humiliated. It felt like Betty had kicked my ego from Rye to Hoboken.

Betty's battering was cataclysmic. In time I got over it because that's what I tend to do. I know I probably would not have felt good about myself if I had gotten mad and connected with a few hard swings, but the fact remains that I was afraid to. It was a confusing time. Again, I had a bigger body and a smaller mind. I did not have the confidence to negotiate my way.

———————

During the summers my mother would take us to Santa Clara, California, to visit her mother and our relatives. We had lots of family in the area, and it was always a good time. One of Father's many benefits working with the telephone company was that he received four weeks of vacation each year, which he spent in California in August. During this time my parents would sometimes take me fishing with them. One trip that comes to mind was on the Rogue River in Oregon. My mother was not crazy about fishing, but she was a good sport and threw her line into the water with the rest of us. My sisters were considered to be too young, so they would stay home with a sitter. They may have felt left out, but it seemed perfectly natural to me since I was well on my way to being spoiled. In my defense, taking those excursions alone with my parents was one of the true joys of my childhood and the tremendous privilege of being the oldest child.

The long summer trips to California were opportune moments for us to reconnect with our West Coast family. It was during this time that I became close to my cousin Jack, who was the son of my mother's oldest brother and four years older than I. Jack Pierce and I seemed to find enough trouble to occupy our days, including setting off fireworks in the old family tennis court and shooting birds out of trees. As in Rye, we had free rein to bicycle anywhere, and we were granted access to a tennis court and pool. Jack was the perfect companion. He was a fisherman, a smart but humble sort. Later in life he became a professor at Stanford and then went to UCLA, where he was a tenured professor at the medical school in biological chemistry. Without Jack those summers would have been deadly; we did everything together and became fast friends.

As a child I looked forward to our trips west by rail, as I have always had an affinity for trains. On one such excursion, the train had stopped to refuel in Laramie, Wyoming. In those days, trains were powered by steam engines that required regular replenishment of coal and water. Mother was trying to organize the four of us children, as a stop like this usually involved getting off the train and stretching our legs. When the train started up again, Mother could not find me. Frantic, she begged the conductor to wait, but after five minutes he said there could be no more delays. He convinced her that I would be put on the next train and said that was the best he could offer. Soon after, the train pulled away from the station and headed down the tracks.

I had no idea that I had become a missing person, having wandered into the observation car and become completely mesmerized watching the coupling of the freight cars and the movement of the switch engines, and all the things that went on in an old railroad yard. It had not occurred to me to tell Mother where I was going, and she never thought to look for me on the train. When she did come across me, she was furious. If Father had been there, I am sure she would have made him spank me. Fortunately he was not on board, so I received a verbal lashing instead.

One of the last summer trips we took to California happened in the mid 1930s, when I was 12. As the time came to return to New York, I had an idea that I wanted to cross the country alone. I do not recall if there was a debate on the subject, though I know Mother was concerned, but they finally came to the conclusion that I could take my first solo trip. Before I stepped on board the train, my father gave me safety advice and money to cover my expenses.

I had a berth in a regular Pullman car, and fortunately, it was a lower berth. In the olden days there was a long hammock-like holder that the porter would assemble across the windows when he made up the bed at night. You could put your things in there and it was said to be secure. Dad showed me how to wrap my wallet in the hip pocket of my pants and then roll my pants up and put them in the holder. He explained that if I followed his instructions, no one would steal my money and I would not lose anything. That turned out to be good advice. The cross-country trip happened without incident. I did not lose my money and I had enough to cover my expenses.

Before World War II there were no through coast-to-coast trains. We traveled across the country on the Overland Limited, from San Francisco to Chicago, and then changed trains and stations and boarded the New York Central bound for New York. The switch-over in Chicago was the only issue. I had to navigate my way from the West Side of Chicago to the East Side, and that required a change of stations, trains, and railroads. I do not remember the details, but the technicalities of the transfer took place and somehow I got on a green Parmelee bus and made my way to a new train and berth.

My days were spent on the outside deck of the observation car looking forward into the wind, watching what seemed to be endless country pass by. It was such an exhilarating experience as a young man to lean out the side of the train and feel the cars take corners and curves while watching billowing clouds of smoke rise high into the sky. On big curves I could look ahead and count the cars on the train beginning with the engine. When I was not occupied with the landscape, there were conversations with the conductors and brakemen or anyone else who would talk to me. I do not recall ever feeling alone or scared because there was always something to fill my thoughts. By the time I arrived in Harmon, New York, I had been given a taste of independence and a love of travel that has endured for a lifetime. That trip across the country became one of my fondest childhood memories. Later, when I was in the army, I found out that not all train travel was as pleasant as my summer trips.

My first years at school were spent at Rye Country Day School. I do not remember much about those early years, but there was one memorable event that took place in the third grade. My teacher at the time was Mrs. Foshay, a smart, accomplished woman. She taught me many things, but the lesson I have never forgotten was the one having to do with telling the truth and cheating.

One day Mrs. Foshay passed out math workbooks. We were to do the multiplication problems, making sure that we showed all of our calculations. I have always had a tendency to search for ways of beating the system, and this time was no exception. I soon discovered that the answers to the problems we were working on were at the bottom of the next page. I could not believe my luck. Of course we were not to show the answers without the necessary calculations, but that did not stop me. I was moving ahead feverishly, jotting down those answers, when Mrs. Foshay tapped me on the shoulder and said, "Dick, you are cheating. You cannot solve the problem without doing the work. You are two pages ahead of the class and into double multiplication. We have not done that yet. It takes two lines of figures that have to be added together to get the answer. Your page is full of one-line answers, which shows you are copying them from the answer sheet."

Then she gave me a lecture on cheating and how I was hurting myself by trying to take a shortcut. She was right, and I was mortified. In the third grade she taught me a lifelong lesson that has never left me. And I learned the right way to do double multiplication as well. Thank you, Mrs. Foshay.

Later I attended Iona School in New Rochelle, New York. It was an old, conservative school run by the Irish Christian Brothers. The method of teaching followed the doom-and-gloom, fire-and-brimstone philosophy that seemed to be coming out of the Catholic Church at the time. We learned to think about our behavior as it related to God's law and to understand the consequences of doing sinful things and ending up in hell.

While at Iona School I became acquainted with Brother Finch. He had an uncanny ability to see straight through me and many other students. Even though he knew I had strong athletic ability, he also recognized that I was timid. The idea of being considered cowardly was horrifying to me. I had the body and the skills, but not the attitude to go with them. In my early years, as well as later in life, I had to learn to overcome my anxieties.

Brother Finch asked me one day, "Why do you always back up before you go forward?" It seemed to me that he was onto my fears. I had something to overcome, and I worked at it for a long time before it ceased to be a problem. With Brother Finch I broke my nose running into a grandstand. I was chasing a football and I forgot about the grandstand and ran smack into it. My nose endured two more breaks on the football field, so it's not surprising that it does not rest on my face as it was designed.

Just before my 14th birthday, the Iona School coaches discovered that I was a good kicker. One afternoon they took me out on a field and asked me to attempt as many points-after-touchdown kicks as I could, and I kicked 19 in a row before I missed. No one had done that before, and I was in the ninth grade and weighed only 125 pounds.

I had been playing on the junior varsity team, not with all the gigantic upperclassmen on varsity, but after that kicking exhibition they suited me up for the big varsity Thanksgiving

Day game against All Hallows, our traditional rival. I was called to kick a point after touchdown and I missed. It was devastating. Back in the locker room at halftime, the coach was saying something about that kick and he turned to me and said, "How old are you, Dick?" I told him I was 14, and he said, "Oh, I thought you were 13," at which point I muttered something about having had a birthday recently. Suddenly pure terror overcame me because that day was my birthday and I did not want anyone to know it for fear of what they might do to me. I do not know what those big guys would have done, probably nothing, but I could hear their deep, cracking voices taunting me. That was one of the first times I can remember being one of the youngest and involved in something that was over my head. In many ways it struck me as a disaster, but in time I learned to cope with it. Now I am older than everyone else, so it is easier to look back on it and be amused.

———

Through his job at the telephone company, my father became acquainted with Bruce Barton. Mr. Barton was a partner in a New York advertising firm, and he had been elected to Congress, representing the so-called Silk Stocking District of Manhattan's Upper East Side.

One day my dad came home after listening to one of Mr. Barton's addresses with a quote: "The Greatest Adventure in Life Is Doing One's Level Best." Father had the words printed in bold font, framed, and hung over my desk. He often told me that everything would work out fine as long as in my heart I knew I had done my best.

I'm not sure if the quote was the deciding factor for my departure to boarding school, or if my father had taken issue with my pastime of listening to Jack Benny and Fred Allen skits on the radio instead of devoting time to homework. In the ninth grade my school marks had fallen slightly, and he blamed the airwaves for my movement in the wrong direction. He was also thinking about college, whereas I had not even considered it. Although it must have been a financial hardship for my family, my father decided that I should go to Portsmouth Priory, a boarding school that housed about 95 boys built on a 500-acre site on the idyllic shores of Narragansett Bay in Rhode Island. He felt that at Portsmouth, which was known for its superior education, strong supervision, and discipline, I would have plenty of time to focus on my studies and ultimately increase my chances of getting into a good college.

Portsmouth Priory was founded in 1926 by a group of English Benedictines as an appendage to an abbey in North Yorkshire called Ampleforth. The Benedictine Order began over 1,500 years ago with what Saint Benedict called the Rule. It later became the basic outline of the monastic principles of love and work. The Benedictines are accredited with carefully copying books by hand and preserving Western culture during the Dark Ages. Through their dedication and perseverance, they were able to protect the intellectual and cultural history for generations to come. Committed to higher education and reverence for God, the Benedictines at Portsmouth Priory translated these values to students by teaching that if you work hard and love God, then everything else takes care of itself.

The curriculum provided for a six-day-a-week class schedule with athletics at the end of each day. Academics were demanding, but we were encouraged to stay physically fit and play sports. We learned about teamwork: how to win and lose, the importance of good sportsmanship, and the kind of effort it takes to excel. At such a small school, students were able to join almost any team if they showed reasonable talent. You might not become an expert at any one sport, but at least you were given the opportunity to play. I had considerable natural athletic ability, so I was able to join many teams such as football, soccer, basketball, baseball, tennis, golf, and basically anything else that was offered, with one exception.

One night I tried out for boxing. I did not know anything about it, but I thought I should give it a try. Bob Glennon was the star of the program. I got in the ring with him and basically he just knocked me all over the place, from one side of the ropes to the other. He was bigger and one year older than I. He understood a lot about boxing.

Bob taught me that you should never go into a ring if you do not know what you are doing.

That probably applies to a lot of other things as well. I can honestly say that this lesson did not have to be repeated. Boxing was off my list.

Life at Portsmouth Priory seemed confining and dreary. I found that at boarding school there was little else to do besides study, and that did not suit my personality at all. I felt isolated and a long way from home. The freedom that I had once experienced in Rye was gone, and I was anxious to get it back. I knew that Portsmouth was a first-rate school, but I was too young and immature to understand the nature of the opportunity. Instead, all I wanted to do was rush through my high school years and move on to college.

Looking back, I realize that all the things that Dad expected happened to me while I was away at school. I did receive an excellent education, and I became more religious. I learned to love God and began to understand what love meant in the religious sense. I could see that there was more to it than the fear of the Irish Catholic church. In hindsight, it was a fine place to spend two years. I met some great friends, both on the faculty and in the student body. Actually, some of the friendships I made at Portsmouth have lasted longer than those I made in college. What I regret is that I did not enjoy the experience to its fullest. Instead

I pushed ahead, reading the various college brochures that were available on campus for seniors. Even though I was only a junior, I was determined to find a loophole. I wanted to get on with life.

At Portsmouth I made friends for life, and I remember them daily when I review my prayer list. They include Peter Flanigan, Jerry Dwyer, and Gordon McShane. My mother, Helen Cooley, became Peter's mother's godmother. Peter's mom was not Catholic by birth, but Peter's dad was, and their four children were raised in the Church. Mrs. Flanigan remained independent until one day she decided to become a Catholic. That's when my mother became her godmother, and like Peter, these two mothers have a prominent place on my prayer list. When I left Portsmouth a year early, Peter stayed on and graduated before attending Princeton. While we never lost our closeness in a general sense, our lives went in different directions. Peter was busy. He went to work in the investment banking business, and after World War II he worked for the Marshall Plan in London. He had a great experience there, finding out how things worked in England. He went in and out of government jobs during his career. In between times he was an investment banker. He has always done very well.

The Flanigans were affluent, as Mrs. Flanigan was from the Anheuser-Busch family, and all the kids had a large amount of money. I think Peter handled his wealth professionally and increased his family's financial well-being. I am sure none of them had to work if they did not want to, but Peter always worked. He was eager to improve himself, and he continued that drive for success his whole life. After Peter's wife Bridgid died, he remained lonesome until 2007, when he married an Austrian woman whom I have yet to meet. She is Catholic and has five children, as does Peter, and 15 grandchildren, as Peter does. I look forward to meeting her and hearing the story of how they met and married when he was 84 and she was 68.

John was Peter's older brother, and he became a good friend. He worked for Anheuser-Busch for a while as a distributor and in

the company. He married his first cousin, Lotsie Busch, right off
the bat. Peter and I were both in that wedding. Then he got
tired of the family business and went other ways. They moved to
Southern California and after a while that marriage broke up.
John got married again, to Nancy, and they were together for over
30 years. They had a fine relationship. I did not see him as
much through the years. He and Peter were both members of
the Bohemian Club and they joined the same camp that I did,
Mandalay. I would see him in the summertime, but our paths
rarely crossed otherwise. He left Los Angeles and moved to Reno
and lived there until he died recently. His wife, Nancy, is a star.
She has been a good wife to him, a good mother to his children,
and is an attractive, interesting person.

Jerry Dwyer remains one of my oldest best friends. We went
to Portsmouth together. I roomed with Peter Flanigan, and I
played tennis with Jerry. We were one and two on the tennis
team. I won the Rhode Island State Singles Championship, and I
am sure we won the doubles championship. He was an only child
and lived in Newport, Rhode Island. We have maintained a close
friendship that has continued to this day.

Gordon McShane was at the Priory with Peter Flanigan,
Jerry Dwyer, and me. In our older age we became closer friends.
Gordie was married to three widows. He outlived the first two,
but with his recent marriage he was not as fortunate. They were
on a trip and he died of a massive heart attack. So I pray for
Gordie in his new life, and I pray for his family and his kids,
hoping they are all doing well.

———————

Rye was considered a New York City commuter town, and many
of the boys in the area went away to boarding school. If they
had gone to private school for the first eight grades, then the
only option to continue would be boarding school or transfer to
a public school. In Rye, most of the people who went away
to school attended Ivy League colleges, and specifically Yale, but

from Portsmouth Priory the majority of boys were accepted at Harvard. (Both Robert and Ted Kennedy attended Portsmouth before entering Harvard.) Naturally I looked at the entrance requirements for both colleges, and there was one thing in particular that caught my attention. Yale required the standard 15 solid credits and passing college boards, but no high school diploma. That was music to my ears!

I had earned only 10 credits from Portsmouth, so I continued to search for the last five credits needed to fulfill Yale's requirements. I had to go back to my ninth-grade work at Iona School, where there were four solid subjects like English and mathematics, but the fifth was a class called Civics. I was afraid it might not meet Yale requirements even though it was a good course. The class taught how the U.S. government worked, how smaller and larger districts functioned, how Congress was composed, and what differences existed between the executive, judicial, and legislative branches. These are facts that have served me throughout my life. I don't think my children ever took such a comprehensive class on the inner workings of the government. To my way of thinking that is a shame because it is the sort of practical knowledge that would generate more interest and participation in the political system. At least Yale recognized its value.

Portsmouth Priory had an excellent English department, and I was able to get a score of 620 on my college boards. It was an honors-level score, but not earthshaking, though I think for a high school junior it showed the Yale acceptance committee that I was able to read, write, and comprehend. It may have helped offset my language boards, which did not turn out as favorably. In preparation for my German boards I studied words and vocabulary all spring, and although I received a score of only 450, apparently it was enough to pass, or at least the Yale people thought it would suffice, giving me credit and accepting me a year early into their freshman class.

When the acceptance letter arrived at the end of my junior year at Portsmouth, I was elated. It was at this time that my father discussed another scenario. Since Yale had given me the option to defer enrollment for a year, he proposed a trip around the world. My uncle, who ran a steamship company, graciously offered me the owner's cabin and the privilege of bringing a friend on what would have been a remarkable adventure. Unfortunately, the timing of the trip coincided with the outbreak of World War II in Europe, shelving all plans to travel the world.

With the trip on hold, I had another discussion with my father. In the heartless way that kids do sometimes, I said to him, "Okay, if I'm going to get killed in the war anyway, I might as well go to Yale and get as much done as I can beforehand." It was a terrible thing to say to my father, but I did not know it at the time. I was a difficult child in a lot of ways, spoiled and headstrong. I did not mean to push and insult him by telling him I was going to be killed as if he would not care. Of course he cared and he was worried, but he did not show it. He knew that I had to accept going into the army and I had to accept that I might lose my life. That was a fact that most young men had to live with at the time.

———————

I arrived in New Haven in the fall of 1940 at the age of 16. Out of the thousand students who were enrolled in Yale's freshman class, I was the second youngest. The youngest happened to be a 14-year-old genius, which I was not. Although no one knew that I was underage, I was keenly aware of it. As I walked through the campus amidst a sea of unfamiliar faces, all my insecurities might as well have been written on my forehead.

I applied for a Catholic roommate and by a stroke of good fortune I was assigned Jim Buckley. He came from Sharon, Connecticut, and like me, he had attended a small boarding school, one called Millbrook. Although Jim and I were quite different in our pursuits, a lifelong friendship ensued. He was much more intellectual than I. Serious minded and bright, Jim became a member of the *Yale Daily News* staff and was chosen to join the best senior society. Jim remains an immense talent, and my deep regard for him has lasted through the years as our paths have continued to cross with his marriage to my sister Ann. We did not see much of each other for many years, as we lived on opposite sides of the country. After a serious accident that involved my sister and Jim's exceptional care of her during her recovery and paraplegic life, he earned a top place of honor on my prayer list. . . . I, on the other hand, favored athletics. I was entranced by the intellectual opportunities offered at Yale, although my grades did not reflect my enthusiasm. If I passed with what we called "gentleman's C's," that suited me fine.

The first year, Jim and I roomed together in Wright Hall, a five-story Gothic brownstone building on the northwest corner of the old campus. Our dorm room had two bedrooms separated by a sitting area and a john that was shared with two students who lived across the hall. I remember sitting on the brick bulkhead outside Wright Hall dangling my feet off the ledge while watching a swarm of campus activity all around me. There were students flocking in and out of wonderful old buildings, stacks of books in their arms, inspired by newfound knowledge and an undeniable determination to succeed.

For me, Yale had an intellectual, physical, and emotional energy that flowed like the Mississippi River. For anyone to think they can change its course or its mission, or want to for that matter, is ludicrous. Over 300 years, Yale has proven to be an institution where geniuses and scholars share their knowledge in classrooms and research labs, and coaches inspire and motivate athletes to achieve their highest potential. That day it dawned on me that no matter what I did during my college years, it would never leave an indelible mark on this grand, well-oiled machine. I had to decide how I wanted to spend my time there and what I wanted to get out of the experience.

Seventy years have passed since I first stepped onto that campus, and although there have been a lot of structural changes, my initial reaction is the same. The momentum lives on at that campus. It's a feeling of excellence, a feeling that all of life is about putting forth one's finest effort. Their goal remains the same — to give each and every student the opportunity to become a full and contributing individual instilled with the knowledge that it is an honor and a responsibility to help others.

Yale was challenging. I have always been a curious type, and in my freshman year I felt as if I were being pulled in all new directions. There did not seem to be enough hours in the day to dedicate to all the interests that lay in wait. Although I appeared to be settling into the routine of classrooms and homework, sports and practice schedules, there was one subject that I knew would be my downfall — German.

It should not have come as a big surprise to me because I had struggled with it at Portsmouth, but there did not seem to be a way to get around the fact that all Yale freshmen were required to take a foreign language. Naturally I signed up for the only language of which I had some working knowledge. As I sat in the back of the class the first three weeks, I realized that I was never going to pass. I was not up to the level of performance and sadly, it was the lowest course level offered. I began to explore the requirements for graduation and found that there was only one course that did not require a language to earn a degree — it was Industrial Administration and Engineering. Fortunately, it was early enough in the year that I could apply for a transfer into the scientific school.

Although my initial reason for becoming an industrial engineer was to escape the language requirement, it turned out to be the perfect major. The course was designed for industrial management, but it offered a broad range of knowledge about a lot of different fields. Years later when I entered the banking world, I found that banks lend money to all types of commerce and in order to be a good loan officer you have to understand how different businesses work. You may lend money to a farmer to harvest his wheat crop, or to someone who is starting a chain of drive-in movies, or someone who wants to build an automobile dealership. Bankers must be diverse in their knowledge of the community they serve, and understanding a little bit about everything makes it easier to relate to clients' specific needs.

Industrial Administration and Engineering required that I take such classes as chemistry, physics, and calculus, with one allowed elective per year. My first exposure to Shakespeare was in an English 101 class taught by Professor Wimsatt, a statuesque man who instilled a love of this great word-master in the basement of Strathcona Hall. I learned about art history and psychology (or as we referred to it, "Sex 63"). Looking back, my only regret is that I was not allowed to take more classes outside my engineering curriculum, as there were so many subjects that interested me. There was only one elective that my mother forbade me to take, and that was not to be disputed.

Before I entered Yale, my mother had made a deal with my father. If I attended Catholic school until college, then I could attend any university I wanted. When I selected Yale, she agreed on the grounds that I did not enroll in any philosophy courses. Mother had built in me the idea that I had to fight for my faith. She did not want the materialism of Yale to make my religion seem unimportant or falsify it in some way. Her thought was that I might become distracted from my faith, and Nietzsche and other philosophers might challenge my Catholic belief. As it was, I was not drawn to their ideas at the time. Instead, I started to go to daily Mass.

I attended Mass not because I was so holy, but because I felt I needed it. I was young and impressionable, and I did not think I could argue with my classmates about my beliefs. If they were going to make fun of my religion, which they might have, I needed to be able to stand up for my convictions. Sometimes you find yourself in an adversarial climate. There were a lot of people at Yale who did not believe in God, people who said it could not be so. I had to be grounded in my faith and actively living it. It started out as a protective device, but to keep my faith as the core of my principles, I had to work at it. Listening to God's word and talking to Him every morning became a ritual, one that I have no desire to forgo. Daily Mass continues to give me structure and guidance in how to serve God and others better.

I suppose it was a stroke of luck that I was diverted to engineering. All the things that had to do with the course requirements had nothing to do with God and challenging my belief system. By accident I got into a nonconfrontational environment, all the while building up my defenses so I could clearly be a Catholic without having to worry if I was right or wrong in my faith.

Playing on the Yale football team was one of the biggest highlights of my college years. It all began in September of 1940, when I tried out for the freshman team and made the second string. I do not recall much of that year except that I played as a linebacker and blocking back in the old-fashioned single-wing formation. I was playing behind Jim Whitmore, who was a fine athlete and well regarded by the coaching staff. I spent enough time on the field that season to make friends with the other players and realize that I wanted nothing more than to work my way up to the starting varsity team.

Sophomore year I tried out for the varsity squad and made the fourth team. One of the jobs for the third and fourth teams was to learn the basic plays of the coming week's varsity opponent and run them against the first string so they would have an idea of what they would be facing the next Saturday. During early training we were doing a lot of changing around, and at the end of each practice we had to sprint 100 yards down the field as fast as we could. Invariably, I was the second fastest on the squad.

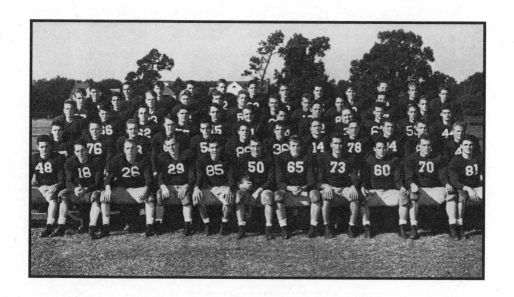

YALE'S VARSITY FOOTBALL TEAM IN 1942.
Left to right, Row 1: NOYES, TALBOTT, TOWN, POTTS, GREENE,
MOSELEY, DAVISON, DEBEER, SMITH, STACK, MILLER
Row 2: OVERLOCK, OGILVIE, ALLDERIGE, FURSE, WARFIELD, SARGENT,
FERGUSON, HOOPES, WHITRIDGE, DENT, JENKINS, MEYER
Row 3: GRAHAM, MACOMBER, O'ROURKE, WHITE, MILES, DIETRICH,
WHEELER, CONSTANTIN, WHITMORE, RYAN, PALMER, KNOWLTON
Row 4: LYNCH, BURKE, WALKER, GREER, COOLEY, COLLINS, RUEBEL,
KIRST, STOCK, LE BOUTILLIER, GOODENOUGH
Row 5: CHAMBERLAIN, BURNHAM, BLAKE, FRANKENHOFF, WILSON,
COUGHLIN, ELLIS, MAHONEY, SCOVIL, DWYER, CONNELLY, ATKINS

Nelson Talbott consistently beat me. He was not as big as I was, but he was a wingback and he could run. After witnessing our head-to-head sprints, the coaches decided that I would be better off playing end, where speed was more important. The switch was made, and I began a new and different training.

After World War II began, Yale established a year-round academic schedule with three semesters instead of two. That meant that I became a junior in June of 1942, and was able to play football in the summer. I had reached a playing weight of 195 pounds, I had a bull neck, and I trained rigorously for the end-position, eagerly practicing the steps and moves that the coach taught us. The principal action consisted of charging forward two or three yards, remaining strong on your legs, hands out and ready to ward off anyone who came at you while you pushed the play back into the middle of the line. Above all, you were never to allow anyone to get around you. That summer I put on my football pants and practiced running sideways, back and forth, and throwing myself on the ground over and over again in the warm Connecticut dust. It was conditioning as well as technique.

By the time September rolled around, I was on the second varsity team and for the most part I was backing up George Greene. The coaches would play me at left or right end because in those days football players covered defense and offense, so they needed to understand both positions.

The first game went well. I got to play almost the whole last quarter as they put in the second string since we were beating our opponents handily. The second game was different. We played Navy at Franklin Field in Philadelphia. The kickoff went to George Greene, who was knocked out cold; KO'd on the kickoff and out of the game. The coaches sent me in and I played almost the whole game. I don't know how I did, but at least I held the position. George returned for the rest of the season and even though I was behind him and on the second team, I began to play more and more.

At one point in the Cornell game I was playing the right-end position. They were using a single-wing attack, which meant there was a wingback outside their end, then the blocking back behind the guard or the tackle, then the fullback, who was back a few yards, and the tailback, four or five yards back. Usually the ball went to the tailback, sometimes to the fullback. If they start an end run and I am playing right end, they're trying to run around me the conventional way. To do that, you pull a guard and the guard goes out and leads the attack, followed by the blocking back or the fullback, then the tailback with the ball, who tries to skirt the end. They attempt to knock the end in and then get around the corner so the ball carrier can run and hopefully get around fast enough so he can make a large gain down the field. That was this particular case. I remember it as clearly as if it happened yesterday instead of 68 years ago.

I charged in just the way they told me, hands out, legs firm, and I rammed the first guy who came around. I do not know if he was a guard or the blocking back, but I hit him with every-thing I had. The world was beautiful at that moment because all the Cornell backfield was lined up one behind the other, like stars in the heavens. They should never have been in that forma-tion, but there they were. When I hit the first man I knocked him off his feet and backwards hard enough so he bumped into the player next to him, who hit the man behind him. It was like a bunch of soldiers falling down. I got probably two or three of them all at once and suddenly the ball carrier was naked. He was out there all by himself and he was swarmed. It was such a big thing to me. No one ever commented on it, but it was so satisfying because that play was exactly what I had been practicing all summer.

The experience taught me that if you are told what to do and it makes sense, then work at it until you become competent and someday it will pay off.

That's what happened. It's a great lesson on life. I wish I could watch those film clips and see if it really happened the way I remember. Regardless, I got to play more in the Cornell game, and then the coaches thought I was doing well enough that I was bumped up to the first team. I was playing on the left side of the line as an end with two sophomores, Cottie Davison, a guard, and Bolt Elwell, who was the tackle. (Bolt served in World War II and returned to play football again in 1945 and 1946.) The three of us started the Princeton and the Harvard games, which is a big thing at Yale.

Being on the first string and starting both of those big games that year was the greatest thing that happened to me at Yale. A lot of wonderful things took place during those years, but playing football at that time in my life meant everything.

On many levels, working my way up to varsity was a major accomplishment. I learned how to play for the sheer pleasure of the sport, for the fun of winning and the disappointment of losing. I discovered the importance of teamwork and working together to achieve a common goal. Maybe more important, I learned to overcome my physical fear of the game and compete for the pure joy of it. Conquering that fear early on in my life helped me face some of the challenges and obstacles that came later.

When I was not playing football, I played tennis most summers, and squash in the winter. Growing up in Rye, I entered a lot of tennis tournaments, and while at Portsmouth Priory, I became the Rhode Island State Champion, which is the smallest state and the smallest champion you can be. Tennis and squash came easier to me than football. I had grown up playing tennis and it felt natural to pick up a racket. At Yale, I played on the freshman tennis team and then on the varsity team starting my sophomore year. We were a good group and even better friends. We were probably not the best players that Yale produced, but we were not bad. I was number one most of the time, though once in a while I would lose a challenge and drop a notch.

At the end of my sophomore year we had a tennis banquet. It was held in one of the fraternities by some of the players, one of whom died in the war and a couple who have died since. They were older and "more sophisticated" than I, having experimented with drinking, smoking, women, and New York stuff. This particular night they were drinking Tom Collinses. I had never had a drink or a cigarette, and I was a virgin to boot. All those were things on which they were planning to shed some light. They gave me a lemonade, and I do not remember if I knew what it was, but it tasted pretty damn good. I had one and then another, and pretty soon I was high as a kite. All that I can recall about the rest of the night was that my doubles partner, Bobby McKenna, who is no longer with us, took me home. We must have been a sight! I was probably six inches taller than he was and maybe 30 pounds heavier. I was sort of wrapped around him while he struggled to maneuver me back to Timothy Dwight College.

We got back to my room and no sooner did I get there and into bed than I was sick. There was no time to get to a bathroom so I rushed to the window, opened it wide, and let it go. That should have been the end of it, but the screens were on. What a mess! When I got home to Rye the next day I was feeling lousy. That hung-over feeling lasted for three days. It gave me a lot of respect for alcohol as I tried to work it out on the golf course. I kept walking around, inhaling fresh air in hopes that it would revive me, but to no avail. I have never been able to drink a Tom Collins since.

In 1941, I got to the National Intercollegiate Squash Finals at Yale. Princeton had the best player at the time, Charlie Brinton. I played him in the finals and he beat me decisively. In 1942, we had a National Intercollegiate Tournament at Yale, and right before the tournament I got the measles. I was released from the infirmary just in time to watch my teammate win it. Sometimes things work out that way, and I was happy for him. But for me, life was about to change.

Three proud warriors in 1944. Shown from left are
U.S. Army Air Corps Second Lieutenant Richard P. Cooley,
U.S. Navy Reserve Midshipman James L. Buckley, and
U.S. Marine Corps Cadet Francis G. Dwyer.

THE CRASH, LOSS, AND RECOVERY

My daily prayers include a man I never met. He picked me out of my parachute shrouds and carried me to a field hospital in France. He saved my life.

I was a fighter pilot, a second lieutenant, a replacement pilot assigned to the 9th Air Force. Our squadron was flying P-38s out of a newly established base next to an airfield we had recently taken from the Germans near Florennes, Belgium. It was toward the end of World War II, only a few months after D-day.

The Lockheed P-38 Lightning was a large twin-engine aircraft designed to fly long-range bomber support missions at high altitudes. Our squadron's initial assignment was to defend the 8th Air Force bombers as they flew in and out of Germany. We would rendezvous with them at various locations and escort them deep into enemy territory. In all, I flew 17 missions but only one to escort the 8th Air Force because by the time I arrived, the Army Air Force command had started to transition the use of P-38s from bomber defense to dive-bomber. Our emphasis was not the frontline or foot soldiers because this particular aircraft was too big and fast for that. Instead, we were there to break up the German supply chain.

For extended range, the original P-38 design included two auxiliary fuel tanks, one under each wing, that could be jettisoned when empty. When it was reconfigured into a dive-bomber, the drop tanks were replaced with thousand-pound bombs, which we dropped onto railroad tracks, marshaling yards, supply depots, bridges, roads, and basically anything that would ultimately dismantle the German war effort. The only hitch in the plan was the P-38's limitations. It was not designed to be a dive-bomber. It was nose-heavy, and when a pilot put the aircraft into a dive and dumped its bomb load, the plane tended to invert, with sometimes tragic consequences. In addition to the P-38's aerodynamic failings, we had been trained as fighter pilots, not bombardiers.

My transformation from a student and athlete to a pilot began in March 1943, when I was called up for active duty. I was in my senior year at Yale before six of my classmates and I left for basic training in Nashville, Tennessee. We traveled coach, with three people sitting in a space that was designed for two, en route to the army indoctrination. The first and most important things I learned in basic training were the three acceptable answers to every comment or question directed at you by a senior officer — "YES SIR," "NO SIR," and "NO EXCUSE SIR." Those answers were all inclusive.

From Nashville we were sent to Santa Ana, California, for basic training in the Air Corps cadet program. Those same three answers were very much in use there as well. Looking back on that period of history, it seems like an era gone by. It may be hard to relate to today, but if you were in it, I do not think you could ever forget it. The things we saw and did will remain with us forever. In the service there was little variance in what you could do. There were rules and a regimen that had to be followed. Every soldier was assigned to a specific unit in alphabetical order by last name. We did not have smart bombs or precise directed artillery, but we did have discipline. It is a quality that I hope will always be in the forefront of my mind. It is important for our country's well-being and for the survival of human nature.

The direction that comes from discipline applied not only to the military during WWII, but to the civilian population as well. We experienced shortages and the strict rationing of gas and household items such as butter, sugar, coffee, and beef. Travel plans were limited, and we found that we could not do everything we wanted to do. That kind of discipline has not been felt by the general population since that war. The fact that we had to sacrifice together as a nation and as a world pulled us closer. Currently we have the military, their families, and the government in Washington involved in a war. We give lip service to it and attach bumper stickers to our cars, but it is not the same thing. As a country we are not involved in the same way. Today people are able to escape the sacrifice that others are making for the whole.

World War II was a time of camaraderie. We entered the war together in pursuit of a common goal. There was the drudgery of the army and a lot of waiting around, but we came to appreciate one another. We found commonalities and ways to connect. Sometimes during recreation breaks we would play basketball. It was fun and I used to look forward to those pickup games a great deal. I learned so much and in the process started to mature. I had spent my youth in a nice suburb, where I attended the "right" schools and had the "right" friends, but the army prepared me for life. I learned how to get along with people who came from different backgrounds, had different opinions and ideals, and had their own ways of doing things. Serving in the military made me realize that God and our constitution gave each one of us the same rights. We all had as much claim to live on this planet as anyone else. Everyone was equal in the army and no lines were drawn.

Three friends stand out from my army days. Rodney P. Colton was a farmer from Eastern Oregon. The two of us did everything together. While in Portland waiting for the weather to clear, he met a young girl in a dance hall. They married and I was his best man. I didn't have any personal knowledge of sex, but it turned out that Rodney had even less than did I. Before his wedding I gave him the facts-of-life speech that my mother had given me years earlier. Rodney became an auditor for Portland Gas and Electric, and fathered six children, so he must have figured it out.

Seymour Crofts was another friend from the army. He was a bright Jewish man from Chicago. I saw a lot of him during the war, but our paths have not crossed since. Seymour introduced me to handball. I had never played it before, but it was similar to squash and I enjoyed the sport and his company.

Bob Anderson was my roommate when we were stationed in Belgium. His father was a well-known Hawaiian entertainer and the family played in his band. Bob was a nervous type, moody at times, but he was there when I needed him.

After two months in Santa Ana, spent mostly in class work and physical training, we moved on to Hemet, California, where I received my basic air training and soloed as a pilot. Fortunately my instructor did not give up on me, as it took me 14 hours to solo. That was a lot of hours to get that little PT-19 off the ground and back in one piece. I was close to washing out. After two and a half months, the next stop was basic training in Hanford, California, where the planes grew in size and the flight instruction became considerably more detailed and demanding.

In Hanford, groups came together from many of the smaller primary training fields and the cadets were divided into platoons. The officers did not know much about us and we did not know each other. There was much more marching and military activity, and for this they needed to have platoon leaders, who were selected in an interesting way. Cadets were allowed to volunteer for the position, and I decided to try for it at the tender age of 19. There were several of us competing for the job. Whatever else they used as determinants, it seemed to me that the principal thing they were looking for was the ability to command with a loud voice and march the platoon from place to place on schedule. I was one of the last to try out for the job. By then I had observed that the platoon responded better to orders that were shouted loudly and clearly. Weak-voiced cadets could not keep the platoon in line and step.

The best cadets performed like the proverbial drill sergeants we had encountered during our basic training. So when it was my turn, I let the platoon have it, shouting my commands as if I had been in the army all my life. It must have been okay because they made me platoon leader even though I did not have a clue about how to run things in the army, and it showed over the next two months. Today, I see that this experience was important to my early leadership training.

The seasoned cadets who had been in the army before knew better than to volunteer for a job like that. It was all part of the "army experience."

Advanced flight training took place in Chandler, Arizona. There we were introduced to the AT-6, with retractable wheels and a variable-pitch prop. That was my first experience with night flying and long cross-country trips. In February 1944, we graduated, got our wings, became second lieutenants, and received our assignments. Some in our class were headed for the Bomber training. I joined the Fighter group and was sent to Portland Army Air Base for more training. I was there for three months, and that was the longest time I spent in any one training location. Our class attempted to complete our flight time requirements, but the weather was so awful that we spent most of our time on the ground waiting for a clearing. In order to log our hours, we were finally sent across the Cascades to Redmond, Oregon, and for 10 days we flew all the time and got caught up with the program. I remember that occasion with great satisfaction. It was an exhilarating time.

After Portland I was sent to Santa Rosa, California, where I learned to fly the P-38. I flew all the time, practiced gunnery, and learned about formation flying. It was serious combat training. We were officers by then and when we were not flying or going to classes, the time was our own. We found that San Francisco was only 80 miles away and quite accessible. With my newly purchased second-hand Ford, I was able to make that trip many times. I had family and friends there who made the time very enjoyable, and a good break from army life.

After we completed our training, our group was ready to go overseas as replacement pilots. Instead of sending us out to the Pacific, they put us on another train bound for the East Coast. For six days we slept two in a bunk until we arrived in Jersey City to board the *Ile de France*, a classy old French ocean liner. At the time almost every large passenger ship had been taken over for military uses. The *Ile de France* could not be used by the French as its ports were occupied by the Germans, so in 1941 she was turned over to the British as a troop-transporter. The *France* made many crossings before she was decommissioned in 1945 and then handed back to the French line in 1947. Along with 4,000 others, we sailed on board the *Ile de France* to the port of Southampton, England. From there we were transported by truck to a training facility close to Sheffield. It was soon clear why additional flight time in Europe was needed. We could fly, but we found navigation challenging as the topography there was flat and unchanging. It was easy to lose your bearings. From the air, the ground looked like one little farmhouse after another placed on a checkerboard of different-colored fields.

Four weeks later we took a boat to France and were driven to Paris for our final assignments. I was loaded onto a truck with a dozen other soldiers and driven to a town in Belgium called Florennes. There were three or four very large homes in the area that were owned by wealthy Belgians and royalty, but the army had appropriated everything for military housing. Our particular unit stayed in a chateau owned by a count and his family. They were moved to the basement and our squadron took over the second floor. The count did not like the fact that we had moved in, but he had little choice. He had a pretty 14-year-old daughter and that might have caused him concern. After settling in, somehow I got hold of a bike to check out the countryside.

Although they were inconvenienced by our arrival, the count seemed to take a liking to me. He learned that I had been a Benedictine schoolboy, so he took me on a ride of about 10 miles to a nearby Benedictine monastery. It had a magnificent church and a truly breathtaking setting, and the monks were warm and welcoming. After our bike ride, the count and countess invited me to dinner in their basement. The night turned out to be quite stiff because no one could speak English except the countess. I often wonder how I communicated with the count during those long bike rides, but we got along fine.

I was considered an experienced pilot when a brand-new P-38 was delivered to our squadron in December 1944, and I requested permission to test fly it. Everyone wanted to fly it, but I had just celebrated my 21st birthday, and I was chosen to evaluate the updated aircraft. My selection came with a firm lecture from my commanding officer. During the flight I was to take notes concerning temperatures, pressures, speeds, and anything pertaining to the performance of the plane. As it was a test flight, I was able to fly away from German lines in the other direction toward France. The idea of flying out of formation and not being shot at was exciting.

Having completed all the checks and with all systems performing beautifully, I took the plane up to 20,000 feet, enough altitude I figured to test the P-38's newly designed dive flaps. One of the joys of flying was letting the wings drop and feeling the plane fall away. With the plane purring across the sky with precision and ease, I let the wing dip and dove toward 10,000 feet. It was then that I pushed the dive flap button. Nothing happened. I pushed it over and over again, but it would not engage. The last thing I remember was watching the altimeter go around and around and knowing that I was in terrible trouble.

What happened next I have to leave to hearsay, as I was not in any condition to recall the events that followed. I was told that a French black man saw the plane spiraling toward the ground, saw a chute open, and found and carried me to a nearby hospital in Chambray, in northern France. I was never able to thank him.

My right arm was dangling by threads of skin. The hospital staff cleaned me up and wrapped me tight in hospital blankets. I do not remember much about the next few days except I do faintly recall an ambulance ride, which involved serious pain and seemed to last forever. All I know is that when I did eventually regain consciousness a few days later, the pain had eased, but I had no idea what had happened or where I was. I felt groggy and I was hurting. I did not know that I had lost my arm.

———

The Battle of the Bulge began on December 16, 1944, and German troops were advancing toward our location. I had received the last sacraments in a hospital ward lined with soldiers in the same miserable state. We remained on the top floor of the hospital while the staff and all transportable patients evacuated to the basement. Being immobile, we looked up at the ceiling, wondering when the bombs were going to come through the roof or when the German paratroopers would break in and shoot us. As the battles raged, all we could do was lie there and listen in the dark. Fortunately, the Germans never got that far into France.

It took a while for my base to find me because in those days there was no instant communication. When the plane did not return, questions were asked. They had no way of knowing I was 100 miles away in France, fighting for my life.

Maybe three or four days later, my squadron had received word that I was in a hospital in Reims. My roommate, Bob Anderson, packed my personal items and along with a few other men drove down to see what was left of me. They told me that our squadron's P-38s were being replaced with P-51 Mustangs. That was welcome news for them. The single-engine P-51 was faster, more maneuverable, and more versatile than the P-38. Although I have not seen Bob for many years, I will always remember his kindness. After the war he returned to Hawaii and later moved to Southern California to raise horses.

Just before Christmas I was moved to a tent hospital between Paris and Le Havre. For someone to be sent to that tent hospital, it had to have been decided that the mortal danger from shock or wounds had passed. Being on the other side of Paris, it was safer and quieter. It was there that I faced the fact that I had lost my arm, and many diverse thoughts began running through my mind. Coping with the loss of a limb was a mental process. I needed to overcome my profound feeling of loss. It may sound odd, but even though I was faced with a life-altering debilitation, I knew I would survive and would be okay with or without the arm. I would make a living. I would find a wife. I would be happy. But I would probably never play football again. The challenge of football, and particularly those years playing at Yale, had been huge. Getting over the fear and being able to truly enjoy the game and all that went with it meant so much. Sometimes during my recovery I found myself dreaming about returning to Yale and playing varsity football. When I realized that I was no longer physically able to accomplish my goal, I cried and cried. There was no consoling me. It was one of the first times in my life that something I desperately wanted was taken away.

I had to learn to let go and accept, to understand that when dreams are gone, you have to rise above the pain and self-pity and go on with life.

Although it was a difficult time, that lesson has served me well over the years.

During other moments of lucidity, I tried to reconstruct the crash and speculate on how my arm may have been torn off. I came up with only two scenarios. The first was impact with the plane's horizontal stabilizer. The P-38 was powered by two huge engines with counter-rotating props that kept the plane from pulling to one side or the other. Behind the engines were two long booms that were joined at the tail, equipped with a horizontal stabilizer. All this was located right behind the cockpit, and many pilots were injured, and some lost limbs, when they were forced to bail out of the plane. It's easy to imagine going down at 300 miles an hour, opening the canopy, and having the full force of the wind suck you from the cockpit and ram you onto the knife-edged stabilizer. My second theory was that in releasing the cockpit canopy, my arm hit the armor plate located directly behind the seat, which protects pilots from getting shot in the back. There will never be a conclusive answer to what happened. All I know for certain is that there is a part of me resting peacefully in France, and that might somehow make me slightly French.

I have reconstructed the events of that day over and over in my head and what I could have done to prevent it. It all comes down to a life-altering assumption. When you are a replacement pilot, it sometimes feels as if you are just going through the motions. I am a much more knowledgeable pilot today. Back then we were taught how to fly and how to follow orders. Our instruction had less to do with the mechanics of a plane than the instructions of a mission. We were told that when flying into Germany, we were to keep our planes next to the captain and be his wingman. As long as he did not get into trouble, we were fine. The day I went out for the test flight, the captain told me to be careful, but he did not tell me to do something that I should have done.

I should have checked the dive flaps on a level flight before I tried to use them in a 300-mile-an-hour drop to 10,000 feet. I just assumed they would work, since everything else did. Lesson: Never take action, big or small, on assumptions when it is not necessary.

I had been raised and educated as a Catholic, and my faith was an untested part of my life until the crash. One thing that remains a mystery I have since credited to divine intervention. Every Army Air Force pilot wore a parachute, and we were drilled in how to use it. It buckled around our legs and shoulders, and it

THIS P-38 LIGHTNING IS THE TYPE OF PLANE I WAS FLYING
WHEN I HAD MY ACCIDENT.

had a red handle on the left side that you pulled tight across your chest to open the chute. Amid pain and pity, I tried to figure out how my parachute was deployed. I had lost the arm that I would have used to pull the red handle, and it seems highly unlikely that, under duress and with limited seconds, I could have pulled the handle across my body with my left arm. My crash, I have since concluded, was totally in the hands of God. My parachute opened just a few hundred feet above the ground and just before my plane exploded into a ball of searing heat and razor-like shrapnel. God saved me for some reason, and all these years later, I still don't know why. I am working on that one. It has been 66 years since the crash that should have left me dead.

Eventually I was put on a boat bound for England and sent to another medical facility between Southampton and London. It was the time of the buzz bomb. The Germans were firing the V-1 at London and we were on the flyway. They were aiming for densely populated areas in London, but nevertheless, we held our breath each time a buzz bomb passed over. There was little else we could do besides pray that the buzzing sound of those motors did not stop.

In February I was considered well enough to head back to the States by ship. Our ship was an old Italian cruise liner, some 600 feet long. We were stacked in old staterooms five levels high, and I was on the bottom bunk because of my immobility. Our cabin was on the middle deck, which would have been better in the summer, as the North Atlantic in February is not an easy place. We could see those 40- to 50-foot waves rising up behind us, then feel them crash down over the stern of the ship. The water often washed into our room, and that made being on the lower level pretty damp. As our ship struggled up and down the waves, we often feared it would split in two, but we landed in New Jersey after a long trip. My mom and dad were there to meet the ship. The great heavyweight fighter Joe Louis was there to greet all the vets. I remember seeing him and then taking advantage of the free long-distance phone call the army granted returning soldiers. I called a girlfriend in Portland, Oregon.

I spent a little over a year in the hospital. Along with the amputation of my arm and dealing with a concussion and shock, there was a big slice out of my right leg and much discussion about how to patch it. The hospital staff sent me to the plastic hospital in Indianapolis, where skin was removed from the inside of my legs to cover the hole. In those days it took time for grow-ing and sometimes it did not take, which was the case with me. There was more review, and it was determined that they had not gone deep enough with the initial skin graft. Eventually my leg mended, so the doctors were able to focus on my arm.

I was experiencing severe phantom pain. It's a fairly common occurrence among those who have lost a limb because the nerve endings are still alive. For some people these pains never go away, but I was fortunate. Mine lasted for only a few years. There were many operations. They tried to pull the nerves out of my spine or from my neck or inject Novocain into the nerve, but nothing seemed to work. That was bothersome in the sense that it is an odd sensation to know that you can have feeling and pain in your finger even though it is not there. When I retired from the mili-tary, we had another go at it. My father knew a specialist in St. Louis who was able to operate under my arm and pull the nerve down in such a way that he deadened it. After that operation, things improved. The war was over and it was time to look ahead.

Once you become an amputee, you enter a different world. You have problems that other people do not have. They are not any worse or any better, they are just different. From the very beginning the important thing is your attitude.

The first thing an amputee has to do is learn to accept it. If you cry about it and feel sad for your luck, it does not solve any problems. You have to deal with it and learn to live with what you have.

An amputee who loses an arm quickly realizes that one arm does most of the things that you need done. The other arm usually is a holder. You put a piece of paper down to write your name and the other arm holds it still. Or you try to thread a needle, and one hand holds the needle and the other pushes the thread through. So one arm keeps the object secure while the other arm takes on the active role. I was right-handed, so losing that arm was more of an obstacle. I had to learn how to write with my left hand, throw, shake hands, and everything else. I still think I'm right-handed, so I continue to write the same way as I did with my right hand. I do not curve my hand across the pen the way that "lefties" do. Though the slant is slightly different, my handwriting is much the same as it was before the accident. That is one of many things. Basically you have to learn to do everything again in your own way. You are always thinking about it.

Getting dressed. Putting on socks. Tying shoes or a tie. Tucking a shirt in behind you. These can be hard things to do unless you have systems in place. You can get by without two hands if you learn new ways of doing things. For instance, charging a cell phone. If I put the charger between my legs then I can put the cord in with my left hand. Does not sound like much, but it is. You constantly have to learn to adjust. Your brain realizes that the normal function is gone, and it looks for a new way to tackle the issue. One great substitute "holder" is your teeth. I use mine as a replacement for my arm all the time. It can sometimes look a little funny, but it works and saves me an infinite amount of time. Imagine going to Starbucks to get a latte and scone on the way to the office. The little bag holding the scone is clamped tightly between your teeth and you pick up the latte with your hand. You walk out and nobody cares.

If you fit in easily, sometimes people will say, "Do this" or "Do that" because they have forgotten that you cannot do some things. This is success from an amputee point of view. For instance, you cannot row a boat with one hand, but you can paddle a canoe with great care. Tennis is not a problem. You have to throw the ball up to serve, so you place the ball on the racket and toss it up. Everything you do has to be analyzed and modified.

The amputee does not want to appear different. You want to do whatever the task is and be a part of the group. I will admit that it is hard to play baseball. Catching the ball in a mitt and then throwing it is difficult. You might learn to throw again with your left hand, but how do you get rid of the mitt? There are certain things you cannot do as an amputee, and you want to accept those and not dwell on it.

Golf takes patience. Most golfers will tell you that it is a left-handed game anyway. With practice, you can hit the ball quite well. The majority of golfers are right-handed, but you can learn how to hit with the left hand because of the way the wrist cocks and does not snap like the right hand wants to do. When I was a kid playing at the Apawamis Club course, I remember playing 18 holes with a score of 82, but the best round I ever played was at Pebble Beach on Cypress Point when I was 35 years old. I scored 80, and if I had not ringed the cup on the 18th hole, I would have broken 80 for the only time in my life. For a while I managed to play tough courses and maintained a handicap of 18. With patience and practice you can gradually do most everything. It takes an analysis of the situation to look at it as an amputee and decide what you can do, and accept things that cannot be changed.

If you are an amputee, you have to get used to people staring at you. Today I rarely wear my prosthesis, and how many amputees do you see? The point is, I do not look at people's curiosity as a negative. On the contrary, I can walk down the street and about 90 percent of the women smile and it is a pleasant feeling. There could be some interest and maybe some pity, but I am not worried about that — it is just nice. Most of the men turn away. That could be the nurturing side of women, but at least I can enjoy it. Why wouldn't people stare? When I see an amputee I think, "He only has one arm" because I do not see myself as being like him. I see myself as a perfectly normal man.

As a young man I used to feel that I had to be independent, but I found out that it can be very nice when people help. You know that you can do it, but maybe not as quickly as someone else can. I began to realize that it is not bad to ask someone to help you. For instance, things like cutting your meat. People look at me and say, "Oh, let me cut your meat." Initially, I refused help and cut it myself. And I can do it if I have a sharp knife, but what I have found is that it is nice to let people do things for me. The only thing I have to be careful of is that they do not try to cut the meat into small portions like those of a child. I sometimes get 25 little pieces and it drives me nuts. It spoils my appetite. On the other hand, it feels nice to accept the help. Nothing wrong with that, but you want to be able to do things by yourself if you can.

Of course it would have been nice to have my arm all these years. However, at this stage of my life, after more than 60 years without it, I do not want it back. One of these days they might be able to transplant arms like other vital organs. Right now the research is not sufficient for that, but I would not be surprised if it becomes available in the not too distant future. More than likely I will not be here, but I am not sure that I would want it even if the procedure became available in my lifetime. I think I am okay as I am. I do not feel different. Being an amputee is not the end of the world. You just have to learn to deal with it, and the way you do that is to give thanks for living through the trauma and enjoy the life that you have been given.

When you have been through an experience like this, it is natural to want to share what you have learned. Other amputees are the ones you can help the most. Over the years I have been in contact with other amputees on request by different medical groups or personal friends who knew someone who needed help.

I have never tried to make an official counseling service out of it. Doing this kind of helping has been more like mentoring. It is easy to do and I like doing it.

Not long ago I had the opportunity to be with Will Guyman, a young man who had recently lost his right arm in a boating mishap. His story was extraordinary, and terrifying. When I shared my experience of losing an arm, he responded with a thoughtful, gripping description of his life since the accident. It is such an extraordinary piece of writing that I am including his essay, with his permission, as an example of what it takes for an amputee to accept his condition, adapt to what is a new reality, and carry on with life in a productive way. It is the very best example one could read to understand how to successfully deal with the loss of a limb, and it shows the depth of Will's character and his immediate understanding and acceptance of the changes that were to take place in his life.

WHAT HAPPENED TO ME
By Will Guyman

Flying along, smelling the fresh pines in Canada's Desolation Sound Marine Park, I sat comfortably in the front seat of a motorboat, content and tranquil. I had no idea that a freak accident was about to change my life forever. The water rushed under our 15-foot speed dinghy as my dad piloted our joyful evening cruise. Although my life would be painfully tormented during the next four hours, and would hang in the balance for the next week, I had no idea that this experience would actually better my life, making me more resilient, grateful, positive, and hardworking.

Suddenly our dinghy lurched as it hit a submerged log, and I hurtled headfirst over the bow and under the boat and confronted the dinghy's 60-horsepower propeller head-on.

Immediately, I was thrust deep under the surface as the accident happened quickly, but the image would forever play back slowly in my mind. Sharp electrical sensations gripped my entire body. I felt myself fade from reality as I hovered seemingly neutrally buoyant under the water. Running out of air, I needed to surface, but the strange command of "kick" didn't seem to be working because my body couldn't communicate through the overwhelming electrical sensations. Somehow, thanks to my life jacket, I managed to break the surface, and my gasp for air was met with another excruciating pain, which emanated from my rib cage. I found out later that one of my seven fractured ribs had punctured my right lung. Furthermore, a crimson cloud surrounded my body, and as I looked at my dad, I spoke in a different voice, a high-pitched, shrill cry.

My dad approached me in the dinghy, his face streaming with tears and stricken with a distinctive look of horror. I followed his gaze to the source of the underwater blood cloud and suddenly realized that the propeller had completely severed my upper right arm. My mind could not compute that my arm was no longer there. My dad grabbed me by my life jacket and heaved me into the boat. My back screamed with pain, the result of a cracked scapula. My dad slammed on the dinghy's throttle to take us back to our anchorage, and within minutes we roared into the isolated small harbor.

Kind, caring people rushed out in small boats to help us as my dad and I fashioned a tourniquet around my arm. The next two and a half hours, as we waited for the Canadian Coast Guard, were the longest and most painful hours of my life, but amazingly I never lost consciousness.

Throughout this horrifying accident, I had this overwhelming instinct that I just needed to get through it and survive, and this perception became my mentality throughout the most difficult aspect of my recovery in the weeks and months ahead. As I was transferred to the small and intrepid Coast Guard super inflatable, an inexperienced crew member accidentally dropped me in the icy water. Utilizing a skill that I later learned to master, I reached up with a burst of energy and pulled my entire body out of the water using only my left arm. Now that I was hypothermic, it took more energy than ever to survive the turbulent journey to the Coast Guard cutter for the helicopter lift rescue. I am told that I was nearly dead when I arrived at the Campbell River Hospital, where I received a blood transfusion and the first of many surgeries. However, the worst was over, and miraculously, it looked as if I was going to survive. I eventually learned that this grace was all I ever needed to live happily.

The first two sentences I remember uttering when I woke up in the hospital were "When can I go back?" and "I'm screwed." I had been strongly right-handed, and now my right arm was gone. As soon as I started thinking about the future, I became mentally chained to the same hospital bed that was physically restraining me with bandages and tubes. I became so overwhelmed with worry and sadness; however, I began to understand that I just needed to focus on the next task in order to recover and resume my normal life. This goal became the paradigm for my recovery: to return to the same level of competency that I was at before the accident, in incremental steps that could be checked off.

After two and a half weeks in the hospital, I returned home. My friends and family members had visited me in the hospital and provided incredible moral support. At home, I was often able to power through the coming adversity by reasoning that somebody had it worse than I did, so I had no cause to complain. Although this reasoning alleviated much of my pain, it was still hard to truly accept myself, or who I had become. My doctors and other strangers were already profiling me as an "amputee," and I was labeled as someone with a disability; however, I never allowed that label to become a limitation. My quest for normality began by beating my doctors' estimates as to when I would return to my normal life. I did every physical therapy and lung exercise more frequently than they required, even if it meant more pain. Despite my back and rib injuries, I tried to walk around as much as I could. I was also determined to get rid of the pain medications as soon as possible so that my brain could be sharp again. I attacked all the one-handed challenges with fervor, especially writing and typing with my left hand. Most of all I wanted to return to school.

Three weeks after my accident, my sophomore year began, and I wanted to prove that I could start on time. In reality this task was practically impossible, considering the complicated schedule of prosthetic, doctor, and physical therapy appointments throughout the week. However, my school administrators gave me the opportunity to return, and I was excited to take it. I started with three classes, which was half my regular load, and went to doctor's appointments in the mornings and classes in the afternoons. Sometimes, I struggled to pay attention in class as the morphine or occasional intense phantom pain in my arm clouded my brain. I soon realized that maybe I had taken on more than I had bargained for, but I couldn't let the school, my family, my friends, or myself down. To combat these challenges, I went in after class to see my teachers about topics that I had not understood. Furthermore, writing and typing were a gargantuan problem for me. Despite practice, writing and typing one-handed with my non-dominant arm took forever, and my handwriting was almost illegible. So I drew upon the powerful combination that gave me strength, my love of technological innovation.

Although I had always been interested in technology, I would have never foreseen its use in my recovery. I seemed to bond with and become energized by technology on a new level. After that accident, with all my newfound limitations, I searched for technology that would make my life easier. Not only did I find and use important software and hardware, such as the Windows Dvorak one-handed keyboard, the Tablet PC, and Dragon

NaturallySpeaking's voice-recognition software, but I also discovered how much I love technology. I immediately joined the school's Artificial Intelligence Club, and the following year I helped run a Mac Support Club. I became passionate about technology, and this passion drove new skills. My accident was really giving me newfound discoveries that worked to my advantage. Without that important technology, I would have never been able to keep up in school in the way that I did.

By November, two and a half months after my traumatic amputation, school was going well and my physical recovery was maintaining a steady pace. My rib and scapula injuries, however, still inhibited most of my regular activities, and the coordination of my left hand was still not up to par. When I entered school it was obvious that I would need to find a way to resume my fluid coordination, and I knew just the game. Before my accident, Ping-Pong had been just a recreational pastime, but during my recovery, it became a competitive physical therapy. Playing left-handed, and with only one hand, was one of the most frustrating challenges I encountered. I often broke down in dissatisfaction, but I also understood that repetitive play was the only way to resume normality. I also found a table tennis gym, where the best player in the United States, Yiyong Fan, coached. I began training with him, and within a month I surpassed my table tennis skills before the accident. Not only had I become a better table tennis player, but I had also built better hand-eye coordination, which helped me with writing, typing, daily activities that required hands, and sports. Table tennis also palliated my rib and scapula injuries because I healed much faster than my doctors had expected. Table tennis taught me that with strong persistence, I could overcome my frustrations. Given my recent progress, it was looking like I might be able to play squash again.

I had lettered in squash my freshman year as a right-handed player with both arms, and because of my success as a table tennis player, I had high expectations for squash. I began playing early, before the season, but I erupted in tears after my first time on the court. It was hard to serve with one hand, and my gross-motor-skill coordination was pathetic in my left arm. However, I decided that if I focused on achievement, I would be able to resume my spot in the top 10 on the team. I played multiple times before the season and reached the point where I could serve one-handed and keep a rally going. I worked with the coach personally, and my skills rapidly grew throughout the season. There were substantial setbacks and disappointments, however, such as defeat at the hands of players whom I had easily disposed of before my accident. I pushed on, though, and tried extra hard on the court. My learning curve was steeper than that of my opponents, and amazingly, at the end of the season, I lettered and regained my spot in the top 10. That season I learned that resilience gets results. Some sports, such as basketball, were harder to resume. My friends stopped inviting me to pickup games, so I played when it wasn't competitive. Most importantly, though, since my recovery, no activity or sport has been entirely walled off because of my accident. I have learned that my accident did not give me a disability, just an opportunity to improve.

Halfway through the year I picked up another class, and by the end of the first term I energetically resumed my regular course load. I worked harder than ever that term to surpass expectations, and I earned some of my best academic results. My accident introduced me to the height of academic success, and from then on I was determined to maintain that apogee.

The most valuable lessons that I learned from my accident are those of gratitude and appreciation for life.

Throughout my recovery, I felt as if I needed to give back in exchange for my saved life, which was another motivator to succeed. At the start of my junior year, I joined our school's "blood team," which organized our blood drives. In order to attract more donors, I volunteered to speak about what blood donations had meant to me, and most important, how I would not be alive today without blood donors. When I talked in front of the whole school, I was nervous; how could I convey the significance of donating a little time and blood to save multiple lives? It was difficult to talk about my personal experiences, especially to my friends, but I understood that candidness was a small sacrifice if it would motivate people to donate blood. After my speech, a record number of people donated blood, and I was soon recruited by the Puget Sound Blood Center to give a similar talk at their annual fund-raiser for blood donations. Giving my speech, I reflected on the irony of my motivating some of the same people who had potentially saved my life. Every time I tell my story, I am reminded of how fortunate I was to live, and how there are others continually suffering from adversity far worse than mine. I now know that my accident led me through a set of challenges and opened my eyes to new skills and opportunities that I would have otherwise ignored.

This spring, my new passion for technology culminated in the starting of my own online business: www.WebWeaverWill.com, which received over 2,000 hits in the first month. During the development of my business, I realized that my interest in technology and entrepreneurism was a significant, positive result of my accident. I now look forward with optimism to my future, and hope that my experience continues to motivate others and myself.

There is nothing to add to this picture. Though I have had the privilege and pleasure of meeting and working with many amputees, I have not seen an account and a bravery to equal it. Will earned an early acceptance to Stanford University and started the next phase of his life last September. He will do well there and is sure to take advantage of the great opportunities to learn about the world and himself.

I COULD NO LONGER PLAY FOOTBALL, BUT I STILL LOVED TO COMPETE,
AND I GOLFED, SKIED, AND PLAYED SQUASH AFTER RECOVERING
FROM MY WAR INJURY. IN 1953, THE PACIFIC COAST SQUASH TEAM WON THE
NATIONAL CHAMPIONSHIP. WE'RE HOLDING MARTINI SHAKERS,
THE TROPHIES PRESENTED TO THE TEAM MEMBERS IN RECOGNITION
OF THEIR VICTORY. SHOWN FROM LEFT: TED CLARK, GENE HOOVER,
DICK COOLEY, BOB COLWELL, AND WALTER PETTIT.

PEACE, DECISIONS, AND A CAREER

J ust as I had studied the college brochures in my junior year at Portsmouth, I began to analyze my options for a quick graduation from college. I learned that Yale would give one semester of credit for time spent in the service, so I would need only another semester to complete the requirements for a degree in Industrial Administration and Engineering. For my arm to have the necessary time to heal and the nerves to grow, I was given three months' leave from the army in May of 1945. I applied for an additional month's extension to my army leave, which was granted without a hassle. That gave me four months: time enough to fulfill all course requirements necessary to receive my degree.

My right leg was still weak, but I was ambulatory. I had been off it so long that it was down to skin and bone, but my left leg was strong. During the months at the hospital, I had been confined to a wheelchair, where I spent a great deal of my time traversing backwards through the endless corridors with the help of my one good leg. It was like poling a boat. But I would be able to walk to my classes.

Before I was called into active duty I had completed one month of senior classes and had looked forward to playing on the football team. That dream did not die easily. There was some dis- cussion with one of the coaches about finding a way to rig me up so that I could play, but the idea was complicated and eventually dropped. I would have been known as the one-armed football player at Yale. Since that option was not available, the best thing seemed to be to finish school as soon as possible. In hindsight, I wish I had not been in such a hurry. In the summer of 1945, I returned for the final semester at Yale. I roomed with a star running back on the football team, Vandy Kirk. We shared rooms in Timothy Dwight College, the same residential college where I had lived in my sophomore year. Unable to play football like Vandy, I turned my sights to relearning tennis, squash, and golf. These were sports that had always come easily to me, and I was hoping I could regain my ability with time. I also bought a bicycle.

During this time I met a young lady who lived in the hills seven miles west of town. Every day after class, I would hop on my bike and make the strenuous trip, eventually ending up at her door. Our meetings were usually just long enough for me to catch my breath and share a Coke. I do not remember how we met or even if we dated, but I do know that by the end of the summer my leg had filled out and was fully functioning.

My classes were organized so that I had one day off a week. On my free Thursdays I would head for New York and enjoy a date in the Big Apple. We would usually go to the theater or to dinner and sometimes dancing. I splurged, spending all of the $1,200 I had saved from the army pay. It was a great summer and oddly enough, my grades improved. I attribute it to growing up and being thankful for the opportunity.

As I was preparing to finish school and review career options, my father offered to send me to the Harvard Business School. He revered education, making sure that my sisters and I attended the best schools possible, regardless of the fact that he was not wealthy. Every penny he earned was spent on our house, school tuition, and all the rest of the household expenses. He was never able to save and died a relatively poor man. I do not know if he ever wanted to do anything else, but I do know that he spent generously on his family and gave us every chance to succeed. That being the case, I knew that whatever was going to happen in my life, I would have to do it myself. Although

Harvard Business School was a tremendous offer and would have been a fine choice, I was impatient to start a career where I could earn my own money. What an MBA degree from Harvard could do for one's career was not on my radar screen.

Again, charging ahead somewhat impatiently was my style, which accounted for some missed opportunities.

Once I had been working for 8 or 10 years, I was mad at myself for not accepting his gift. I considered Harvard's Advanced Management Program, which was a fine course for those people who were already in the workforce and were interested in developing skills for higher levels of management. Unfortunately my boss thought that I would learn more staying put on the job. In his opinion I would not need education in a classroom for what I would be doing. Although I did not know it at the time, I was being groomed to run Wells Fargo Bank and my own management course had already begun.

At the end of October 1945, I graduated from Yale in the class of '44 in Industrial Administration and Engineering. Stepping onto the platform to receive my diploma, I was the only one in army uniform, while everyone else wore the ceremonial caps and gowns. It was a mixed-up time. People were coming and going during the war, and most of my classmates were still on active duty. As it worked out, I graduated ahead of my class and missed all the camaraderie after the war. To this day I am not sure I allowed myself the opportunity to feel the sadness of that missed football dream. Instead, I focused on what I could, moving ahead and finding a suitable career.

After graduation I returned to the hospital in Indiana, where the doctors checked the growth of the nerves and the status of my leg. Soon after, there was a clearance and in November, I was sent to the final stage of the amputee recovery program at Thomas England General Hospital in Atlantic City. During the war Atlantic City had essentially been transformed into a military medical facility with the takeover of a large number of local resort hotels. It was there that they reshaped the stump surgically and prepared me for the prosthesis.

Nothing had been done with my right arm since the initial healing, so the stump was prepared to fit a false arm that would be comfortable and useful. There were some side issues that had to be cleaned up as well. Before I could be legally discharged, there was significant training with the new arm and proficiency tests to be passed.

After the revision operation and time to heal, I was fitted with a prosthesis. January became an instructional period in which I learned a host of new techniques on how to maneuver the limb, the proper care, and the donning and doffing of the prosthesis. After a few weeks of practice I was getting the hang of it, not with the greatest expertise, but enough to pass the tests to prove I could manage on my own. At the end of January '46, with the prosthesis and my overall health cleared, I was able to retire from the Army Air Corps as a first lieutenant and return to civilian life. I celebrated with a short ski trip to Vermont and went to work in mid February.

My father had taken me to the Johnson O'Connor Research Foundation for an aptitude examination. For a few days I went through a battery of tests that we hoped would shed some light on my strengths and weaknesses, and give an indication of what kind of job I would be best suited for. When the Johnson O'Connor advisers reviewed my scores, they found that I would generally be adept at a wide variety of endeavors, not expert, not great, but generally competent in a number of fields. To further illustrate (and confuse) their message, the results in the various skills were put on a bar graph, which illustrated straight-line profiles. It was explained that I was one of those individuals who did not fall into a specific category. Instead they suggested a wide range of career choices, such as lawyer, accountant,

or salesperson. Their view seemed to be that whatever I chose
to do, I would be a success. Their answer did not give the specific
direction that I was looking for, although once again I was
thankful for the preparation and broad-based background of the
Industrial Administration degree at Yale.

Different options surfaced. The founder of Portsmouth Priory
believed that I could be a monk at the Priory and offered to help
me get a dispensation so I could perform the duties of a priest
with one arm. That was an issue because many of the rituals in
the church involve two hands. For instance, administering
Communion during Mass requires the priest to hold the chalice
with one hand while giving out the Host with the other. You
could get by without it, but then you might be leaving out some
other specifically important part of the ceremony. I did not seriously consider the priesthood. Feelings of guilt or obligation are
not enough to support a vocation for that life. I was too material-
istic and heterosexual, and I suppose too selfish, to be a priest.
Instead I went to work for McCall Corporation in New York City.

McCall's was a publishing company run by Marvin Pierce, a
golfing friend of my father's. They offered me a job in the commercial printing department. It seemed like a good opportunity,
so I interviewed, and shortly after took the position. In looking
for that first job, money may not have been the primary incen-
tive, but it was always a welcome moment each Friday when
the woman paymaster came around and paid me $65 in cash.
In three years my salary grew until I was making $135 a week.

McCall's had a large printing plant in Ohio and owned its
own magazines such as *McCall's*, *Redbook*, and *Bluebook*. They
also handled other magazine printing for properties like *Reader's
Digest*, *Newsweek*, *Mademoiselle*, *Glamour*, and *Popular Science*.
My main accounts were *Mademoiselle*, *Glamour*, and *Popular
Science*. There were many trips back and forth to Dayton making
sure that each publication date was met exactly as required with
perfect quality and on time. In those days we used the letterpress

printing process on enormous web-fed printing machines, which meant that the huge rolls of magazine paper went on the end of the press and came off the other end perfectly printed up in magazine-size pages in groups of 12-, 18-, or 24-page signatures (sections). We had to learn how to diagram each plate on the rollers so that all the pages lined up in the right place. Since that time they have come up with different and better technology with improved economy and quality.

My first boss was Clayton Westland. I had tremendous respect and affection for him because he taught me a great deal about how to work in an office, commercial printing, and many other essentials of the workaday world. He ran the business carefully and turned it into a moneymaker. The three of us who worked for him had the responsibility of keeping the clients, editors, and production people happy. Production of each magazine had to be done in a precise, clearly defined way. When changes were made, we had to make sure any and all substitutions were accommodated precisely. If the color on a Revlon ad did not quite exude the exquisite shade of red that the art director envisioned, we would catch hell. To amend a failed situation often took a three-martini lunch with the magazine production man, which was typical New York style back then.

Producing magazines was a highly stressful and multi-faceted job. It is a big business, but a quiet one. There is a lot at stake. Each week there was the pressure of time deadlines and feet-to-the-fire decisions. We were on our own a lot and responsible for the outcome of many publications. It was a good job that I held for a little over three years, until I decided to leave New York and move west.

The job at McCall's was interesting and challenging and typically took place during the Monday-through-Friday work-week. McCall's Manhattan office was ideally situated directly over Grand Central Station, making it easy to be in the office before nine. I would usually catch an evening train shortly after five that would arrive in Rye well before seven. For many New Yorkers, this would be considered an ideal commute.

Life began to shape into a general pattern. Rye was a quiet community during the week, with most of the social life concentrated on the weekends. As time went on, my squash game improved enough that I started playing in tournaments during the winter season. With the Yale Club just a block from the McCall's office, I could meet opponents on the squash court during lunch break. My tennis game did not return to form as quickly, but golf showed improvement, and I was able to play with my old friends on the weekends. As I was a former Yale varsity player, tickets to the season games in New Haven were easy to come by. Two-week vacations often resulted in a week skiing in winter and a golf outing in summertime. This sounds better than it was. I was 25 years old and I could see the same routine repeating itself when I was 50, and I hoped that there was more to life. I began thinking about moving to California, where the family had its roots. Going west sounded exciting, but I had no idea what I could do. I would need a job right away because I had practically no money and the postwar recession was taking hold.

In the winter of 1948 I began seeing Sheila McDonnell. Dating turned into courting, which turned into marriage in January of '49. The year of engagement taught me how the McDonnells lived with their 14 children and enormous extended family, and it was different from any lifestyle I knew. They were strong Irish Catholics with powerful connections. Mrs. McDonnell's father had been a partner of Thomas Edison. In the winter the McDonnells lived in two spacious apartment floors at 72nd Street and 5th Avenue. The older seven lived on the main floor with their parents and the younger seven lived a floor below. Sheila was number 10, and so marrying me put her close to being in the upper seven. Normally the younger seven came up to the main floor for a social time before dinner but did not stay for dinner with the older members of the family. In June they moved to their summer home on the beach in Southampton. That was a spectacular setting. Everything was organized and beautiful. I was totally impressed with the lifestyle and how great it would be to be part of it all. In a nice way my father tried to tell me that the McDonnells were much wealthier and were out of our class, but I did not hear him. In a way, the caution flags he raised only increased my determination to make it work.

The first real lesson on what I was getting into occurred when Sheila and I were thinking about decorating the garage apartment we were planning to rent from our great friend and supporter, Mary Harris. The Harris family, Mr. and Mrs. Basil Harris, lived in Rye, New York. Mr. Harris was the chairman of the United States Lines, a transatlantic shipping company, in his working career. They had a big house overlooking the Apawamis golf course. Over their garage was an apartment that Sheila and I moved into for three months after we were married. Mrs. Harris was like a godmother to me. She was always helping and advising me on what to do. She was a great friend and a good supporter. Before I was married, I had lunch almost every Sunday at their home. It was always a wonderful meal, with her famous peanut butter and bacon appetizers. Life above their garage would be comfortable.

The two Harris children whom I knew best were Basil Jr. and Dick Harris. Dick was married to Charlotte McDonnell, who was number four in "the upper seven" of the McDonnell family. The Harrises were great. Mrs. Harris was a very holy Catholic woman who was a big support to our family.

The Harrises, Flanigans, and McDonnells became related to the Cooleys by marriage, but the connections between them were ages old. Mrs. Flanigan was not a Catholic by birth, but she married Mr. Flanigan and their four children were all raised in the church. Initially she did not join the church, but later on she decided to, and my mother became her godmother in the ceremony of bringing her into the Catholic Church. It gave them a special connection and brought our two families closer together.

Sheila's mother offered to decorate the Harris apartment for us as a wedding present, and she sent us to McMillen, the well-known decorator that all the McDonnells used. Sheila was immensely pleased. When I finally saw what they came up with, it did not look good to me, and I said so. At that point in my life, I knew nothing about decorating and even less about compromising. It showed, and this dismayed Sheila. After a couple of unsatisfactory visits with the McMillen people, the difficulty of pleasing me got back to Mrs. McDonnell, and she informed Sheila that I could please myself, but I would have to pay for it. Unfairly, Sheila had been caught in the middle and must have had some misgivings about the kind of person she was getting involved with. I wish I had been more tolerant at that time.

I decided that the chance for a successful married life lay in getting away from the family and from the New York area. The honeymoon was planned for the West Coast: Los Angeles, Carmel, and San Francisco, where I intended to do some job hunting. Life was not going to be so independent living in the clan, and the thought gave impetus to making the westward move.

———

I found two employment opportunities in the Bay Area, pumping gas at a Standard Oil station or a training program at American Trust Bank. Before then I had never thought of banking as a career. At the time American Trust was looking to hire 50 people to rebuild its ranks after the war. I was offered the 49th slot, but at a substantial 30 percent cut in pay. At McCall's I was making the great sum of $7,200 a year, while the American Trust training position offered $5,000. Although it was a decrease in salary, I was hell-bent on moving to California.

Despite my longing to relocate, I did not accept the job immediately. My plans were met with a somewhat mixed review.

*Father had his doubts. He did not think a bank was the place
for a man with gumption and drive. He expected me to do
something meaningful, and he was convinced that a bank
would do little to foster my ambition.*

We discussed it back and forth for a few weeks, but he knew
that when my mind was made up, I could be bullheaded. Sheila,
now pregnant, was feeling uncertain about the move west and
the separation from her family and friends. She was young and
inexperienced when it came to putting her foot down with me.

It was at this time that a wonderful and unexpected safety
net arrived. Horace Flanigan, my friend Peter's father, was running Manufacturers Hanover Bank at the time. When he heard
of my plan to take the trainee position at American Trust Bank
in San Francisco, he offered to hire me at Manufacturers
Hanover for $50,000 a year. It was a huge sum of money and a
tremendous, tempting offer. Mr. Flanigan made few conditions
with his proposal, and in fact he left it open-ended. He told me
to take the position at American Trust, but if I did not like it,
or living on the West Coast, to call him and he would hire me.
With Mr. Flanigan's attractive safety net in my back pocket and
a young bride by my side, I took the job at American Trust
Company and we moved to San Francisco.

Before moving to San Francisco, Sheila and I took a six-week
vacation in Europe. I had convinced myself that if we did not get
to Europe before I started work in California and the baby
arrived, then we probably would never get another chance for a
very long time. I had saved $3,000, which was all we had, and
planned to spend it on the trip. I purchased a guidebook and
underlined everything. In my travel naiveté, I mapped out every
minute and calculated every stop so that we never spent more
than one or two days at a location. I tried to be sure we saw
everything important, but in the end the whole trip was a blur
because we had raced from place to place.

Our first stop was Rome, where we had the good fortune of meeting Pope Pius XII. Mrs. Harris, the wonderful family friend from Rye, had become acquainted with the Pope when he was a cardinal. Her husband, Basil, had been appointed to escort him around the United States when he visited in 1936. The trip covered a great deal of the country, from the Brooklyn Bridge to the Golden Gate Bridge. When Mr. Harris died in 1948, Mrs. Harris wanted to visit the Vatican and speak to the Pope. That is quite a feat, as the general public usually cannot get that close to the Pontiff, but because Pope Pius remembered his trip to the United States with Mr. Harris favorably, he graciously granted her an audience, and she took us with her.

We were taken to the Pope's office, where he was seated behind a little desk. The same desk where I knew he did his work and made a lot of his decisions. Mrs. Harris was crying and the tears were running down her face. She spoke to the Pope about her husband and he listened intently to every word. I too was crying, but with tears of joy. I observed the kindness that Pope Pius extended to Mrs. Harris, and then he turned to me and took my hand. He said a blessing and I could feel God's presence surging through me. Although the time spent in the Pope's company was probably no more than 10 or 15 minutes, it is something that I will never forget. It was so precious, like God was talking to us. Pope Pius noticed my arm and asked about it. Then he gave me a special blessing. It was one of life's great moments.

Sheila had suffered from morning sickness, but we both assumed she was over the worst of it and was fit to travel. After we left Italy, we were on our way to Austria and into Vienna and Salzburg. We were driving a European Ford that my brother-in-law Henry had arranged for us to use. The car did not have a lot of power, and we were trying to get over the Grossglockner Pass. The Austrian countryside was magnificent but rural, and I knew that if we had trouble crossing over the pass, it might be difficult to find help. Eventually I made the decision to turn

around and head back down. By this time Sheila was feeling
horrible, so we ended up in a chalet on a Tirolean hillside. Lienz
was the next closest town en route to Salzburg, but there was
little more than picture-perfect farmhouses along the way. At the
sight of an inn we pulled to a stop. No one spoke English except
for one woman in the area, and we communicated through her.
At that moment I cursed myself for opting out of my foreign
language class, as Sheila was getting worse by the minute.
The young woman who was acting as our interpreter called an
Austrian doctor, who arrived shortly after to examine Sheila.
He, too, was unable to speak English, though we were told
through our lone interpreter that she would be fine, although it
was imperative that she rest. For one week we stayed at the
chalet while Sheila regained her strength.

The main thing I remember about that week was there was
very little to do. While Sheila recovered, I walked the Tirolean
countryside, smiling at the locals, which seemed to suffice for all
those I encountered. Though I could not speak to anyone, I found
the people to be incredibly hospitable. As Sheila regained her
energy and her appetite returned, the only thing that tasted good
to her was chicken soup. This presented a small problem for the
owners of the chalet, as every day they had to go out to the coop
and kill one of their hens. It was a frightening time. We did
not know where we were or what we would find if a hospital was
needed. After a daily dose of soup and much rest, we left the
chalet. I don't suppose Sheila felt absolutely on top of things
when we drove away, but at least she could manage.

We returned to New York and prepared to move. Given
Sheila's condition, there was no question of her driving west with
me. Instead, I drove to St. Louis alone and stayed briefly with my
family that had moved there from Rye right after World War II.
In the latter part of July, my sister Ann drove with me to
San Francisco. I started work on August 1. Family and friends
were wonderful and helped in so many ways. When Sheila

arrived in mid August we were staying with my Uncle Wake and Aunt Maggie until we could find a place of our own.

Sheila was brave and gutsy. The last thing she remembered before leaving New York was her father saying to her, "Now Sheila, if I write you a letter, do you think you will get it?" For some older New Yorkers, the West begins when you cross the Hudson River.

When we arrived in San Francisco, the Phlegers were there to greet Sheila and me. The family relationship between the Phlegers and the Cooleys went way back. All through my father's life, Herman Phleger was his best friend. When I moved to San Francisco, Herman became a great friend to me. He was a director of the American Trust Company and gave me good advice as I joined that training program in August of 1949. All through my career he was very supportive. He was still on the board when I became the bank's chief executive. He was a strong man, the bank's lawyer, and no one challenged him very often. He told me when he got off the board, and his son Atherton went on, that Atherton would be a good friend and a big support to me, and he was right. Atherton was a member of the same camp I belonged to at the Bohemian Grove called Mandalay Camp. We saw each other more and more. He asked me to be godfather to his son Peter, which was an honor. Unfortunately Atherton became ill with cancer and did not survive it for more than a couple of years. I think about him all the time. He was even-minded, fair, bright, and an outstanding person. He is one of the people that I miss in life, and I pray for him every day as well as all his family. I am sorry that we did not get closer sooner, because my years with him were limited.

A FAMILY VACATION, CIRCA 1960, WITH MY CHILDREN,
FROM LEFT, SHEILA, PIERCE, AND LESLIE.

BECOMING A PARENT
AND A BANKER

I n August of 1949 I began a two-year training program at
American Trust Bank, California's second-oldest financial
institution. It was largely a retail bank, and every two or
three weeks, trainees would be sent to different departments or
branches, where we would learn the various functions of the
banking business. First stop was the collection department, then
the bond department, followed by the property division, and
so on until we had systematically gone through essentially all
the departments and received a general overview of the bank.
The theory was that if we were going to be branch managers, we
would need to know where everything was located and how it
was managed. After moving through the departments, I spent the
final year of training in the credit department learning about
the larger credits and how they were approved and cleared with
the board of directors.

The following year I became a junior loan officer, making
small commercial loans, and an assistant to the head loan officer,
Ransom Cook. This position would lay the foundation for a long
period of mentoring and a friendship that would mean a great
deal to me, both personally and professionally. I was his assistant
so I would do his flunky work, if he had any, and then he would
occasionally let me handle a small account. I remember there
was one person who came in who had a string of drive-in movie
theaters. He would always come in to see "Rans," and after their
visit Ransom would turn him over to me and I would get his
numbers and find out what he was doing. It was not big money,
but in banking you take care of your customers. It doesn't matter

if they are borrowing $25,000 or $500,000, you have to take care of everyone equally. I was called in for the small loans, but I did the paperwork for the larger loans. Most of my banking and business know-how came from Mr. Cook, who shared his knowledge and experience generously.

My bank responsibilities were clear, but what was expected of me at home was a different matter. We had a baby girl, Leslie, in 1950.

I was not only a new banker but also a new father. When Leslie would cry I would sometimes kneel outside her door and say the Rosary that she would stop crying. I had a lot to learn about both children and banking.

Two years later, on December 27, 1951, Richard Pierce Cooley Jr. was born. He was a natural athlete, but we were not able to understand his academic challenges until much later in his life, when more became known about dyslexia. He struggled. Sometimes it is hard for the son of a successful father to succeed. If I had been around more and traveled less, I might have helped him more. I never cared what career he chose as long as he was happy and was using his abilities as best he could.

Another two years passed. I was well up in the ranks of the bank managers. I traveled more and was home less when Sheila was born. Named after her mother, she was delivered one day after my birthday. She has become a hard worker, and my father always thought she was a star. She is a star. All of my kids are stars.

Long before I was in the upper management of the bank, a senior vice president asked to speak with me. I went to his office. "Dick," he said, "what do you know about the zoo?" I told him that I knew very little. In fact I was not that big on animals in general, having never had a pet growing up. He said, "We have had the zoo account for a long time, and they are looking for a treasurer. How would you like to be on the zoo board?"

I said, "Sure. Be glad to." Even though I did not have much experience with animals, I wanted to represent the bank and become a part of the community. It turned out that the zoo board was fascinating. It was composed of scientists and businessmen. The scientists worried about the care of the animals, how they developed, and everything to do with the biology of it, and the businessmen were interested in charging the right amount for the hot dogs, keeping the place clean and open, being sure that the admission fees were adequate, but not too much, and other issues of that sort.

The San Francisco Zoo was an interesting organization. Its board would meet one night a month. I learned a lot about animals and made many friends. One of the more interesting discussions we had was when one of the elephants became ill and the scientists knew he was not going to last very long. They decided they had to put him away because they did not want him to die on a Sunday afternoon with 150 schoolchildren watching. It was carefully thought out and I do not remember all the facts, but I do recall that it was a big deal deciding how to take the elephant down peacefully without upsetting anyone. They ended up giving him a sleeping sedative and then they put him away on a Monday night. I believe the zoo was closed that night so they were able to move him out without disruption, or an audience. It was a big concern for the board and some of it was over my head. The discussion helped me to understand the problems involved with keeping the animals healthy and maintaining a zoo that the city and county could be proud of, and the San Francisco Zoo was that kind of place.

The bank decided that I should continue working for Mr. Cook, but split my duties with Senior Vice President Harris Kirk. He was in charge of the bank's business all over the country.

At the time there was a growing feeling that someone young was needed to meet the up-and-comers in other banks and clients. I was selected for the position as I came from the East Coast and had connections that they hoped would promote strong ties and new business partnerships. That gave me two bosses, one who managed loans and the other who was in charge of business development. My job changed significantly. It involved a considerable amount of travel.

All through the 1950s I traveled through the Midwest and Northeast, calling on accounts in New York, Chicago, Detroit, Pittsburgh, or anywhere the bank had customers. The first title I received was assistant cashier, but as I traveled more they pushed me up to the rank of assistant vice president. This was not because I deserved it, but because I was representing the bank in different cities and they felt I needed a certain kind of title to get recognized. Eventually the assistant VP position turned into VP for the same reason. The bank had a load of vice presidents who had worked in the bank a lot longer and knew a lot more than I, but the title gave other banks and clients the impression that I was important enough to talk to.

Our national business was growing, so Mr. Kirk brought two more people into his department and divided the country into thirds. I was given the East Coast. Consolidating my focus helped me to develop a network, and I made connections with people in other banks with whom we could exchange business and share in large credits.

In the 1950s, banks depended on each other to arrange large loans. No single bank had a sufficient legal lending limit to handle the needs of the big national corporations. Bankers were more cautious then and more interested in spreading large risks. It sometimes would take 50 banks to join in one loan agreement to provide the credit needs of a big borrower like the Aluminum Company of America or General Motors. Our relationships with other banks in the country were key to being invited to participate in those large credits. Many of the large loans were initiated and managed by the big eastern banks that were better compensated than we were. The regional banks were able to get the scraps, the local accounts of those borrowers.

———————

During the late 1950s and all through the '60s, money was tight at home. Our family had grown and there seemed to be endless expenses, which were beginning to exceed our income. We discussed my leaving the bank and finding employment elsewhere that would meet more of our financial needs. At the time we had three children who were nearing school age. Private school was a strong consideration, but it was not in our budget. I did not have a clear idea of what else I could do, and Mr. Flanigan's safety net seemed a long way away. I had been working hard to build a career in banking and had no desire to start fresh somewhere else when I could see potential for management in the future. Still, something had to be done to supplement my income.

Sheila's older sister Ann was married to Henry Ford II. His father had died when he was 21, and he took over the Ford Motor Company. It was a tremendous responsibility for such a young man, but he worked hard and did a fine job managing the business. Henry was a humble and generous man. After he married Ann, he continued his kind ways by giving some of the older McDonnell children Ford dealerships. I discussed the topic with some of the fortunate siblings, and then I broached the subject with Henry.

I had only one conversation with him about my strategy, though he did not show much enthusiasm. Instead he gave me the name of a kind and wonderful man in San Francisco named Arthur Hatch. He was the West Coast regional sales manager for Ford. Soon after, it became apparent that Henry had given us an opportunity to create extra income from owning dealerships with no strings attached. His only desire was that we make money and operate the business with integrity. This chance to become monetarily solvent would not have been possible without the McDonnell connection with Henry Ford and Sheila's financial support in signing the guarantee, based on her modest family trust, for the necessary loan. If these two things had not happened, our lives might have played out in a totally different way.

Our first dealership was in the San Fernando Valley, in a town called Reseda. Mr. Hatch set us up with two experienced auto dealers in Los Angeles who had dealership operations in the area. Once a month I would go down to check on the dealership, and to learn as much as I could about the automobile business. During those years auto sales were profitable, so we eventually started a second one in Sacramento. Both of these dealerships were successful. Each dealership provided the Cooleys with a new demo car and a salary of $1,000 per month. That meant I was taking home $2,000 monthly from the dealerships and $1,000 from the bank. It seemed like an enormous sum and allowed me to keep up with the day-to-day expenses of running the household.

What a gift of gratitude I owe Henry Ford. Through his generous support I was able to continue my career working at the bank. Over those years I saw him occasionally and he never mentioned the dealerships, but we did talk about business. I will never forget some advice he gave me on one of our visits.

"Dick," he said, "everyone I work with is smarter than I am and I know it. That is fine with me, but when they want to do something, I make them tell me in five-letter words what it is they want to do and why. I don't approve anything unless I understand it."

In 1960, Wells Fargo President I. W. Hellman III and Harris Kirk negotiated the merger of Wells Fargo Bank with American Trust Company, and it became the 11th-largest banking institution in America. It was a time of adjustment for many reasons.

The merger was dominated by American Trust, which was a $1.7 billion bank, whereas Wells had assets worth $700 million. Harris Kirk became the president and chief executive officer of the new bank. With a clear majority on the board controlled by American Trust, the merged bank in time assumed the historic name Wells Fargo. At the time of the merger there were many excellent young employees at American Trust. Wells lacked young talent, sapped by the Depression and World War II, and they subsequently had not invested enough in training programs or people.

Not long after the merger Harris Kirk died, and Ransom Cook was next in line to become the bank's chief executive.

————————

One Friday morning Ransom sat me down and said, "Dick, you have to learn this business. There are not many people who are eligible for management, and all you have been doing is traveling. We need to put you in a training program." That training program began the following Monday morning, when I was told to report to the Matson branch office as its manager. Mr. Cook felt it was imperative that I learn the day-to-day operations and be aware of how the bank really worked.

I did not know how to balance the books or do much of anything. In those days bookkeeping was a laborious system of hand entries and punch cards. Computers had not yet been significantly employed by banks. Books had to balance to the penny every night, and we could not go home until the books balanced. I was fortunate to have a skillful assistant manager, James Houser, who knew the ins and outs of the operation, and he steadfastly taught me the ropes. The office was well managed before I arrived, and it was my job to learn how it worked, not to mess it up. Sometimes there was not a lot to do besides make sure clients felt that they were being cared for and their money was secure and that the staff was happy.

The Matson branch served as my classroom, and it was there that I began to understand management principles such as taking care of the customers, office policies, servicing accounts, and supervising employees.

At the time I supervised the Matson office, I did not fully understand that I was being groomed for top management. Still there were times when I sensed that there was some sort of design for my future. One such example came the day that Chase Manhattan's chairman, David Rockefeller, walked in and introduced himself to me. He had been told that I was showing promise and that he should make my acquaintance. Later, we would have more opportunities to meet, including a dinner he gave for me when I was promoted to chief executive officer and president. I was at the Matson branch for less than two years.

In 1964, Ransom Cook decided there was need for a reorganization of the bank. He restructured the branch system, separating it into three divisions: Metropolitan, Sacramento, and Valley. There was one manager for each division. The number of branches in each depended on the geography of the area. I was made head of the Metropolitan Division, which was the largest of the three. They moved me into the old Wells Fargo building and gave me a staff that managed business development, loans, operations, and property. It served as a mini-bank within a bank. Part of my job was to visit all the branches and call on customers, but mostly it was to work with our own people to make sure they understood the programs and that we were efficiently taking care of existing customers and growing with new business. I was young to have such a position, and everyone working for me was older and more experienced.

I managed the Metropolitan Division until Ransom Cook moved me back to the main office, where I was given responsibility for the Property Division. I was in charge of buying new branch sites, building, redecorating, and maintenance. This was considered a large part of the learning process by Ransom, who thought it was the only job in the bank where I would receive practical business experience making the sort of decisions that clients made with architects and contractors, choosing locations and negotiating prices. This, Cook reasoned, would help me to better relate to customers as well as learn about management.

I stayed as head of Properties for nine months before I became head of the bank's personnel department. There were a lot of technicalities that I needed to learn. We did not have unions at the time, but we still had to worry about our people and how they were doing their jobs, plus all other aspects of human resources. A year or so later, I also became the head of the branch divisions. Now I had the Metropolitan, Sacramento, and Valley districts reporting to me, while remaining as head of personnel. Early in 1965 my title was changed to executive vice president, and in 1966 I was elected to the board of directors. My future as a banker was cast.

INSPECTING AN ICE SCULPTURE OF WELLS FARGO'S
ICONIC STAGECOACH WITH ERNIE ARBUCKLE.

CEO

I n the 1950s and onward, the bank had a problem. Its senior managers were nearing retirement, and their juniors were young and mostly inexperienced. Survival came before succession planning, and during the Great Depression the bank was not hiring. During the war there was nobody to hire, so there was a decade-sized age gap in our management. As my boss got to be 65, there was no one there to take over. I was on a fast track, and I had run several different departments by then. I entertained clients several evenings each week. Sheila was wonderful with people, and she was great at entertaining. One day the boss told me, "People are defenseless against a young couple like you two . . . you have got to make friends." I began to meet people from all over the country.

When Ransom Cook became chief executive of Wells Fargo Bank American Trust Company in 1961, he and the board grew concerned about management succession. He was a fine, intelligent man, and he taught me almost everything I knew about banking. Like my father, he believed in succession planning from his first day on the job. The board tried to hire a New York banker who had roots in San Francisco to line up behind Mr. Cook. He turned them down. Then they tried to hire Tom Killefer, a Stanford graduate and a Rhodes Scholar, who was at the time Chrysler's chief financial officer. He also turned them down. At the time I did not think I was a candidate for the job, but Ransom asked me to talk with Killefer, whom I knew socially. I did, and when Killefer turned down the job, Ransom thought I had said something or in some way expressed an unwillingness to work with Killefer. That was not so, but for a time it put me in the doghouse with Mr. Cook.

If I had to do it all over again, I would go back into the banking business. It was a good place for someone like me whose talents are evenly distributed. I was just 40 when I became Wells' executive vice president, and a member of its board. The board put me in line to succeed Mr. Cook and Mr. Chase, but in 1965 they were not totally sure that I was ready. My boss, Ransom Cook, talked to me about becoming the bank's president and chief executive officer, and I told him that being president was enough. He said, "No, the board wants you to be the chief executive officer. They want to build for the future. I'm over retirement age and Steve Chase has only one year until retirement. I'll stick around for a year and Steve will probably stay for a year, and then you are on your own." That was fine.

The next conversation we had was about money. At the time I was making $50,000 a year being executive vice president. Mr. Cook told me that I would get a raise and go to $75,000, and that Steve Chase would be making $100,000 a year. He was making pretty close to that anyway, and I did not know what Ransom Cook would be making as chairman of the executive committee.

I told Ransom, "You do not have to make me chief executive officer. I'm happy to be president and I'll work just as hard, but if you make me chief executive officer, I think I should be paid as much as anyone in the bank, which means I should be paid $100,000 if that's what you're going to pay Steve."

Either way, it was a lot of money to me, but I just did not think I should be the bank's chief executive in name only, so to speak. The way you keep score is with your salary, and I would not be chief executive officer that way. I stuck to my guns and I think Ransom was a little surprised and miffed, but he talked with the board members, the compensation committee I suppose, and they decided that I would make the same salary as Steve.

The board named me president and chief executive officer in November 1966. Steve Chase became chairman. He was already 64, and they expected him to retire the following year. I was a young chief executive at the age of 42. When that change took place, Mr. Cook moved off the executive floor and upstairs to the boardroom floor, where he had a beautiful office. But he was by himself up there. He would be chairman of the executive committee for a year and then he would retire from that position. Steve Chase would become chairman of the board and would hold that position until retirement at 65, and then he would be gone. In the beginning I would be president and chief executive officer, and upon Steve's retirement, if everything went well, I would also become chairman of the bank's board.

It all seemed to happen quickly. One day they moved Mr. Cook upstairs and I moved into his old office, which was on the 12th floor of the old Wells Fargo headquarters. Imagine that. I did not know what to do, so I moved his desk from one side of the office to the other. I was sitting there trying to process the change. I was now running the regular meetings I had always attended. It was difficult, but I got along the best I could and tried not to make too many mistakes. I made some, but nothing disastrous. At the time the bank had assets of about $1.8 billion. In Northern California, Wells Fargo was second only to Bank of America in terms of size, and Wells was still the 11th-largest bank in the nation.

I remember that things changed and yet they didn't change. I cannot recall what day I was put in charge, but I remember sitting at Mr. Cook's desk. Ransom and Steve Chase were sitting there in the room, and three or four senior and executive vice presidents were also there. We were having a senior management meeting about buying bonds, and I was supposed to be in charge.

At the time I did not know much about buying bonds, so I was taking the advice of the senior bond officer, Dwight Chapman. He was a good man and he had been in the business for 40 years or more. He explained what we should do. People were asking questions. It was a swap, changing some maturities for others, and hoping interest rates would go a certain way and therefore we would make some money. I said that's fine, but did not have a clue what they were talking about. I trusted the men and the combined judgment of the group.

I had been working with all those people for years, but that day Mr. Cook took a seat at the back of the room and I took his desk. It was really something. Sweat rolled down my back. In fact, it rolled down my back for almost a full year, sitting in that office trying to be the chief executive with all these older people around me. No one was mean to me. Everyone was kind, but it was clear that I was not one of their group, and yet I had to do it. It was the hardest thing I had had to do as a banker. I never had confidence in it, but I just went along day to day. Eventually it worked out and I gained confidence in my abilities, and eventually I understood what needed to be done. Watching a chief executive officer lead and actually doing the job are two very different realities.

In addition to the small senior management meeting that took place in Mr. Cook's former office, we had a larger weekly management committee meeting downstairs in a larger room for roughly all the department heads, 25 or so people. Part of my job as the new chief was to run that forum. It was mainly for com-munication, so that all the managers would be aware of what was going on in the bank. It was another big sweat for me. After the first one was over, Mr. Cook took me aside and gave me a few ideas on how to improve. His net thought for me was to keep control of the responses and keep them moving. Not to let anyone drag it out and provoke questions that had to be answered, saving those for another more appropriate time. He thought that I had let it get away from me. He was correct. He told me that I needed to be more assertive with each person as we went around the table. That first time we ran 15 or 20 minutes over normal, but thanks to the criticism it did not happen again.

———————

Banking relationships led to personal friendships, and one example was Robert Watt Miller. He was chairman of the compensation committee. I had to go see him shortly after I became the chief executive. We were talking about some business deal for which I had to get his approval. Then we talked about his health, as he had a weak heart. When I went to see him, he had an operation scheduled at the end of the month. I was giving him a pep talk, telling him that I knew he'd be fine. He said, "No, I won't. I'm probably not going to survive this operation." He'd had problems before, and I think this was one of those operations that they had to try in order to save his life, but they could not guarantee that he would survive the operation. He was so brave about it. He had a feeling that he wouldn't survive, but he knew he had to do it. It seemed like such a paradox to me that he had to make that kind of decision. In the end, he did not survive. He had the operation and died on the table. He was so dignified and such an outstanding gentleman.

His son Dick Miller became one of my best friends in San Francisco. He was married to Ann Miller, and they had 12 children. Dick was godfather to one of my children, and I was godfather to one of his. We lived within a block of each other in San Francisco for many years, and he was always a good friend. Dick and Ann were both Catholics and very religious. When Dick was diagnosed with cancer, they took trips seeking cures and prayed, but nothing worked. Somewhere along the way they made a religious promise that after Dick died, Ann would enter the Carmelite convent in Illinois. Three years after Dick's death, with the children mostly grown, Ann entered the order and began to fulfill her promise to become a nun. Ann Miller was a live wire in San Francisco. She liked to run things. If it moved, she knew about it. If you needed to know someone, she knew them.

If you needed help, she could do it. She is the one who introduced me to Father Egon and got me started with Woodside Priory.

She was the only child of Donald Russell, who was head of the Southern Pacific Company for years and a dominant person in town as well. Ann had the ability and the foresight, and after Dick died she kept her vow. She had an enormous party just before she went into the convent, and there she has been ever since. People keep in touch with her. She doesn't seem to be totally cloistered since she is able to communicate with her children. Her mother was angry with her because she felt that Ann had all the children to take care of. Still, Ann entered the convent, and she went ahead to fulfill her promise. I have read about such promises in books, but this is the only example I've seen in real life of someone's commitment to God. Very moving.

I'm not a good godfather because I cannot remember who they all are, other than that they are children of the Phlegers, the Millers, the Kilduffs, the Willoughbys, and others. I became a godfather because a lot of people we knew were Catholic but did not move in Catholic circles. In a sense I became a link to the Church. There were not that many people they could ask to be a Catholic godfather for their children. I think that is one way I got to have so many, because some of these families that I became involved with as a godfather were not that close. I understand the situation. We had the same problem when looking around with some of ours. If they weren't Catholic, they couldn't become a godparent, so that made it difficult sometimes to come up with the right people. I pray for them as a group each day. I pray that they know God and love God and that God gives them the gift of faith and blesses them in their lives.

A year later, Ransom and Steve Chase retired on schedule, and the title of chairman was added to my office. I immediately started to search for a new chairman. I was uneasy with the directors and wanted someone older than I was to take the job, and that was when I got Ernie Arbuckle to join the bank's board. He was an incredible person who had been in business in San Francisco for a long time and had many friends on the board. Ernie was finishing 10 years as dean of the Stanford Business School. He had a theory about staying too long in one job. After 10 years in a position, he thought, you might be getting stale and should seek another challenge. It was his "repotting idea," and that was why he was leaving the Stanford Business School. He had committed to the position for 10 years and that was it. Initially, he turned down my offer because he had already accepted another position, but that fell apart for some reason, so he came back six months later and asked if the chairman position was still open. I could not have been more pleased.

I hired Ernie Arbuckle at exactly my salary for several reasons. We were going to be partners, and I never wanted monetary means to become a factor in our partnership. I was the bank's chief executive officer, but it was understood between us that his help with the board and the general business community would be important to my success and the success of the bank. Ernie was a great cushion between my office and the board. The directors were older than I was, and they were clearly watching to see how I was progressing. Ernie became a good friend. He was a fine man and helped me all the way through. I tried to make sure that I never made any big decisions without talking to him first because I wanted him to feel that he was always important. I figured he would go if he did not feel he was needed. He was good at dealing with people, and that was not always easy for me. He was on several outside boards and was in a great position to advise me on many things that came up and on matters in which I had little or no experience. He attracted people from Stanford, giving us access to the best people that the Business School produced. We put a lot of them to work, sometimes hiring them without even knowing what they would do.

*We just wanted good people and we had this particular
pipeline, which I think made the bank.*

———————

It was one thing to acquire a stream of young talent from
Stanford, or anyplace else, but it was another thing to utilize,
challenge, and keep them. As I have said elsewhere, commercial
banks often behave like a herd of sheep. They operate in the
same bureaucratic manner, and when something new is started,
they often ape each other in following a trend. As the money
center banks began to do more international business, they
sought clients from the larger regional banks around the country.
This posed a threat to the regional banks' major accounts, which
resulted in the regionals establishing offices in places like
London, Tokyo, and New York. In a few years there were more
American banking offices in these key international cities than
there was business to support them and allow them to be profitable. At the peak of this trend, there were 144 American
banking offices in London. There are other examples of this
herdlike behavior in the 1960s and 1970s.

However, there was one thing that became clear. The old
stuffy ways of banking were beginning to loosen up, particularly
as deregulation appeared on the horizon. To keep up with the
opportunities, and with the competition, a successful organization needed new ideas and new minds. That is how we sought to
use the new talent that came our way. There were better ways to
run the bank and newer ways to help our customers. With technology advancing at such a pace, there were infinite possibilities
to offer new products that could help and benefit our clientele.

One concept that appealed to me was the mathematical
computerized approach to investing. We were able to attract
some of the early researchers in the index fund field and produce
significant index-type investment products. I have always been
intrigued by good ideas, and I found their research totally con-
vincing. Some of our directors were not as enthusiastic, holding

firmly to the idea that superior investment counselors could always outperform a computerized program over time. That did not turn out to be true, and the bank did well on its indexing products. Ernie was open to new ideas as well. I think the young people who came to us felt that Wells was a place where creativity was welcomed and encouraged. That may have helped us keep the talent that we were able to attract. We wanted to challenge them, and I think the kind of people who came our way responded well. As commercial banks were tightly regulated, there were clear restrictions that limited what could be done. Still, within that framework there were many possibilities for new ideas and ways of doing business.

Most banks watched their published quarterly reports carefully. The growth in deposits, loans, and assets always got close attention. Earnings were important, but often did not seem to get the attention that growth did.

As the quality of earnings came under analytical scrutiny, some banks began to look at it more carefully. Wells was one of them, empowered by the young MBAs. They thought of banking more as a business, not a profession. This began to have a positive effect on our costs and budgeting.

We were willing to take risks if the idea was good enough. It was another area where good and imaginative thoughts were received and welcomed.

———

Perhaps it was Sheila's need to fill space left in her life as I spent more time tending to the bank, or maybe it was just God's will, but as my tenure in the bank's management started, we had a fourth child, Sean. He is now in his mid-forties and works in commercial real estate. He has done well, and if I had to guess, I would say he has done better financially than anyone else in the family, including me. The current real estate market has been hard on him, but he will be successful as the cycle evolves.

Then shortly into my term as Wells' chief executive came another son, Mark Cooley, in 1964. He went to Robert Louis Stevenson School. He was goal directed and capable from the start. He graduated from the University of California-San Diego, and shortly thereafter received his MBA at Santa Clara University.

With the added pressures of the chief executive's job, I became tense and unhappy, and I began to consider a divorce. Sheila did not want the divorce. She did not believe in it. I did not believe in it either, but I felt strongly pressured by Sheila, the family, and my job, and I was struggling to keep everyone happy. Gradually the bank and the business became the enemy to her, and when I began to run the place, I turned into the enemy. We had a difficult time. I had been traveling a great deal, and she seemed to think that I was being urged to work hard by senior management. In fact I was pressuring myself to do my best. She may have hoped that there would be more time for the family when I ran the bank. That was not going to be the case. I probably worked longer hours and traveled just as much or more.

If I could relive those years, I would not have divorced her. I would have learned to live with the situation and become more accepting. Even though I told myself that family comes first, looking back, it hardly seems true. I was selfish and self-directed, and I would be better about that. I would be more patient and not so gung-ho for my work that I did not fully experience my children. I made sure they attended good schools and all those things, but I missed being a scoutmaster or a soccer coach. I wanted my own life, and I did what I thought I had to do to manage the business. I did not want it to run me. It was like holding the tail of a tiger, and I did not want to live that way. I wanted to control it. I could not imagine failure. Failure was the worst thing. I could not accept that. In a general sense I had never not succeeded at anything that I tried hard to achieve, and I was not about to start with the bank. It was another example of having a big responsibility too early in life. No one should take a job like that when there is a young wife and five children at home.

After 20 years of marriage, Sheila and I went in different directions. I became head of the Wells Fargo Bank and was busy with that. In the matter of expectations, there was a lot left to be desired, both at home and at work. The combination of the two things was very difficult. When it got to be too much, or when I thought it was too much, I decided to leave. It was not a good decision for any of us. Sheila died in 2008. I never had the opportunity to tell her how in retrospect I felt about our marriage, and that for all those years she was a key part of my daily prayers.

———————

Putting the customer first implies many things. It sounds like an oxymoron for a large retail bank, but it is not. When one truly commits the total thrust of an organization to always putting the customer first, many choices are made, some of which may not seem to benefit the shareholder or the staff. It is possible to make compromises on corporate activities that seem to favor the customer, but may not do so in certain circumstances. At Wells, and afterward at Seafirst, putting the customer first always seemed the best way to go for me. While for a time, one or two of the other stakeholders might have appeared to be hurting under this policy, in the end all of the bank's constituents benefited.

Generally at Wells, we started the week with a management committee meeting. It was held around the meeting table in my office. There were usually the various division heads plus the chairman, vice chairman, and president — all of whom had their offices on the executive floor. We would talk about the state of each section of the business so everyone would be aware of what was happening throughout the bank. It was important for communication, but also for dealing with the problems and challenges facing us. Sometimes decisions were easily made and sometimes not.

When there were different approaches to be considered, I would speak last and either make the decision there and approve the course of action to be taken, or put it off until we had more information and could find a better way to attack the problem. The chief executive makes those decisions.

We tried to adjourn that meeting before 10 o'clock, after which everybody could retire to the coffee room, where other staff members would join us. The coffee room provided an informal way of communicating and keeping everyone on the same page. It was also a place where we could introduce new and/or special people to the group. Occasionally we used the time and place to be sure that some of our most important customers could meet other members of the senior management. There was no espresso, or fancy coffee carts, as this was basically in the 1970s, before the Starbucks culture took over.

The rest of the morning would be devoted to one-on-one meetings with various division heads concerning things relating to their particular business. Typically before lunch, corporate people might bring customers by my office to meet the "boss," or it might be a branch manager from downstate with some people important to him. The chief executive officer's job requires a lot of meeting and greeting all kinds of people who are working for or with the bank. Almost every lunch was taken up with an occasion of this sort. Usually we would take them to a local luncheon club for businesspeople.

Dinner entertaining was different — more expensive and time consuming — and good restaurants were used. In the early days of my banking career there was considerable lunchtime drinking, but it was gradually phased out in the '70s and '80s. Even VIP dinners became more subdued, with cocktails and dinner followed by coffee and going directly home. Occasionally we would go to the theater or a baseball game after an early dinner, which was usually good fun. The West Coast was more laid back than the New York area, where the evenings were more formal and structured. In the West we did more home entertaining than they did in the East. On the weekends there were golf games and socializing at your club.

Back at the office after lunch, you might be lucky enough to have some personal time to catch up on your phone calls and correspondence. Sitting down with your assistant and going over what was happening that week was important. For the rest of the afternoon, your schedule would be full of various appointments with people who had called and were given time by the most important person in the office — your skillful assistant. Though it did not necessarily happen on Mondays, there would often be some committee meeting scheduled outside the bank for one of the community nonprofits like United Way. After that, if you were fortunate, you could take the briefcase full of necessary reading and go home for the evening.

The above was a typical day. On other days of the week there were meetings for specific purposes such as going over the company budget or reviewing the controversial or larger loans. Almost every week there would be a short trip away from the office that would take the entire day. Sometimes there were banking association meetings, or sometimes it would be customer calling with some of our people. The longer trips east or overseas would take more time, and you might be gone for a week to 10 days. Many people thought that bank chief executive officers and presidents did too much traveling. It was thought that they should stay home more and tend to their local knitting. I was as guilty as any, and in fact I traveled extensively trying to expand our international and foreign connections.

Fortunately we had strong division heads running their business sections successfully, and we had a superb operations head in Jim Dobey, who was the number-three person in the bank after Ernie and myself. Jim had started out in the branches after World War II, and he was a tower at successfully managing bank branches and also became an excellent loan officer. He was one of the 50 trainees hired after the war. His judgment was very good and was based on years of experience. When I was away, I had complete confidence in Jim making the day-to-day decisions for the company. To run any large organization, you need to have good people and then stay out of the way and let them do their job.

Banking is a people business. Whether it is a group of employees or an important customer, you spend your day talking to people. That is why successful bankers have to be high-energy people. Each day your calendar is filled up like that of a lawyer or doctor. There is little time to think, as each unallocated time slot will be filled by your assistant, who knows about your relationships with the various people who want to see you. That is why having an intelligent, detail-oriented assistant is key to your ability to use your time wisely. It is also why I have made it a point to get to know the assistants of my peer group. These remarkable, talented people are the ones who allocate the majority of a chief executive's time. If you need to get something important done, and have to presell a new idea or project, you always run it by the assistant for input on the appropriate way to proceed.

Each month there was the regular board meeting and the committee meetings that accompanied it. We would prepare carefully for those meetings, as they often represented a complete review of the business for the directors. We would practice our presentations after taking great care with the making of the various agendas. The directors were our bosses and we treated them accordingly. One of our more important and senior directors was Ed Littlefield. He was chairman of the compensation committee, a job he seemed to like and one I found hard to rotate him out of, which made him a very important director.

In general, Ernie and I liked to rotate the board members through all of the committees so they would each have a good general grasp of our business. Also, we did not want anyone to have an overly strong hold on any one part of the bank's management. As I have said elsewhere in this book, all directors should be equal. Ed was bright and highly respected in the business community, and having sold his company to General Electric, he had become the largest individual shareholder of that company. Occasionally there was a conflict in the dates of those meetings, and Ed told me that if I wanted him to come to the bank's meeting, it had better be more interesting and thought-provoking than the GE board meeting agenda.

Board meetings can be dull and uninteresting, particularly when they don't make use of the experience and intelligence of the directors attending.

(I have sat through many of them.) It was a good wake-up call, and we tried hard to have each meeting be informative and clearly describe what was going on in the bank's world so the directors would go away having learned something useful and interesting that they might apply to their businesses. We also tried to find ways to tap into their expertise to solve problems that were not clear or easy for the bank to fix. They had to feel that they were needed and that they were contributing.

I always tried to have a one-on-one breakfast or lunch with each director a minimum of once a year. It was a time to find out what they were thinking about, which perhaps would not have come up in the meeting itself. Certain directors are uneasy bringing up controversial points of view in a setting with their peers, but they will level with you when it is just the two of you.

You work for the directors. Any chief executive officer forgets that at his or her own peril.

The board meeting used to be on a Tuesday morning. After the meeting the directors and senior staff would lunch together in the board dining room. When the lunch was over and things had gone as planned, I would go back to my office and breathe a big sigh of relief. It was like I had passed an examination and could feel secure in my job for another month.

When you are in the midst of making daily decisions as chief executive, you sometimes cannot see how it will play out, but you know that it is the best for the company now and in the future. Years after I left Wells, I read *Good to Great*, a book written by Jim Collins. It was first published in 2001, and it has stayed on the business bestseller list for a very long time. Collins mentions the companies that possess Level 5 Leadership. A Level 5 leader, according to Mr. Collins, is a person who is very humble, but has the indomitable urge to succeed and who is perseverance personified. When you put those two attributes together, according to the book, it leads to greatness in leadership. A great leader, according to Collins and his research team, is self-effacing, quiet, reserved, even to the point of being shy. "The good-to-great leaders never wanted to become larger-than-life heroes. They never aspired to be put on a pedestal or become unreachable icons."

Collins picked 11 core companies out of thousands that over a 15-year period maintained a good-to-great standard. Wells Fargo was one of them, but Collins picked a period after I retired, so I did not get or deserve credit for it. Carl Reichardt put it together and did it. The Collins team took those companies that were selected and compared them to another competitive company. The companies they chose to highlight were Abbott, Circuit City, Fannie Mae, Gillette, Kimberly-Clark, Kroger, Nucor, Philip Morris, Pitney Bowes, Walgreens, and Wells Fargo. The match for Wells was Bank of America for the study.

Collins found that "Wells Fargo began its 15-year stint of spectacular performance in 1983, but the foundation for the shift dates back to the early 1970s, when then-CEO Dick Cooley began building one of the most talented management teams in the industry (*the* best team, according to investor Warren Buffett). Cooley foresaw that the banking industry would eventually undergo wrenching change, but he did not pretend to know what form that change would take. So instead of mapping out a strategy for change, he and chairman Ernie Arbuckle focused on 'injecting an endless stream of talent' directly into the veins of the company. They hired outstanding people whenever and wherever they found them, often without any specific job in mind. 'That's how you build a future [Cooley said]. If I'm not smart enough to see the changes that are coming, these people will. And they'll be flexible enough to deal with them.'"

Collins noted, "Cooley's approach proved prescient. No one could predict all the changes that would be wrought by banking deregulation. Yet when these changes came, no bank handled those challenges better than Wells Fargo. At a time when its sector of the banking industry fell 59 percent behind the general stock market, Wells Fargo outperformed the market by over three times."

Collins interviewed a former president of Ford Motor Company and a longtime director of Wells, Arjay Miller, who found the Wells Fargo management team to be similar to Ford's "Whiz Kids" who had been recruited right after World War II. "Wells Fargo's approach was simple: You get the best people, you build them into the best managers in the industry, and you accept the fact that some of them will be recruited to become CEOs of other companies." Bank of America recruited so many Wells Fargo executives during its turnaround in the late 1980s that people inside began to refer to themselves as "Wells of America."

"Carl Reichardt, who became Wells' CEO in 1983, attributed the bank's success largely to the people around him, most of whom he inherited from Cooley," concluded Collins. "As he listed members of the Wells Fargo executive team that had joined the company during the Cooley-Reichardt era, we were stunned. Nearly every person had gone on to become CEO of a major company: Bill Aldinger became the CEO of Household Finance, Jack Grundhofer became CEO of U.S. Bancorp, Frank Newman became CEO of Bankers Trust, Richard Rosenberg became CEO of Bank of America, Bob Joss became CEO of Westpac Banking (one of the largest banks in Australia) and later became dean of the Graduate School of Business at Stanford University — not exactly your garden variety executive team."

Paul Hazen was also part of our management team during my tenure. He was a little younger than the others, and he succeeded Carl as Wells' chief executive in 1995.

"They stick with what they understand and let their abilities, not their egos, determine what they attempt." So wrote Warren Buffett about his $290 million investment in Wells Fargo despite his serious reservations about the banking industry.

The lessons that Jim Collins and his team analyzed and wrote about were good ones. They make sense and are well worth studying and using. That is why the book stayed on the top of the bestseller lists for so many years.

When you sit in the chief executive chair, you make decisions. You make the best ones you can. Rarely is it easy or black and white. A chief executive makes those decisions and lives by them.

If your judgments are half right, you are probably pretty successful. I used to agonize over my choices, but now I realize you have to make a lot of decisions if you are running an organization.

You cannot worry about what others think, or the consequences of crossing someone, because inevitably you will. It is human nature to want others to respect and approve your judgment in management, but being in charge means setting the tone and making decisions for the good of the company. You make big choices about buying millions of dollars' worth of bonds and hope that the interest plays will be favorable to you.

That is a big decision, but there can also be a decision on what color the new decoration in the coffee room should be. Silly things like that. You decide too much, in my opinion.

Sometimes there are contemporaries in the bank who offer good advice on how to handle a certain situation. There are also associates who would rather have you make any questionable decision so they will not have to. Making these choices can rattle nerves when you are only 42 years old. That is how I started out as president and chief executive of Wells Fargo Bank.

My first major decision after becoming chief executive officer was to expand the bank to Southern California. It seemed to me and to my confreres, the younger part of bank management, that we had to expand our territory south in order to compete statewide. Besides, there was a lot more money and economic activity in the southland. We had always been one of the top banks in Northern California, and our principal competition was Bank of America, which was the largest bank in both ends of the state. Security Pacific was ranked number two in the South, and Wells Fargo was ranked number two in the North. At one point we started merger talks with Security Pacific in an effort to provide statewide competition for Bank of America. When we got to a discussion of feasibility with lawyers, they told us that the antitrust department of the federal government would not allow it. Likely, Bank of America would see that such a merger did not happen. We dropped that idea and continued on alone, planning to build slowly and methodically, one branch at a time. But we knew that de novo banking would be expensive.

Early in 1967, we made the decision to open a branch on Pershing Square, in the heart of downtown Los Angeles. Wells Fargo has long had its stagecoach trademark, so we took the coach down and rode around the square in our stagecoach wearing western hats. The little bank branch opened in a modest locale,

CLOCKWISE FROM TOP: TV ACTOR JAMES DRURY OF *The Virginian;*
HOLLYWOOD ACTOR DALE ROBERTSON; JACK BREEDEN;
DICK COOLEY; AND WELLS FARGO MANAGER BRAD DAVIS.

not classy at all and with little business to speak of, but it gradually grew into something. I remember one of the directors said to me, "Dick, this is going to take you 15 years before this becomes anything at all. Hope you do not lose your shirt in the process." We knew that it would take a long time to get off the ground, but we had to start. We did not think it would be a profitable thing, but we thought for the growth and future of the bank in the decades ahead, we simply had to be in both ends of the state.

We had begun what would be an expensive de novo plan for developing a system of 50 branches in Southern California when we had an opportunity to purchase Los Angeles-based First Western Bank & Trust. It had 54 branches in Southern California and assets of about $1.1 billion. It was owned by World Airways, and bank regulators had ruled that banks could no longer be owned by nonbanks. At the time we had assets of not quite $8 billion, and most of our 285 branches were in Northern California. It could have been a great marriage for Wells, but the Department of Justice denied the union, claiming the merger would reduce competition in both lending and customer service. Had it been completed, it would have been one of the largest mergers in U.S. banking history.

Although de novo banking was expensive, it turned out to be a good plan 40 years later. But those early years were hard. I can remember that decision, which was approved by the younger people and worried about by the board and the older management. It was something that we thought was inevitable. During my early years as president and chief executive officer, we kept looking around for new merger candidates that might pass the antitrust tests, as well as new branch locations. Some people in San Francisco did not think much of Los Angeles in those days, but on the other hand, it was an economic powerhouse. LA was where it was all happening. People in San Francisco were more conservative and not quite as open as they have since become.

Moving south was probably the biggest decision that I made. Mr. Cook and Mr. Chase were not enthusiastic at this stage of their careers, but the idea was well supported by the younger bank managers. Although it was challenging and difficult to launch, it was a strategically positive move. Today the bank is well established in both markets, and it offers strong competition to all the other banks.

California's growth over that period far exceeded the vision we had when we started. The growth of the bank was a combination of mergers and de novo branching that is too lengthy to detail here. We needed more capital, more people, and a tremendous amount of energy to keep up with the opportunities in Southern California. It was exciting and stimulating and demanded much hard effort from all involved.

As we built the branch system, we had another major problem — senior management and representing the bank to the Southern California community. In our corporate business we already had many important customers in the area that we serviced out of San Francisco. We needed to build on that base and be able to service that business in the south. A very senior presence was required as we began to build a Southern California headquarters. Jack Breeden, who ran our corporate business from San Francisco, volunteered to go to Los Angeles as our executive vice president in charge of Southern California operations. Jack took early retirement when he turned 60, moved to Hawaii, and for a time worked there as a consultant. Years later his place was taken by Bill Barkan. He took early retirement after a medical scare.

Carl Reichardt, having joined Wells Fargo & Company to start our Real Estate Investment Trust business (REIT) in 1979, was made president of the bank. He had grown up in the south, working primarily for Union Bank. He knew Southern California well, and as a potential successor to me, we wanted to move him north so he could become familiar with both ends of the state.

To accomplish that and to convince people in the south that Wells Fargo was serious about becoming part of the community, I moved myself to Wells' Southern California headquarters, though the bank's headquarters remained in San Francisco. By 1980 we had 383 branches statewide, and 125 of them were in Southern California. Carl moved to SFO as president. He was ranked fourth in executive management, behind myself, Ernie, and Jim Dobey, who was vice chairman.

While I was officially in Los Angeles, I usually spent two days a week in my San Francisco office, which meant constant travel back and forth. I bought a home on the beach in Orange County, and the bank provided me with an apartment in San Francisco. Getting to know people in the south was a challenge. Bank of America's chairman lived in Los Angeles. Security Pacific was second in size to Bank of America in the Southern California market, and always a possible merger consideration for Wells, but we were starting from scratch. Our competitors were already entrenched. The Southern California market became a tremendous source of deposits, and there were many opportunities to loan money. I went on the boards of the symphony and the County Museum of Art, as well as a few others. Civic dinners in Los Angeles were as important as in San Francisco if not more so, leaving me plenty to do.

Looking back on it over four decades, I know that it was the right choice and one that ensured the future of Wells Fargo & Co. As I mentioned earlier, chief executive officers make a lot of decisions, some good and some bad. If you make some important ones right over time, the mistakes will not kill you. I will forever be grateful and glad that we moved to Southern California when we did.

DESCENDING THE STAIRS FROM A HILL OVERLOOKING HONG KONG
IN THE COMPANY OF IAC REPRESENTATIVES IN 1971.

INTERNATIONAL INTEREST AND INVESTMENTS

N ew York City banks traditionally handled international transactions, but as businesses grew in the West, Wells Fargo accounts more often needed services that required international banking relationships. In the beginning we would fulfill these needs through Citibank or Chase, but as the volume of this business increased, we looked to establish our own international banking connections. Wells was not alone in banking beyond U.S. borders. Bank of America and others were also shunning the costly services of New York banks, choosing instead to establish their own relationships.

———

Carlos Rodriguez Pastor was our man at Wells Fargo in the International Division. He had been the finance minister of Peru, but then his politics got caught in Latin American volatility and he had to leave the country permanently. During this period he began to explore the possibility of working in the U.S. financial sector. It happened to be good timing for Wells, as we were in a building mode internationally, and we hired him. Carlos was experienced, and because of his numerous connections all over the world, he could open doors anyplace in Europe or Latin America. He also could play the piano beautifully, and everyone enjoyed his company.

Through Carlos we got to know Miguel de la Madrid. He was a senior credit manager at the Banco de Mexico, the Mexican central bank. We visited him regularly and watched as he advanced politically in the PRI, the dominant political party in

Mexico at that time. It seemed like a short time before he
became his party's leading candidate, and ultimately president of
the country. Carlos felt that Miguel de la Madrid would be the
candidate who would clean up the corruption in Mexico.

How much he accomplished in his six-year term I am not
sure, but I liked him a great deal. He was personable and well
educated and the only president of a foreign country I have had
the pleasure of meeting. One evening we were invited to his
house for dinner, and we ate around the table with his family.
Everyone was speaking Spanish except me. Miguel spoke English
well, as he had gone to graduate school at Harvard. Although I
do not know for sure, as I did not follow his presidency closely,
I do not recall any horrendous media stories during his term.
Miguel was a gracious, intelligent, and sincere man.

When Miguel de la Madrid became president, Carlos took
me down for the inauguration. We liked the fact that Miguel
would be the president, as we thought he was a competent tech-
nocrat more than an old-style PRI politician. We were eager to
support his efforts. As we went through the reception line, he
was speaking in Spanish to hundreds of his guests. When it came
my turn to shake his hand, he shifted over to English and said
warmly, "Hello, Dick. I'm so glad you came down." Out of that
mass of people, he recognized me and made the adjustment to
speak English. It was something that I will not forget. I have
always prayed for his success in running the country, and even
though he is no longer in office, I have not stopped.

There was a time when Carlos thought doing business in
Spain would be a good connection for our Latin American business. He hired a young, attractive, well-connected man in Madrid
to represent us. Our new young man was a cousin of King Juan
Carlos. In 1976, a trip to Spain was arranged, and Carlos and I
went to Madrid to make ourselves known to the bankers and the
business community. It was the only time I have ever been
there, and it was memorable because of our new representative.

Amidst the regular calling, he arranged a personal visit with the king for the three of us.

The king and queen were popular there, and were considered to be doing a good job. We were invited to go to the palace in the late morning for coffee and a personal visit. When we arrived we were taken upstairs to a large room that had the appearance of a comfortable family room here in the United States. There was a large chaise against the wall in front of which was a wooden coffee table. Two easy chairs were at each end of the coffee table.

After we were ushered in, the king arrived from the opposite side of the room, informally attired in short sleeves, with a smile and a welcome in English. He sat in one of the easy chairs, was relaxed, and appeared to enjoy seeing us. Having his cousin there seemed to give the visit a pleasant family tone. He wanted to know about the bank and what we were hoping to do there. No problems of state came up, and the time passed easily as we had our coffee. He was cordial and friendly, and you could not help but like him. That was more than 30 years ago, and it gave me a good feeling to see his picture with Queen Sofia in the *New York Times* in more recent years. Whatever political problems they are having in Spain right now, they still have their popular king and queen.

I have always found that smaller, more intimate groups suit my personality better. I was never good at going through a cocktail party and shaking hands with everyone in the room, and I never found small talk particularly captivating. I know it is a technique that you can learn, but it has never been my style. I would get someplace and start talking to someone and stay there. I was always better at standing in one place and visiting with whoever was around me. Having a good conversation was easier and more pleasing than moving about the room.

You meet a lot of people in the course of a career. One of the basic things in life is the wonderful people you encounter along the way.

Some may be around for a while and then they tend to fade. What I have found to be true is that even the richest man in the world may be grumpy in the morning. You cannot be a star every day. If you are in a position in life where you meet many people, it does not change anything unless you find each other agreeable and you do things together as friends.

The mere fact that someone is famous does not make that person more of a human being.

One memorable occasion took place when David Rockefeller offered to host a business dinner for me in New York City. I was both flattered and pleased. The impetus behind the dinner was that I was a young bank president and he wanted his bank, Chase, to be our principal New York bank. He informed me that there would be several important executives there, but I told him that I would rather have a smaller dinner with some people he found interesting. That might have surprised him because I am sure he probably had to organize this type of dinner every night of the week. David invited his wife and daughter, the president of Rockefeller University, a few professors, and the U.S. Secretary of Health, Education and Welfare, John Gardner. They were all fascinating people in their own right.

The dinner was held at one of his old New York clubs. It was the kind of place that would not make the newspapers. New York has many such clubs that people do not know about where families who have lived there a long time can have a private place to entertain. It is not that it was so fancy, although it was a fine place and the food was very good, but the protocol is the same. If your manners have been taught to you by your mother, then you can enjoy these events and be at ease. David Rockefeller was always to be found at the upper level of things, so for him to have a dinner for me was quite an honor. I hope he enjoyed himself, because it was not just another bank dinner. Maybe he was glad to find someone who wanted to do something different. David was a kind man and for me, this evening was most enjoyable.

David Rockefeller and Walter Wriston of Citibank ran the two largest banks in New York, and they were known to compete. Everyone liked David Rockefeller, although some did not think he was the same caliber of businessman as Walter Wriston. Regardless, David Rockefeller was an impressive man who was known by kings and queens, and all the Saudis. On the international scene he was without a peer and enormously well regarded as a person. David spent much of his time as chief executive officer of Chase making connections for the bank. Wells Fargo had a long-standing relationship with Chase by then, and David's interest in our West Coast bank was gratifying for us.

Walter Wriston wanted his bank to be successful, and he was more aggressive about it than Chase. He decided that Citibank had made a mistake when it started in the credit card business with the Everything Card, and he made a classic Wriston move. He did not stick with something simply because he had created it. The Everything Card was not a good name. It did not work for Citibank, so he made a 180-degree turn. He decided to dump it and asked to join our MasterCard Association. That was fine. We were glad to have Citibank.

Our bank had started MasterCard with three other California bank partners to compete with BankAmericard, Bank of America's early Visa card. Jack Elmer of Wells was the organizer of the original MasterCard, and he ran the project with the three partner banks, Security Pacific, Bank of California, and Crocker.

By the time the research, planning, and organization were done, we had 70 banks belonging to the MasterCard Association. Adding the biggest bank in New York to the association increased our critical mass, and we welcomed Mr. Wriston's interest and Citibank.

Asia became another part of my global banking experience. In 1965, when the board decided to make me the head of the bank, they put me in a special training program. It was during this time that Mr. Cook took me and our wives to Europe so introductions could be made to the proper bankers in London, Paris, and elsewhere. He also took me to Japan to visit the bankers there, introducing me as the man who would succeed him. That was the old-fashioned way, but it was important in building relationships and keeping the bank's connections intact.

In 1965 I started going regularly to Tokyo and Osaka. Those were the two principal cities, but I also went to Nagoya and Kyoto to see the temples, plus the traditional tea service and how it was performed. For 20 years I made business trips to Japan. The bank had a small office in Tokyo. It was not quite as successful for the bank as they had hoped. Unfortunately, it was another example of bankers acting like sheep and falling into the herd mentality. If one bank decides to go in a certain direction, the rest tend to follow. If one decides that it is important to establish a business office in London or Tokyo, then they all set up an office. Often there is not enough business to support everyone. Being a West Coast bank, we had customers who did business in Japan and we wanted to serve them. The Bank of America was everywhere, so we were trying to hold on to our customers and compete with them. We thought it was something we should do, but it did not work out well, and was eventually sold to a Swedish bank.

The Tokyo office had only four people, one American and the rest Japanese. One of the men in the office was an old Japanese fighter pilot named Sidney Shimizu. He had been shot down five times in World War II. His English was excellent, as was his knowledge of Japanese banks. He arranged everything and would accompany me wherever I went.

The Japanese trips were always business related. There was an interpreter on each call, and as it turned out, there was more calling on banks than corporate calling. If the bank had an important relationship with a client, they would entertain them. If you had 10 major banks that you were dealing with, most would entertain you, particularly as a new young bank president. Not only were you entertained graciously, but there also were welcoming gifts. In time they got over that, but during my early years in Japan it was still very much a part of the protocol.

I was told by Mr. Cook that I should always bring bottles of Johnny Walker Black Label. Recently, I was told by a Japanese friend that that preference was still alive and well in his country. Since that is what they liked, I brought some with me on each trip. It was a courtesy. They used to say that Japanese bankers did not make a lot of money, but they had a huge expense allowance because they ate most of their dinners on bank money. All the entertaining was a large part of their job. They would get home late, and that was viewed as normal as their wives ran the households.

One of the interesting aspects of their traditional entertaining was the dinners. They were always formal and lengthy. We would go into a private room in a restaurant and sit across the table from the man who was hosting the dinner. He would have a geisha on each side of him, and I would be flanked by two geishas. They would fill your sake cup or your glass if you were drinking scotch. I was always terrified to drink the sake because I did not want to over imbibe with these bankers. Usually it did not bother the Japanese men, who helped themselves generously. They drank the scotch copiously, as they probably did every evening with clients or others who came into town.

Sidney told me that they had geisha parties nightly. Since he was the one who arranged the dinners, I knew this was probably true. We played childish little games, and sometimes the geishas would dance for us and sing in Japanese. The music must not hit the American ear as it does the Japanese. Dinners usually consisted of 10 or 12 courses. I always tried to do my best with the portions, but the dessert course was always a welcome sight because I knew that I could leave soon and get into bed. It was not our kind of food, but there were never difficult things to swallow. The Japanese presentation is very important, so the food looked appetizing but was not always warm and excitingly edible.

There were formal calls at the banks, but never drop-ins. The dinners were always separate and not a place to discuss business. Geisha dinners involved party talk. Nothing was ever solved. It was a time to form a relationship and a friendship. In time I became acquainted with one of the bank chairmen, but I was never invited to his home. It was always a dinner party out at a restaurant.

On one trip I did bring my wife, and she was invited to a dinner. She was seated at the main table and was given her two geishas. My friend the chairman, who was hosting the dinner, broke precedent and brought his wife. She sat in the row behind us and was not allowed to sit at the table. His wife had never been invited before, and she was happy to be included, even if it was in the second row. That is how they did things back then, but I am sure that as time went on, the entertainment became more modernized.

One time a Japanese bank took me golfing. Afterward, we had a steam bath where people scrubbed our backs. It was an all-day affair. They love their golf. The caddies were women, and what I found impressive was that they never lost a ball no matter how bad you were or where it landed. We played nine holes and then stopped for a wonderful lunch, followed by another nine holes. I am sure things have changed now with the younger westernized managers. Being part of a golf club is important to the Japanese banker, and the banks pay enormous sums for those memberships.

The Japanese were big at forming societies when they wanted to deal with a problem. I belonged to a few of them. Each one had a meeting once a year. Bank of America participated and so did we. They were interesting in a lot of ways. I am not sure how much they did to enhance trade between customers or countries, but we certainly learned about Japanese culture and how to do things. It was also a chance to be close to some of the American businessmen with whom I wanted to establish a relationship.

I went there many times because our bank was a member of the Japan-California society. One year we would meet in the United States and the next in Japan. All the heads of the largest businesses in California — some 20 or 30 important executives — joined the society. It was a way to try to be friends and do business with them. The meetings were conducted in a very gentlemanly way, but not much came from the discussions. Topics fluctuated between imports, tariffs, and exchange rates. The thing that was bothersome to the Americans was the Japanese yen. It was a controlled currency, and it was so low at that time.

Despite my 20 years of travel to Japan, I have yet to take a vacation there. Once in a while there would be the odd day off when I could go exploring or possibly a weekend free in which the office would organize a room at an inn on the side of Mount Fuji. It was a nice way to see the beauty of the area as well as walk and take the steams. If it was the right time of year, they might arrange a golf game. Only once or twice did I ever stay in one of the Japanese inns where they pull the mattress out of the wall and you sleep on the floor. The rooms usually had a hot tub, which added to the ambience and made it totally different and fun. On the occasions when I could get away for a few hours, I was able to see some of the temples and beautiful meditative gardens. These exquisite sites offer time to think and reflect about what is going on in the great cosmos. My Japanese friend told me it was a time for prayer.

In 1976 we initiated the Wells Fargo Bank Advisory Council (IAC). Through Ernie's connections we were able to get Lord Roger Sherfield to take on the chairmanship and help us to gather an extraordinary group of talented people. Many American banks had established special boards or advisory groups to aid their becoming more international in scope.

Lord Sherfield was an active member of the House of Lords, and had been the United Kingdom's ambassador to the United States. His wife of more than 30 years, Alice, was American. His experience, not only in the United States but also in Europe, made him an ideal person to help us build our IAC.

The council had two major purposes. First, its members were to keep Wells Fargo's senior management apprised of their views on the world economy, particularly in their own countries and regions. Second, the individuals served as experienced senior advisers in discussions of the company's plans and strategies for domestic and international markets.

The first two IAC meetings were held in London in 1976. The meetings were to be held every eight months, alternating between California and a foreign location. When the first regular meeting took place in San Francisco in 1977, there were 12 members from nine different countries.

In addition to Lord Sherfield, Ernie, and myself, the initial members included Göran Ennerfelt. Ennerfelt was from Sweden, and he was president and chief executive of Axel Johnson AB, one of the three major companies in that country. Early in his career he had spent a year with Wells in a specialized bank training program learning about American business. He was smart and attractive, and he fit in easily with this group.

Eugenio Garza Lagüera managed his family's industrial conglomerate, Valores Industriales, in Monterrey, Mexico. He also became chairman of the Monterrey Institute of Technology and

Higher Education. He was one of the important businesspeople behind the PRI government's modernization of the Mexican economy, and he provided valuable insights into Latin American business and finance.

North American IAC members included Belton K. Johnson. He was a part of the King Ranch family from Texas. He owned several ranches and was a beef industry expert and a noted participant in the world of philanthropy. Educated at both Cornell and Stanford, he sat on some of the most noted boards of the day, including AT&T, Signal Companies, Campbell Soup, and the National Cowboy Hall of Fame. And like me, he had served United Way as a trustee, and we were both members of the Bohemian Club in San Francisco.

Ahmed Juffali was a Saudi living in Jedda. While he was not a member of the royal family, he was part of the business elite. He and his brothers owned the Juffali Group, which was a joint-venture partner with international stalwarts such as Daimler-Benz, Dow Chemical, Fluor Corporation, Ericsson, IBM, and others. His inside knowledge provided IAC remarkable insight into both the politics and business of the Middle East.

Lord Lawrence Kadoorie was one of the original taipans, a key English investor from Hong Kong. He and his family owned (among many other entities) the famous old Peninsula Hotel in Kowloon. He advised the IAC regarding China's and Hong Kong's sphere of influence in Asia.

Adolf Kracht was Wells Fargo's German banking friend. He migrated from banking to one of the large old German family firms during the 1970s and then ended up running Gerling-Konzern, one of the largest insurance companies in the country.

Roger Lapham Jr. was a regular Wells Fargo director whose interests were primarily in insurance and finance. His father had been mayor of San Francisco. He was chairman of the Rama Corporation Ltd. in Paris, France. He also represented the bank and holding company boards on the council.

Monroe Spaght was a retired senior executive from Shell Oil Company and a close friend of Roger Sherfield. He contributed his observations from the United Kingdom and his knowledge of the petroleum business.

Jacques Terray was chairman of the Credit Chimique, our French investment, and adviser to the IAC regarding European business and finance. I worked with Jacques on a regular basis as a board member of Credit Chimique, and also on the IAC.

William Turner represented the Canadian business sector on the IAC board. He was chairman and chief executive officer of Exsultate Inc., a holding company for Newmont Gold Company. He was vice chairman of the Carnegie Institution of Washington, and a director of Proudfoot, a Canadian management consulting firm.

Sir James Vernon was IAC's only member from the Southern Hemisphere. He ran the major sugar business in Australia, and was an expert on the Australian postal system, among other interests.

We were looking for meaningful international financial know-how to make available to our customers as the business world became ever more global and our overseas business expanded. Much of the West Coast business went to European, Latin American, and Asian companies, and that business was reciprocal.

Initially we decided to try for one meeting a year in some part of the world that was important economically and interesting in a business sense. It was a large and continuous task. We were lucky to find Jackson Schultz, a retired U.S. Navy captain working in the bank, to take on the job of planning and caring for this group. All of these people were highly placed in their own countries and required intelligent and thoughtful maintenance. Jackson's wife, Rhoda, was a perfect complement to him in this effort, as one of the conditions of each meeting was the inclusion of the members' wives. Their inclusion was important to the bank, as they helped us understand the various cultures we would encounter in making international investments, and it was attractive to the busy executives we wanted to attend our meetings. Our goal was for everything to be first class, and the Schultzes accomplished that.

After the London and San Francisco meetings, we ventured to Mexico City and a year later to Brazil. In between the locations mentioned above, we continued to have our California events but moved them up and down the state. The business part of the meetings usually ran over two days. They were in many ways like a regular board meeting, with the difference being that this was an advisory group with no need for resolutions, votes, and so on. We wanted their help and advice, so we had to make them aware of how the bank was doing and what we were working on. The important thing was that it had to be interesting for them. Often a department head would come and talk about a part of the business that had little or nothing to do with our international efforts. It was essential that these sessions be in sync with member thoughts and experiences. The variety and experience represented on the council was awesome, and these meetings were a great help to us.

My last trip with the council was to Saudi Arabia in 1982. In most places we went, one of the council members acted as sort of an unofficial host, which made it possible to see and visit places that would have been out of reach otherwise. That applied especially to meeting and talking to key persons in government and the economic life of the part of the world we were in. Some of these key people were willing to participate in our meetings, which were often fascinating.

Over the years the membership varied, as some stayed only for their initial term of six years or occasionally less. As new members were added to the list, we more than maintained the high quality of the initial group. Of the original nine, five were still with the council when it was disbanded in 1995.

Jim Collins noted in *Good to Great* that Wells Fargo studied its results and made adjustments. "Wells Fargo had tried to be a global bank, operating like a mini-Citicorp, and a mediocre one at that," wrote Collins. "Then, at first under Dick Cooley and then under Carl Reichardt, Wells Fargo executives began to ask themselves a piercing set of questions: What can we potentially do better than any other company, and, equally important, what can we *not* do better than any other company? And if we can't be the best at it, then why are we doing it at all?"

"Wells came to two essential insights," concluded Collins. "First, most banks thought of themselves as banks, acted like banks, and protected the banker culture. Wells saw itself as a business that happened to be in banking. 'Run it like a business' and 'Run it like you own it' became mantras. Second, Wells recognized that it could not be the best in the world as a superglobal bank, but that it could be the best in the western United States."

"It wasn't a single switch that was thrown at one time. Little by little," wrote Collins, "the themes became more apparent and stronger. When Carl became CEO, there wasn't any great wrenching. Dick led one stage of evolution and Carl the next, and it just proceeded smoothly, rather than an abrupt shift."

In 1966, when I became chief executive officer at Wells, I was clearly the youngest man on the management team. As things developed, Ernie Arbuckle came on board in 1967. I stayed as president and chief executive, and Jim Dobey became executive vice president. We were the three senior executives of the company. Ernie came in at the top. He did not have banking know-how, but he had tremendous business experience. He was busy with policy and helping us to get things done at the upper level. Jim was the operating person. When I was not there, he was in charge of the day-to-day operations.

Ten years later, Ernie retired. There were a lot of changes in between times, but gradually we built a management team of younger people. At the time of Ernie's retirement in 1977, I became chairman and chief executive officer, and Jim Dobey became vice chairman along with Ralph Crawford. We were the oldest of the bank's senior officers. We brought Carl Reichardt up to San Francisco as president from Wells' Southern California unit, but by the bylaws he was number 4 in executive ranks, after Dobey, Crawford, and myself.

Ernie Arbuckle believed that I should never have stayed as long as I did as CEO. He once said, "You are over your limit and that is when you lose your zing and zang. It is hard to be a CEO longer than 10 years in this day and age."

I lasted 16, but I knew what he was saying. He retired when he was 65, and shortly after, unfortunately, he and his wife were killed in an automobile accident driving back to Carmel. It was a terrible shock to all of us.

My personal life was not terrific. Since moving to Los Angeles, I had been going back and forth from LA to San Francisco every week. It seemed to me that lots of problems came up, and we had to handle them face-to-face.

The team around me was good, they were younger, and clearly they had their own ideas of what they would like to do. As the older man I thought they were somewhat impatient to have a new plan, one of their own creation. They were a group of outstanding young people, and I knew they could take the bank in whatever direction it had to go. This should have been comforting for me, but it was not. Although it was unintentional, this group made me feel uncomfortable, like young lions nipping at my heels.

Wells Fargo board, 1976. Back row, from left: Regnar Paulsen, Bob Nahas, Malcolm MacNaughton, Mary Lanigar, Dick Cooley, Palmer Fuller, Jim Dobey, Jack Mailliard, Ken Bechtel, and Bob Bridges. Front row, from left: Dick Guggenhime, Ed Littlefield, Bill Brenner, Jim Dickason, Ernie Arbuckle, Jim Hait, Paul Miller, Arjay Miller, and Atherton Phleger.

WELLS FARGO BANKING
AND BOARD WORK

W hen I started moving up the ladder, the bank made me sell the car dealerships and remove myself from all boards, except for United Way. There I was nearing completion of my five-year commitment to the campaign, so it was not considered to be a problem by my bosses. From the bank's standpoint, it was felt that my overall attention should be concentrated solely on the job and not distracted by outside obligations. Although there were invitations, I turned them down. It was made clear to me that if I wished to join another board, I would have to seek the approval of the bank's directors. I found I had plenty to keep me occupied as president and chief executive officer of Wells. This policy remains a part of Wells Fargo today.

The first invitation to join a for-profit board that I felt compelled to discuss with the board arrived about three years after I became the bank's chief executive. It was from United Airlines (UAL Inc.), the holding company and the airline. One of our directors, Paul Bissinger, had been a member of that board for years and had unexpectedly died of a heart attack. The United people came and asked if I would like to take Paul's place. I was intrigued and talked about it with Ernie Arbuckle, who by then was chairman of our board.

United Airlines was a major carrier to and from San Francisco International, and its ties to the Bay Area were historic. It opened the nation's first flight kitchen in Oakland in 1936. And in the 1960s, United had become the largest airline in the world, with many flights originating in San Francisco.

San Francisco International Airport also was the site of United's maintenance facilities.

The prospect of joining the UAL Inc. board appealed to me because I was interested in flying and airlines, and I also thought I would learn a lot that could be beneficial to the bank. Airlines meet all their customers through flight attendants, the men and women who run those cabins. That is 95 percent of who you see outside your ticket agent. They have a tremendous effect on how you regard and use the service. This is also true of a bank. Other than a few upper-level corporate accounts, most customers meet the bank through its tellers. When people cash their checks and make their deposits, they use a teller's window.

We have money in the bank and an airline has airplanes, but we have similar kinds of opportunities and problems with customer relationships.

Ernie and I talked about it quite a bit. He agreed that my reasoning was probably sound, but he was not overly enthusiastic about my choice. Still, he went to the board and explained to the members that I had this opportunity and he thought I should take it. After all, the place had not blown up, and we seemed to be doing relatively well by most standards. He convinced the executive committee that it would be acceptable, so the decision was approved.

It was early in the 1970s when I joined the United board, and I stayed on it for 25 years. Meetings were held monthly in Chicago, and the board members would fly in from all over the country in time for dinner on the night before the Thursday meeting. At least a couple members of the management would be present on those evenings, and this became an opportune time to discuss relevant topics or some current project that otherwise would not receive adequate time during the meeting. The directors of United were a diverse group who usually ran a major business in one of the key sites that the airline served.

We sometimes had more than one representative from a hub city, but we always had someone from Seattle, San Francisco, Los Angeles, Denver, Chicago, and New York, as well as someone from the Midwest and Washington, D.C.

In the course of these Wednesday night dinners we had some incredible and informative conversations. I would say that most of the board members were Republican, but not all. One of our important directors was Andy Brimmer, who was a governor of the Federal Reserve Bank in Washington, D.C. He was a big Democrat. The political discussions were engaging because we had some heavyweight Republican executives on the board, and then we had Andy. That made it lively. I learned about what other companies were doing, and besides that I made some good friends from all sectors of the business community.

The following morning there would be the regular board meeting and then everyone would go home after lunch. I would return from most meetings with notes in my pocket about ideas that could improve our customer service or make the company run more smoothly. There were ideas about their pension plan, and HR decisions and other corporate know-how. It was different from our board in some ways, but the issues were often similar. There was usually something that United was doing that we could implement at the bank to help improve performance.

At the time I joined the board, there was a significant problem. They were in the process of reorganizing management. The situation came to a head when the airline's chief executive officer made the mistake of coming to the board with a loss budget for the year. The board members could not stand for that, and they wanted someone else to run the company. To his great displeasure, the board replaced the CEO with existing board member Eddie Carlson, who was chairman and chief executive of Western International Hotels, and living in Seattle. United had a holding company at the time (UAL, Inc.) that owned United Airlines, and they had decided to buy a hotel company, and later on an auto rental company, Hertz, to try to get their arms around the whole travel experience. They bought Western International, and Eddie Carlson and Lynn Himmelman came on United's board. Without conducting an expensive search, they moved Eddie Carlson from running the hotel company to running the whole company. Lynn Himmelman, who was number two at the hotel, took over for Carlson and ran the hotel business.

Eddie did an interesting thing as he took the helm. He did not have much experience with airlines, but he understood the travel business. He also did not know about pilots or maintenance or buying airplanes, but he did know about building hotels and taking care of customers. *Fortune* magazine made a stab at humor when they wrote, "Carlson doesn't know much about airlines, but what he's going to do is make hotels out of all the 747's." It was supposed to be a joke, but it wasn't in some ways.

Eddie decided that morale at United was bad. For the next two years, he traveled to the major United employee domiciles to talk with all the employees he could. The pilots and flight attendants were based in Chicago, Denver, Los Angeles, Seattle, New York, and some other locations. The mechanics were concentrated in large operations centers. Eddie met as many employees as he could in each location, answering all their questions. He would tell them what he hoped to do with the airline and how he intended to fix things, raise morale, and give good customer service. His efforts paid off. He was well received. The employees liked him, and ultimately he was quite successful.

I took Eddie's example and applied his tactic to our own management challenges. At times you have trouble in the sense that attitudes shift, and for whatever reason, we had a bad period at the bank. We started having meetings with employees. I would stand in front of the tellers for three hours on a Saturday morning and answer all their questions — whatever they wanted to ask. I did that a lot, and I think it really helped. It was an idea that I got from Eddie and the United board. That alone helped justify the time I used on the board because you should never go on a board if you cannot learn something and offer ideas in return.

The United board did some things that helped alter my views on management style. One thing in particular I noted was how they would take the board on trips to new locations. If they were opening a new plant, say a big maintenance base in Denver, the board would have their meeting there that month and probably stay an extra night when the company would entertain big clients with a director at each table meeting local business owners. It was a public relations event, but it was appreciated. It gave the directors a means to sell the company, and it also helped them to understand what people were thinking about in that part of the country. When you are dealing with an entity like United that goes from coast to coast and almost north to south, there are a lot of different things going on.

It is important to understand that the culture is different in each area and you have to be able to adjust to it.

Wells Fargo was an in-state bank for a long time, and we would take the board on trips to see different parts of the state that we served. We also used the board to sell ourselves to the customers in that part of the state. It was an idea that I was able to take from United and implement at Wells. I saw how effective it was, and I thought we could adapt it to our purposes.

Getting the board together outside the boardroom became basic — something that almost every board chairman under-stands and does. I learned more about that from my experience at United. Whenever there was a chance to do something with the board, like an annual dinner or a meeting, it was good to get the group together in addition to just coming to an 8 a.m. board meeting and finishing by noon. The meeting itself is formal, and you do not have much of a chance to interact. Organizing a luncheon in conjunction with each meeting was something that was useful.

The whole point is that the board needs to be a team, and if that is accomplished, then you have a good chance of running a really strong business because everyone is moving in the same direction.

I was asked to join the board of Pacific Gas and Electric (PG&E), the major Northern California utility. It was an old relationship that was established because the bank signed on their bonds, and my board allowed the participation because it was expected. The bank's chief executive had been on the PG&E board forever, so when the changeover took place, they wanted the active head of Wells on the board. The experience was completely different from that at United Airlines because it was one of those cases where the meetings were run strictly by the rules, and there was little chance to connect with the members in a more neutral, casual setting.

Running an electric utility in a state like California, you would have a lot of lawyers. Lawyers were important in dealing with the state public utilities commission and the state legislature. It was almost equally important to have engineers, although lawyers typically dominated the scene, but not always. The main objective of the utility was how to generate electricity and gas and have it consistently available around its segment of the state. The company had an enormous need for capital expenditures to build plant and equipment to keep increasing the volume of electricity and gas as the population and economy expanded.

PG&E was one of those boards where there was not a lot of discussion and what discussion did transpire was highly technical. I am not a lawyer or an electrical engineer, so I did not always understand the details of the legal or technical issues, but I did gain an understanding of how that board operated.

The executive committee was composed of the older, more experienced people on the board. They would often meet just before the regular board meeting and go over the agenda, seemingly deciding which way things would go. The board, which was maybe twice the size of the executive committee, would then go over the same agenda. It seemed to me that we were voting on subjects that had already been approved by the executive committee. We just ratified their approval and there was not a lot we could do about it, even if we wanted to. There were two classes of directors: those who were on the executive committee, of which there were four or five, and then 12 others who were on the regular board. The board was set up so that people were there to represent a group or a community. I was there because of the bank and our relationship with the bonds. The directors were not circulated annually through the various committees as they were at United or at the bank. In essence there were two classes of directors, and because I was young and coming in, I was part of the regular board, not the executive committee.

At that time the head of the company was Sherm Sibley. He was a little older than I, an engineer, but not an attorney. We had become acquainted through community and social activities. Sherm was well liked, and going on the board with him running it was one of the big pluses as far as I was concerned. Then a terrible thing happened. One summer he was fishing in Oregon and he got caught in the fast water, which flooded his waders and carried him out to sea. No one ever saw him again. It was a great personal tragedy. I knew his wife and family, and everyone liked him. He was a good friend who remains on my prayer list today.

The effect on the company was tumultuous, and the way PG&E handled it was disappointing. The executive committee met immediately to discuss the situation and selected Sherm's successor without talking to the rest of the board. When the subject of succession came up at the special board meeting, the successor's name was already in the resolution. One of the older directors denied that it was true and told us that they were just thinking of this new person to take over. Basically, they had already decided whom they wanted to push up, and they did so without the approval of the whole board. It was maybe a good choice or maybe a bad choice, but it was a clear demonstration that there were two classes of directors. In a business sense you never want unequal directors on a board. Everyone bears the same liability, and if all the decisions are being made by a third of the directors, it puts the other two-thirds in an untenable position. It was the first time I had ever witnessed such a division. It was not good business, and it made me feel uninterested in being on that board.

They have probably gotten away from such practices now, but that was the way it worked 25 or 30 years ago. I clearly remember that day and how incensed I was at the outcome. There was not anything I could do about it except grin and bear it. I could not get up and resign because of the bank's business relationship, although there was nothing I would have liked more. It was apparent that they did not feel the need for the whole board's decision-making abilities. That was my first experience with two classes of directors, and I have talked about it a lot since. If there is such a situation, steps should be taken to change it.

In the mid 1970s PG&E took a big step. A large problem arose because the company decided to build a huge nuclear plant in Northern California. Southern California Edison, the big electrical company in Southern California, had already decided to build one, so we made the decision to do the same. The glitch surfaced when it turned out that the site picked for the plant appeared to be close to the San Andreas Fault. All kinds of safety and media problems surfaced with it. It was horrendous politically and public relations-wise because no one wanted to build a nuclear plant next to a fault line.

It was a big engineering dilemma, which I think the engineers handled well. The project was economically feasible, in fact desirable. The company had hydroelectric power and some coal power and they wanted to go to nuclear, which they thought would be better in the long run. The project took some 20 years to go on line. It has been many years since that happened, so I cannot tell you much about how it turned out or if that plant is still working today. Nuclear power has had its ups and downs (more downs) over the last few decades, but given today's energy crisis and the strong ecology movement, it may be making a comeback.

———————

Let's talk about nonprofit organizations, and United Way in particular. Bankers have opportunities to join a lot of things. Most banks are heavily oriented toward nonprofit community activities. I do not mean the money-center banks in New York or Chicago, but the strong regional banks, which encourage their managers to become involved in all kinds of activities. They are represented on many boards, such as United Way, Red Cross, Boy Scouts, and various hospitals, schools, and colleges. The theory is that if the bank is situated in a healthy community, that is good for the business of the bank. I found that people expect bankers to jump in and help.

My first board work was as a trustee for the San Francisco Zoo, and as I said before, I did not have pets and really did not know much about animals. I quickly found out that I wasn't asked on the board as an animal expert. I was invited to join because the bank had relations with the zoo. It was a gratifying experience and I learned a great deal about nonprofit organizations, which always need money, and animals, which always need caring for.

My association with the San Francisco United Way began when I was a senior vice president. One of our major clients at the bank was the Southern Pacific Company, where my friend Benjamin Biaggini was the number-two man in charge, and the heir apparent. He had moved to San Francisco from New Orleans to take over the operations of the railroad, which he did from 1964 to 1976. Then he served as chairman of the Southern Pacific Company's board of directors from 1976 to 1983.

Ben had been selected to run the Bay Area United Way Campaign. He took me to lunch and said, "Cooley, I want you to head the corporate section of the campaign." I thought he was joking. In my mind I was far too young and inexperienced and did not know enough key people in the area to handle that size responsibility. However, that was not Ben's impression. He said, "You are on the threshold. You can do it and more importantly, I need your help." Ben was a man whom I liked very much and greatly respected. At his insistence and with his promise to keep me on course, I received permission from my bosses and took the job.

The corporate element of the campaign was the biggest part. The campaign was separated into divisions for individuals, homes, geographical areas, lines of business, and the major corporations. There were 50 large companies in the Bay Area that provided the lion's share of the United Way funds. To take that on seemed like a lot to me, but there was no way that I could say no to Ben. He insisted that I could do it. That was the first of five years working for the United Way. We did do the campaign, and though we did not make our goal, we were close. It certainly was not a bad result.

What I remember is that it was like going through the chairs of a fraternal organization. You ran a segment of it, then every year there was a new leader in each division and you moved to a new position. From starting out as a chairman of the corporate campaign you went to vice president of United Way and campaign chairman. Then you made the move to president, and the following year chairman of the board. In your fifth and last year, you became chairman of the executive committee. In the last two years the time commitment was not nearly as heavy as in the previous two. For continuity, one tried to get people lined up to take these positions far in advance so there was a planned leadership team from the community to support this organization each year for two or three years ahead.

The United Way in San Francisco was a big operation, representing five counties. There was a large paid staff who did all the detail work, but they also required a huge number of volunteers. It could not be done without the volunteers. Businesses liked it because the contact was consolidated. United Way at that time represented about 148 agencies in the five-county area. That meant that businesses did not have to pick someone to represent the Red Cross, and someone else for the Boy Scouts, and someone for all the rest of the agencies that asked for help. They got it all done at one time. Only one campaign per year was allowed to take place within each corporate organization.

The company appointed someone to run their internal United Way campaign. It would be organized so that during a certain week in the fall, all employees would be asked to contribute to the United Way. The chairman or the president of that company would have a meeting with the senior people and tell them that they should do this or that, or would ask them to consider making a certain level of gift. Forcing them to give was frowned upon, but there was supposed to be a slight push (sometimes more than slight) to stress what a good idea this was for themselves and the company.

How it worked was that donation money was deducted from an employee's paycheck. The payroll system was set up with only one charity box to hold this money. What made it attractive was that there were not 20 different boxes on the payroll system for different charities but only one that covered the gamut of community needs. Then there was the corporate gift. Each company would decide on its corporate gift and add that to the combined offerings of the staff. It could get pretty large, and they did not allow any other charity in. That was always the United Way problem: how to keep United Way as the only one that was allowed to do an internal campaign. In a sense, they had a monopoly on asking for money from corporate employees. Many years later it broke down, but that was the basic idea in the beginning.

Quite early on, before I got to be executive vice president or chief executive officer at Wells Fargo, I started my five years of running through the chairs at United Way. I had no idea it would end up like that. The year I became chairman of the campaign there was an enormous goal, something like $50 million. It was similar to being in politics: you had to have a stump speech, only I had my United Way speech. I always felt that if you pushed the right spot on my chest, the United Way speech would start coming out. The staff would make appointments all over the area and I traveled around continuously. That year I must have given 60 speeches at breakfasts and lunches, or in-between times. I would give that speech about the United Way — all the benefits to the community, how necessary it was to contribute, what the needs were in the community, and how important it was to have a healthy community — to many different groups.

The United Way was unique. It was established across America, but there was always a local United Way. You could find out what was happening at United Ways in other parts of the country and learn from them. Giving all the speeches was good because I had never done much public speaking and I was nervous on my feet. I could do it, but I did not enjoy doing it. I was timid and not at ease talking to an unfamiliar crowd. When I was discussing the United Way, I knew what I was talking about, and I gave the speech so often that I became an advocate with it. It developed my ability to speak in front of people and to think on my feet. I learned a lot from the experience. It was good for the United Way, and the United Way did a lot of good for me.

From the bank's point of view, Wells contributed my time and my efforts to doing this program, so the bank was "off the hook" from handling other requests. I carried the bank's load for that five-year period. United Way was considered part of my job. There was a benefit from learning how to think clearly and finding out how to present yourself in front of a lot of people you did not know. You also met lots of new people in the five counties. Even if you were not doing business with them, they got to know you and you got to know them. If they liked you, there was always the chance that you might get some business from them someday. It was fun and there were good people involved. The whole business community supported the program. It was an opportunity to spread my wings and become better known in the business world.

———————

Jumping ahead maybe 15 or 20 years, when I moved to Seattle from San Francisco, oddly enough, within six months of my arrival three distinguished elder citizens of the community came and asked me to run United Way in Seattle. I told them that I could not do that because I had already done it in San Francisco. They said to me, "That's just why we are asking you. We want you to do it here. We need you." Again, it is one of those things that happen to bankers. I was new in Seattle and it was a great way to meet people. It was a positive for the bank. The bank had been in trouble and I was hired to fix the problem. I did it. It was just so much work, the speeches, the moving around, the time it took, while there was constant worry about making enough money to keep the bank afloat.

There was one aspect of the Seattle experience that was different from San Francisco. In San Francisco, we had something called Corporate Circles. It was a special name for people who gave $10,000 or more per year. That was a large sum, and it was definitely a large sum in those days. To be successful you had to have major givers, and they were not all going to be rich people. A lot of them had to come from corporations where they made large salaries and could afford that kind of deduction on a monthly basis. In San Francisco the program existed before I got through all those chairs, and there were over 100 people who were giving $10,000 or more. When I came to Seattle, I found out to my horror that there were only three people who gave $10,000 or more to the annual United Way campaign. That was shocking to me.

In time I went to see one of the senior citizens who had asked me to take the job, as it was getting close to my turn to lead the campaign. I asked him for his contribution and told him that I wanted to start a Circle Club where whoever belonged would give $10,000 per year to the Leadership Giving. He looked horrified. He said, "Dick, you don't understand. In Seattle we do not do things like that. If you gave more than $1,000, people would think you were showing off. People just don't do that." I was shocked again. Here was a very wealthy man who was feeling that he could not show his wealth by giving generously to the United Way. That was an idea that we had to break down, and eventually we did. Now, many years later, we have over 700 people in the Alexis de Tocqueville Society who give $10,000 or more each year. In fact, we have a $100,000 Annual Giving Club, which is amazing. People are generous in Seattle, but they do not want to do the wrong thing. There is a lot of money in the area, and they need to be comfortable about sharing it.

That first United Way experience in San Francisco was a wonderful one. I will not forget it. You find out about what is going on in the community that you did not know about before. You find causes and people who really need your assistance, and you help out by contributing to organizations like the United Way.

The United Way is always an annual event. It's not a capital campaign; it is for daily operations in these organizations. If you are going to build a hospital or a gym for a school or a law school, that is a capital project and a different kind of campaign. The United Way goes on every year, and it takes care of the annual needs of the organizations that are helping disadvantaged people.

The United Way has had its ups and downs across the country. There have been some abuses, but by and large, it has done a good job and I am glad to have been associated with it.

Remember the famous firm Hewlett-Packard? Bill Hewlett and Dave Packard were great friends of Ernie Arbuckle. One day, Bill Hewlett came in to see Ernie. This would have been around 1970, and he told Ernie that he was going off the RAND board and he thought it would be a great organization for me to join. In his opinion I was young, and this would be a way for me to learn what was happening in the world. To be honest, I did not think I was intelligent enough to join the board. The members were scientists, physicists, and economists, and I was just a young, inexperienced businessman trying to get along.

RAND is a highly regarded think tank, and it has recently celebrated its 60th birthday. It is involved in the gut problems of the country. It does not make anything, but it uses brainpower to develop solutions and solve problems. Other people construct and run the programs they implement, but RAND provides the blueprint on how to get things done. Its resolutions may not always be the greatest, but it is usually better than anyone else. RAND people are doing so many worthwhile things in the world, and it was an incredible experience to know you could be a participant in what might be going on in the future.

For one reason or another, through Bill's push, I was accepted on the board. It was a 10-year term for a trustee. If you started early enough, you could take two or three terms, but board members must complete their terms by the time they reach their 70th birthday. I learned that most trustees serve one term, but I was fortunate because Bill got me in early enough so that I was able to complete two terms as a trustee, with the standard one year off between terms.

When Bill first spoke to me about RAND, he gave me a report that had been written 20 years before, sometime during the late 1940s. The report described how to put a man on the moon. Twenty years later, it was done exactly as outlined in the report. It was incredible to read the description of the mission.

Like millions of others in the summer of 1969, I watched the launch and touchdown on the moon without realizing that it was RAND's vision put into motion. Every detail was carefully calculated, permitting our astronauts to take the first steps on the moon's surface and plant the American flag. Eventually I met all three of those astronauts, Neil Armstrong, Michael Collins, and Buzz Aldrin. Neil Armstrong was on the board of United Airlines, Michael Collins was on the RAND board, and Buzz Aldrin I met socially after he retired.

RAND is a fine group of approximately 1,600 people (roughly 950 scientists) from more than 45 countries around the world. It has three principal U.S. locations: Santa Monica, California; Arlington, Virginia; and Pittsburgh, Pennsylvania. Others operate from the RAND Gulf States Policy Institute in Jackson, Mississippi; RAND Europe in Cambridge, U.K.; and the RAND-Qatar Policy Institute in Doha, Qatar. Alongside these locations is the Frederick S. Pardee RAND Graduate School, which has 53 professors and a student body of about 100. Graduates of this prestigious school receive a Ph.D. in public policy analysis. After I turned 70 I became an emeritus trustee and served on the graduate school board for several years. It has been a rare honor and a privilege to be a part of such an illustrious group.

A typical meeting consisted of 15 or 16 people, mostly scientists and a few businessmen. I was told that they were interested in my participation from the standpoint of business and what that influence would be on their projects. At the meetings they would talk about the latest assignment, whether it was to help the Air Force be more efficient in getting supplies to the front, or whatever. Usually they would give a presentation or a report, but we did not vote on it. Instead, we would ask questions in such a way that it might help strengthen the report. Then the briefing team would go back to the people who had constructed the findings and make changes before they handed it over to whoever was paying for it. In many cases they ran these reports by the board so the board might see something that the researchers had missed. Or if the material appeared controversial, it was good to run it by the board so they could decide if it was appropriate.

RAND held two meetings each year, one in the spring and another in the fall, and they were two-day meetings. Often they were held in Santa Monica and other times in Washington, D.C., but the location moved to different sites such as New York or anywhere around the world if there was a reason. When I joined, it was hard to justify the time away because there was always pressure to be visible in the bank, but now two days does not sound like much at all. Although the time away seemed difficult to schedule, we all agreed that once we were there, it was an incredible experience and well worth every moment.

During my first term Donald Rumsfeld was chairman of the board. His recent actions are not surprising to those of us who knew him. He is very bright, very quick. He liked to get things done. If he decided that he wanted to do something, he did it. You can see how he implemented things during the Iraq war. At different times Alan Greenspan, Condi Rice, and Brent Scowcroft were on the board. It used to be that most of the programs were designed for the Air Force and the Army, and then they started doing work more broadly for the government itself.

The domestic work of RAND was more interesting to me than the military side. They look at health care, education, and municipal government among many other issues on the domestic side, while having strong programs supporting the Air Force, the Army, the Department of Defense, and other government projects. I still get their monthly reports about what they are currently working on and the scope of their involvement in the Middle East and other parts of the world.

Most RAND members were well versed in what was going on in the government, although they had to be nonpartisan. They were rooting for the country, not a political party. The group itself was not necessarily a secret, but the work they did was. You have to have a top-secret clearance to be on the board, which I had for many years but do not have anymore.

When New York City went through its bankruptcy period in the 1970s, they started a RAND-New York City Institute to look at a way to run the city more economically. Among many projects were two things they did that were noteworthy and helpful. First, they worked on improving the efficiency of the police department. They researched the crime reports to find out when the crimes were being committed. They found out that there was a clear time frame when crime activity heightened. So they reorganized the police force in shifts and accentuated the number of policemen during the peak times when crimes took place. They started to get a handle on it, and police effectiveness improved tremendously. Second, they took a look at the fire department. RAND physicists got involved and invented something called slippery water. They put something in the water that made it go through the pipes faster than regular water, which made it possible to get more water flow to a fire quicker. Slippery water cut costs and minimized fire damage.

RAND often had to spend its own money for research. Recently it organized a fund for its school-development and other money-related projects of importance. Being associated with RAND for over 30 years has been a broadening and fascinating experience. I have enjoyed this affiliation greatly and my friendships with many on the board, including Jim Thomson, who is the head of RAND and came to Seattle to visit.

Here is a list of recent RAND achievements:

■ After Hurricane Katrina, a tool kit of trauma intervention programs was designed for Gulf State schools to meet the immediate need and help to stave off negative long-term mental-health consequences, and also to prepare for the future.

■ Senior economist Richard Neu has been a huge contributor at RAND for the past 30 years. He oversees projects to improve health-care systems and K-12 and university-level education in Qatar. He was the assistant to the president of RAND for Research on Counterterrorism, associate dean of the RAND Graduate School of Policy Studies, and associate director of RAND Project Air Force.

■ International policy analyst R. Kim Cragin studies political violence to give policymakers a richer understanding of issues associated with terrorism such as suicide bombings, terrorist recruitment, and the potential for socioeconomic development to inhibit terrorism. Cragin led a study in 2006 that examined factors that have allowed terrorist groups to successfully exchange new technologies.

■ Michael Kennedy, senior economist, helped lead a very large RAND project team to guide the Air Force's $200 billion decision to replace its aging fleet of aerial refueling tankers. Aerial refueling tankers enable the Air Force to rapidly and effectively undertake important missions in distant places such as Iraq and Afghanistan. They improve our ability to maintain surveillance of U.S. airspace for homeland-security purposes, and can play an important role in aiding relief efforts in the wake of overseas disasters such as the 2004 Asian tsunami.

■ Melinda Beeuwkes Buntin helped policymakers develop effective health-care reforms by understanding the complex interplay between cost, quality, and access to care. RAND analysis found that consumer-directed plans can lower costs by reducing unnecessary care, an effect of high deductibles that we have known about since RAND's groundbreaking Health Insurance Experiment in the 1970s. Explained Buntin, "The effect of these plans on overall health is potentially worrisome, as people experiencing higher out-of-pocket expenses also tend to forgo necessary care, which can jeopardize their health."

■ As director of the military Logistics program at the RAND Arroyo Center, the Army's federally funded research and development center for policy analysis, Eric Peltz and his dedicated team of analysts help improve the military's joint supply-chain system to ensure that American troops at home and overseas have the supplies they need when and where they need them.

■ Jonathan Grant is a policy analyst and recently appointed president of RAND Europe. "Europe is facing economic, social, and health-care challenges as a result of its rapidly aging population and low fertility rates."

■ Angel Rabasa is a senior political scientist at RAND whose research and analyses address problems of international security and religious extremism.

■ Bill Overholt is director of the RAND Center for Asia Pacific Policy. "Asia is undergoing tremendous change," he said, "particularly with the expansion of China's and India's economies, the political situation in Korea, and so on. My ambition is that decision-makers in the U.S., in Asia, and throughout the world respond to these changes not based on irrational fears or ideological or nationalistic agendas but, rather, based on a reasoned understanding of what's going to produce the greatest net benefit for people's lives and for peace."

———————

Among the most interesting outside organizations that I had the privilege to serve as a trustee was the California Institute of Technology, best known as Caltech. It is a private school, although it receives substantial grant money from the federal government. I have been on that board for over 30 years. It is another incredible Southern California institution, different from RAND but equally fascinating. Caltech is in the same category as MIT, but it's about one-fifth the size. Today Caltech has about 900 undergraduate students, with many of them getting perfect scores on their SATs. It also supports 1,300 or more graduate students and the work of over 500 postdoctoral scholars.

Caltech students and staff work on all kinds of scientific endeavors. There is practically nothing you could name that they are not involved in. At any given time they have 12 or 13 Nobel Laureates on the faculty doing research. Usually people who go there for their undergraduate degree do not get their Ph.D. at Caltech. An unofficial rule is that you don't want to get both degrees at Caltech even though it is possible. This is a view based more on the value of a diverse educational experience than on any Caltech inadequacies.

Caltech makes an enormous contribution to science. Jet Propulsion Laboratory (JPL) was established by Caltech in the 1930s to further its development of rocket engines. The noise of rocket motors and explosions prompted its move away from the Caltech campus in 1940, and not long thereafter it began the development of guided missiles. Starting in the 1950s, JPL developed light-gathering instruments, and in 1958, *Explorer 1* became the first American satellite to achieve orbit. It gathered information about radiation banks high above the earth's surface. It was our country's entry into what became a space race with the Soviet Union. JPL interest in space exploration led to the first robotic craft that was sent to the moon, and later units were sent deep into our solar system. Today JPL is a NASA laboratory, and it operates a fleet of 21 spacecraft and nine instruments conducting active missions. It has just finished the first stage of the Mars Rovers, those little buggies that they put on Mars to see what it is made of, what kind of temperatures exist there, what the weather patterns are, etc. A lot more is known about Mars now because they were able to put those two little machines up there in January 2004. They have lasted much longer than anyone expected. It was calculated that if they lasted three or four months, that would be good, but they are still going strong. Jet Propulsion Laboratory employees are an imaginative group and at the leading edge of our solar system studies.

Being on the board there, you are not quite as involved as you are at RAND. You are more involved in raising money. Right now they are just completing a $1.5 billion campaign to build new buildings and fund new telescopes, new labs, and research, as well as increase the scholarships available for students who should be allowed to use those minds to further research and discovery. They do not want to lose anyone who might contribute to the scientific frontier because of lack of funds.

———————

I joined the Kaiser Family Foundation board in 1987 and served as a director through 1994. This came about through Eddie Carlson, who was a friend of the Kaiser family. The term was seven years, and when Eddie went off he suggested that I take his place. There was a family feud going on, a disagreement between the outside trustees and a member of the family. It was subsequently resolved, and the board decided that no member of the family would be chairman in the future, but the title of vice chairman would always go to a family member. As I got involved with board decisions, there were problems. It was not dissimilar to the situation that existed when I arrived at RAND, where they were in the process of changing their president and chief executive officer, and we went through a bit of trauma.

Oddly, that happened to me more than once in the same time frame. At United we had to replace the chief executive and Eddie Carlson was put in, whereas at RAND we replaced a man who was a renowned scientist but not a good manager. They put in Don Rice, who lasted as its chief executive for 17 years. The current head is Jim Thomson, and he has been there for over 20 years. RAND is a well-organized, well-operated institution. Their budget is not big, but their intellectual reach is enormous.

The Kaiser Family Foundation had problems when I went in. I was part of an early group that was trying to keep the factions together and make some changes at the top, which we did. Kaiser's idea was to keep on top of medical policies in the USA and influence decisions, as well as determine what our research should be and how it should be organized to give good health care to all our citizens. It was a little political, and they were not able to be as nonpartisan as the RAND people. I have been off the board for a while, but they always invite retired trustees to an annual weekend to find out where they are going and what they are doing. They have a CEO who has been there for 12 or 13 years and has done a good job. He was barely 40 when they brought him in, like Don Rice, who was only 37 when he took over RAND. It shows you that these boards who are concerned with scientific matters are interested in young minds that have the creative imagination for big leaps and visions.

The Kaiser Foundation has focused its efforts on health-care policy and has been very influential. They have a strong media section and good relationships with the broadcasting companies. I do not know what they are worried about now, but I know they have a focus on Africa. They spent money and time in South Africa to figure out how the change in government with Mandela would affect health care and the local citizenry. They opened an office and put a man there to follow how the change would play out. About 20 percent of the budget went for improving public health in South Africa. They are interested in HIV and teenage pregnancy, and many major medical problems. The board is selected carefully. There is one member of the Kaiser family on the board at all times. The family has passed it around to various members over the years, and I think the system has worked pretty well. The Kaiser Foundation is an interesting and successful organization, concentrating strictly on medical policy.

Board work remained satisfying, but I felt a growing need for a change.

I had been working at Wells Fargo in one job for 15 years, and I needed a fresh start. What Ernie had said about losing your zing and your zang after too many years in the top job appeared to be true. As I thought about giving myself a new challenge, it also occurred to me that Wells was ready for a breath of fresh air at the top of its management.

WELLS FARGO'S EXECUTIVE OFFICERS IN LATE 1980, ABOUT TWO YEARS
BEFORE I RETIRED AND MOVED TO SEATTLE. SEATED ON THE LEFT IS CARL E.
REICHARDT, PRESIDENT, AND I'M IN THE RIGHT CHAIR. STANDING, FROM LEFT,
ARE PAUL HAZEN, EXECUTIVE VICE PRESIDENT, ROBERT L. KEMPER,
VICE CHAIRMAN, AND RICHARD M. ROSENBERG, VICE CHAIRMAN.

TRANSITION TO SEATTLE

In 1966, at 42 years of age, I was clearly the youngest man on the Wells management team. After 10 years of being the bank's chief executive, instead of being the youngest person on the block, I was among the oldest. In 1980, with the early retirements of Crawford and Dobey, who by then had become vice chairmen of the bank, I was the oldest (at 57) on the senior management team. Ernie used to say to me that I should not stay longer than 10 years as chief executive officer. When he retired I had led the bank for 12 years, and he thought I should not plan to keep the job much longer.

Things were not as flexible in the banking world then, and I did not know what else to do. We had a strong succession plan built in, and Carl Reichardt and his team were coming along fine. He was younger than I by the right amount of years and was fully capable of running the bank. I do not think he was aware that he might take it over as early as 1983, but he was ready. And I was ready to leave the bank if I could find some satisfactory way to support myself.

I was 58 when I started to think about what I was going to do at 60. Was I going to make Carl president and chief executive, and then wait around as chairman until I was 65? That did not sound like much fun. And yet, I did not know what kind of job I could get outside Wells Fargo Bank. I did not know what I could do or where I could go, and I was very uncertain. I talked to a headhunter, an old friend, and he told me what I might be able to expect. I had a conversation with one of the significant board members, Ed Littlefield, and he was under the assumption that any job I took at that point in my career would be a tough job. In other words, I would be working for a company that was in trouble and wanted me to come in and fix it. "You could not just expect to move into a comfortable job and add whatever you could add to an already successful company," counseled Littlefield. "Instead, you would have to straighten out somebody else's mess, and put it back on track."

My whole career had been in banking except for those early years at McCall's, and that appeared to be a problem because I did not have the confidence to move into Boeing or Pepsi-Cola or any other business that I did not understand. I was a banker. That was Littlefield's view, and I did not think I could strike out in a completely new direction, even though I had become a little burned out in my job. I had led the bank by then for 14 or 15 years and did not feel that I was in tune with the younger staff as much as I could or should have been. With all these concerns looming, my headhunter friend said that he would look around. In one of our conversations he told me about an opportunity in Hawaii. One of the big five companies there was looking for a chief executive officer, and he asked if I would be interested. It was a food company, which I knew nothing about, but it was something to consider. Ultimately I did not do anything about it.

Seafirst Bank in Seattle got into trouble. It had made very large, largely unsecured or poorly collateralized loans into the petroleum business, and when that blew up in the early 1980s Seafirst's chairman, Bill Jenkins, fell out of favor with the board. The board decided that he had to go, and they initiated a search to find a replacement. The chairman of the search committee was Harry Mullikin, who had been a friend of mine for a long time. We had been on the United board together and knew each other quite well. In the summer of 1982, Harry came down to see me and said, "You've been in this business a long time. What should we be looking for in a candidate to replace Bill?" Harry and other board members were talking to bankers and others who might help them look for ideas on how to forward their search.

I had a good talk with Harry about various people I knew and things that might be important in Seattle. I started thinking about that conversation and more specifically, the job. Harry came back later and talked to me about whom he had in mind and what was going on in the search. By October of 1982 the Seafirst board had whittled its list down to four candidates. Then I started to seriously consider it for myself. Seafirst was about two-thirds the size of Wells Fargo at the time, but it was not as important. It was a good bank, the biggest and oldest bank in the state of Washington. Its assets were a little over $10 billion, but it had problems.

I arranged to see Harry in Vancouver, B.C. It was at this meeting that I said to him, "Harry, what would happen if you put my name in the hat for this search you are running?" I do not know if he was surprised or not, but he said, "Oh, well, that's interesting. I'd be glad to put that down and talk to the other members of the committee about it if you are truly interested." Harry asked why I would consider the job, and I told him that I thought I had gone stale at Wells and it was time for me to make a change. While I had the opportunity to move in another direction, I felt more comfortable going to a business that I understood. I did not know Seattle but I did know the banking business, and I felt confident that I could do something with Seafirst if it was necessary. I will never know if it was my idea or if Harry had subtly put the idea in my head.

One thing led to another. Harry talked to his people and told me that it was good news as far as he was concerned because the committee would like to meet with me. I went to Seattle and met with the selection committee and did some due diligence with the bank's senior staff. It seemed to go well, although one can never know for sure. Toward the end of November, without going through all the details of meetings and such, I was trying to get to the heart of Seafirst's problems. Essentially it came down to bad loans. Seafirst had made energy loans in excess of a billion dollars, and the portfolio was poorly secured. The bank's energy loan department was small, and it had little or no experience with the technical side of contracting perfected collateral, which turned out to mean that they did not have sufficient collateral to support its loans to the oil patch. A significant part of the total exposure related to Seafirst's practice of participating with Oklahoma-based Penn Square Bank. When Penn Square Bank failed in July 1982, Seafirst was left holding an empty bag.

Bill Jenkins thought things were not as serious as they seemed and that the industry would correct itself in time, but the board did not agree. It was a tense time because Jenkins did not think they should be getting rid of him, but they persisted. Things got tougher and the bank had to write off more and more of the loans that went sour. There was an incredible loss looming, and no one saw it coming. No one knew how bad it was going to be, including me.

The search went ahead, and Harry told me that my name had been added to the four finalists. I had been put in front of the executive committee, and eventually the whole board decided that I was their man. I was told that they would be delighted to have me come up and take over the bank. It happened quickly, and that presented some problems. I had to talk to everyone on the Wells board about what I had decided to do and why I was doing it. I suggested that Carl Reichardt take my place. I knew the bank would do well because the key managers were all pros. They were good and aggressive, and the bank would be fine. The board agreed.

I had to talk to every member of the Wells board by early December. The final board meeting of the year was nearing, and that seemed to be the best time to formally announce my retirement. The meeting was on a Tuesday morning, but the Seafirst board meeting in which I would be named as that bank's chief executive was not to take place until the following morning. The Seafirst people did not want the Wells Fargo board to announce my departure for Seattle and Seafirst, but only my year-end retirement from Wells. The timing of the meetings was awkward because I did announce my retirement from Wells on the Tuesday and the change was announced. I was able to leave the bank that day to fly up to Seattle. They kept the secret very well, as no one seemed to know what was going on. Then the Seafirst board made the announcement at the board meeting in Seattle on Wednesday, and I was able to be there. The 24-hour news blackout made some people antsy because they did not know where I was going or why I was retiring. By Wednesday there were only a few noses out of joint over the way it was handled, but by then it was a fait accompli.

The transition was to be made effective on January 1, 1983. Having had dinner with the board of Seafirst, I took a week off and went skiing in Aspen with my friend Mary Alice Clark and some of our respective children. After that I moved to Seattle and was there to take over on the first of January. Those days were a rush of meeting people and interviews. I was excited about the new challenge and establishing myself in a new city.

When Bill Jenkins found out I was the one the board had selected to take his place, he never batted an eyelash. He was always friendly, considerate, and helpful in every way. We had known one another for years and had done things socially together in the past. We had also served on the United Airlines board together. He could not have been more of a complete gentleman and good friend in helping me get started in Seattle. I will never forget how he treated me with the utmost respect and graciousness. His problem was with the bank, not with me. His removal was the board's decision, and I was the one who was elected to take his place. That was the way it was and the way he seemed to look at it publicly. I do not know how he felt inside, but he certainly handled himself well and in a constructive way as far as I was concerned. He did things he didn't have to do, like introducing me to his friends and the town.

There were others who went out of their way to introduce me to the community. Certainly Harry Mullikin and his predecessors Eddie Carlson and Lynn Himmelman were great supporters and good friends. They sponsored me many times and were helpful with the local knowledge that is so essential to getting started in a new city. We had been together on the United Airlines board for years and knew each other well. Another old friend, Chuck Pigott, was also warm and welcoming. Shortly after I arrived, Chuck offered to give a lunch for me at the Rainier Club to introduce me to some of his friends in the business world. The people I met that day became friends for as long as I have been in Seattle. It was a generous and thoughtful event that I enjoyed and appreciated greatly. It was as if he were mentoring me and letting his friends know that I would be able to add something to the community.

In the end it all happened in a short time. The move came about after considerable thought and angst over a year or two while I was still at Wells. Ernie's advice came back to me, as I may have overstayed my welcome at Wells and I no longer felt comfortable. My social situation was not great, and I just did not want to be in San Francisco anymore.

Seafirst's management team was a good one, but the system was flawed.

The bank's structure had been changed in response to a consultant's report in the early 1980s. It became top-heavy and expensive, and many of the bank's well-publicized problems were justified. Still, we hoped that the high level of professionalism at Seafirst and the personal strengths of its employees, combined with the continued support of the bank's customers and shareholders, would save the day.

We revised our corporate mission statement to clearly define Seafirst's new strategy. It read, "Seafirst's primary mission is to be the major provider of quality financial services to profitable segments within the personal, business and corporate markets in the Northwest. Seafirst will also compete within selected areas of the Western United States and Western Canada whenever a significant presence is sustainable. Nationally and internationally, the company will be active in those areas and countries where providing service to major corporations and foreign operations will directly support and enhance Seafirst's primary mission as the leading Northwest regional financial institution." Perhaps this was too little, too late, but it eventually led to the bank's return to profitability.

During my first three months in Seattle, it became clear that Seafirst was in much worse shape than I or anyone had imagined, and each month it got worse. Its book value was fast becoming a negative number. Seafirst's nonperforming loans represented nearly 8 percent of its assets, and they exceeded the bank's shareholders' equity and loss reserves by more than 7 percent. It became clear that the bank had to be sold or it would be taken over by the FDIC. In the latter case, all the shareholders would have been wiped out. Initially to keep the bank in business I had to secure a $3 billion line of credit from the nation's largest banks. The line was collateralized by good loan assets pledged at the Federal Reserve Bank. This credit was not long lasting, and it only gave us time to see what we could do about getting a large capital infusion or selling the bank. The credit line provided Seafirst some assurance that it could withstand a possible run on the bank.

We had launched Westnet, an effort to form a consortium of major western banks that would provide common services and products to customers throughout the West to compete with Bank of America. We were making good strides toward this and other objectives. We exceeded our own expectations when we began to offer Market Rate Savings accounts.

After many trips east and overseas, it became obvious that a sale of Seafirst was the only opportunity short of an FDIC takeover, and Bank of America became the chosen buyer. A special dispensation would be required for Bank of America to acquire Seafirst, or any other bank within the state for that matter. The acquisition was hotly contested by our competitors, who feared the strength of what they understood to be a financial behemoth, but the state law was amended to allow "failing" banks to be acquired by out-of-state banks, and by June 1983 the transaction was completed. By the end of that year Seafirst had written off almost one billion in failed loans.

The deal preserved about 50 percent of Seafirst stock's peak value, and that was better than many had expected. If the FDIC had taken over the bank, its shareholders would have received nothing for their investments and the government would have owned and operated the institution until it could be liquidated or sold.

In theory, the FDIC would have kept the bank's management, including me, until the bank's business was straightened out and resold to the public. From my point of view that would have been a good outcome, but that was not what I had been hired to do. I was there to try to save the bank and protect the existing shareholders as much as possible. Either way, the customers of the bank were going to be protected and the operations would continue to serve the community, but there would be no more participation in the oil business.

Seafirst went through some difficult and perilous times. The board stuck together and was supportive of our efforts. When Bank of America acquired Seafirst, they maintained the board and kept me as its chief executive, and put one of its executives on the board. Subject to little restraint, I was allowed to run the business, plumb the depth of its losses, and continue the effort to return it to profitability. As usually happens in a case like this, the effort to stabilize took longer than I expected. There were lots of changes in organization and policy to be established, and after the first year a large turnover in the top management had occurred. I brought only one key person with me from Wells, Glenhall Taylor. He became our senior loan officer. He took over the immense job of sorting out the loan portfolio while I tried to straighten out the organization that had created the mess in the first place. Those were our two key responsibilities. The personnel for the other management moves came from within the existing staff. It took me a while to learn the bank, its people, and its needs and also to become familiar with the community.

I did not remove anyone for the first year, but then I began to make changes that I hoped would help meet our goals and create a new operating environment. It was a nervous time but also stimulating. As we went through the difficult times, it seemed to me that all I had learned at Wells in those 16 years as its chief executive was being put to good use. I became more confident and comfortable with what to do and how to do it. Best of all, it was satisfying and fun.

Even though the bank was owned by Bank of America, they let Seafirst's board and management plan and run the operations as if we were an independent entity. We were allowed to keep our name and operating procedures without consolidating with Bank of America to the south. The immense financial strength of Seafirst's parent allowed us to move ahead. By 1986 our assets totaled $10.3 billion. We were still the state's largest bank, but we faced increased competition. Washington State banking law again facilitated the merger of prosperous banks, and in 1987 I found I would again compete with Los Angeles-based Security Pacific when it acquired the state's second-largest bank, Rainier Bancorp. But by then, Seafirst had become profitable.

I SERVED THE STATE AS PART OF THE WASHINGTON ROUNDTABLE. SHOWN,
FROM LEFT, ARE SAFECO CHIEF EXECUTIVE OFFICER BRUCE MAINES;
SEAFIRST CHIEF EXECUTIVE OFFICER DICK COOLEY; WASHINGTON
ROUNDTABLE EXECUTIVE DIRECTOR DICK FORD; AND PUGET SOUND BANK
CHAIRMAN AND CHIEF EXECUTIVE OFFICER BILL PHILIP.

I have been retired from Seafirst for almost 20 years. Lots of changes have taken place in the banking business during that time. People who have known me as a banker often ask me if I'm happy that I am not in the business today. I used to smile and duck that question, but of late it is becoming easier to agree with the premise of the question as the conditions in the financial world have become so disastrous.

From 1934 to 1988 there was a clear distinction between commercial and investment bankers. Commercial bankers were regulated carefully, primarily through the Glass-Steagall Act and by the Federal Reserve Bank, the Comptroller of the Currency, and the Federal Deposit Insurance Corporation, while investment bankers were governed by the marketplace. Governmental regulation put strong controls on risk.

Commercial bankers took in deposits from people and corporations and used those deposits to make loans and clearly defined investments. These loans and investments were subject to management review and also to rigid examination by the governmental regulators. Investment bankers had no such restraints and were able to borrow funds from banks, insurance companies, and the general marketplace.

Commercial banks were not able to leverage themselves freely, as they were controlled by their regulators.

A small example of how this worked is the housing market. In the 1980s our bank would be able to lend 80 percent of the appraised value of a $500,000 home, while our savings-and-loan competitors could lend 100 percent, plus a separate loan for furniture and fixtures. As market conditions changed in the 1990s, sub-prime loan packages could reach 130 percent of value. With the economy booming, housing prices went up, which made the loan seem less risky than it was. The success of these loan packages depended on rising home prices and full employment with consistently rising payrolls. If the economy slowed and wages decreased, there was no way to keep the mortgage payments on track. In addition, some lenders applied fewer restraints and made numerous loans at less-than-appropriate credit standards. And as the bubble burst, that is exactly what happened. There was no way to service these debts.

The above scenario is a simplified description of how homes came to be financed in the new century. Imagine bundling thousands and thousands of this kind of paper into collateral for a bond issue that would be sold all over the world as a "safe" investment. The risks involved in the sub-prime bond market were exceedingly high. And this is a simple example that does not even take into account the surrounding vehicles of derivatives, counter-party risks, default insurance, and all the other financial contracts that accompanied investments in general. Putting all these instruments together in an accelerating stream of activity produced enormous profits, which led to cutting corners and fraudulent activities pushed hard by the greedy desire for profits.

After the elimination of the Glass-Steagall Act in 1999, the differences between commercial and investment bankers gradually went away and the media defined all financial participants as "bankers." Whether one was a commercial banker or an investment banker, all were considered bankers. As that happened, the business of the old commercial bankers changed, and I became grateful that my banking days were over. Much has been written about the new financial vehicles that have come to the market in the last few years. Until 2008 the vast increase in risk was not talked about as much as the tremendous profits that were being generated. When the bubble burst, that changed dramatically and the word *greed* was on everybody's lips. The assumption that things could never get so tight that even a firm like Lehman Brothers could not borrow a dollar overnight in the marketplace proved erroneous.

People forgot the rules and cut too many corners, again seem-
ingly pushed on by greed and the assumption that everything
would keep going up. It is hard to buck a trend like that.

Basically it was not the kind of banking I was trained in and in
which I grew up. So even though I missed the big paychecks,
albeit they were small by comparison to those paid to investment bank management, I am glad that this frenzy was not part
of my career.

At the time I came up to Seattle I had just been divorced from
Judy, my second wife. We had been doing the best we could to
iron things out, but I had asked for the divorce and saw it finalized
in the fall of 1982. Our relationship had begun during a period of
great loneliness for us both. I was in the process of divorcing
Sheila when I first found out about Judy Ludwig. She was going
through a set of problems similar to mine. Since neither of us had
formally left our homes, communication was limited to the
phone. Still, through those conversations we became closer. After
a time we both moved out of our then homes and began leading
our individual lives. Separations were accommodated, but after a
few years they led to final separations and divorce. When the
divorces were finalized, we became engaged and then were married before taking enough time to understand all the implications
of what our families and backgrounds would bring us. Judy knew
what was expected of me by the bank, its board, management, and
clients. She had grown up around banking. Her father, H. Stephen
Chase, had been my boss at Wells Fargo, and I succeeded him as
the bank's chairman. She tried hard and was a good person and a
good wife, but the marriage did not last.

About the time that Judy and I married, Sheila, my first wife,
married Dick Collins. He was an equestrian and ran the equestrian center at Pebble Beach. He also was busy in the real estate
business and over time taught Sheila all she needed to know to

be successful in that field. She became the top salesperson in the Monterey area and held that position for 10 years.

Dick Collins was older than Sheila and died several years after they were married, but not before making a tremendous impression on Sean and Mark. He was the father for them that I was not. They loved and respected him, so I pray for him for what he did for the boys and Sheila. By then Sheila was in declining health, and ultimately she sold her home in Pebble Beach and moved back to San Francisco. She died in the fall of 2008, surrounded by our children. It is never easy to see your mother die, but the children all told me it was a happy death.

———————

Before retiring from Wells Fargo and moving to Seattle, I had grown quite fond of Mary Alice Clark. Her husband had recently died, and in fact, she had been widowed three times. Her third husband had succumbed to cancer about a year before Mary Alice and I became friends. She was dating other people and so was I, but the move to Seattle precipitated a change in our relationship. I asked her if she would consider moving to Seattle if I relocated. She thought she might be open to the idea, but it was a lot to consider and she was not sure. We firmed it up in January after I had moved and she had come to Seattle for a visit.

Boeing President Mal Stamper became a good friend. He and his wife, Mari, gave a dinner party for us shortly after I arrived in Seattle. They wanted to introduce me to some people they thought I would enjoy meeting. I asked if it was all right to bring Mary Alice, being concerned about appearances in a city that I had been led to believe was somewhat conservative. As I was new to a very visible job at a well-known Seattle company, I asked Harry Mullikin his opinion regarding any exposure of my personal life. He told me that it would be just fine for me to bring a lovely lady to Seattle. "No one would care, and people would be happy about that," he said. There was no pressure either way, and I was happy to share the evening with Mary Alice.

I was able to say to Mary Alice that if we did get married and she moved to Seattle, she could pursue anything she wanted. I told her that she did not have to join a lot of boards or work for the bank. That was my job. Mary Alice was an artist and she wanted to pursue her education and her art degree, which she was able to do. In January we decided to marry. The ceremony took place in the Westin Hotel on February 20, 1983. It was a wonderful day and just happened to fall on the same day as my parents' wedding, some 67 years before. That is how I got to Seattle and began my life with Mary Alice. Ten of our combined 11 children attended, making it a great occasion. The rest of this memoir will cover my time in Seattle. It is a significant period of my life, lasting more than 25 years and still counting. More importantly, it has been the happiest time in my life.

As the decision to move to Seafirst Bank in Seattle happened so quickly, there had been no time to search for a place to live. The bank gave me three months to get settled and put me up at the Westin Hotel. Initially I was not too concerned about my accommodations, but that changed when Mary Alice and I decided to get married. She had a large classic home in Beverly Hills where she lived with three of her children. There was much to be done, as she decided to rent rather than sell her home. And then there was the question regarding her children. Where did they want to live? We traded weekends at both locations in those first three months, but spent considerable time looking around Seattle for a rentable place. We found a nice penthouse apartment overlooking the harbor and took possession in April at a location less than a mile from the bank headquarters.

We furnished our new place from scratch. Mary Alice's youngest child, Bruce, was the only one of her children who made the trip north to live with us. His sister Anne-Marie had gone off to UC-Berkeley as a freshman. She went straight through in four years, earning a degree in history, and then took a job at a San Francisco brokerage firm. Being a broker did not turn out to be a good fit for her, so a year later she went back to school to get her teaching credential. During this period she married and moved to Hillsborough, California, where she began her teaching career at the Crocker School.

Mary Alice had four of her six children, Karin, Susan, Michael, and Jim, during her first marriage. Anne-Marie and Bruce were children of her second marriage, to Bruce Cordingly. The older three were out of the house and gone before I came onto the scene, and I pray for each of them every day.

———

I gradually settled into my job and my adopted city, Seattle, but there were still many trips back and forth to Beverly Hills. In our first year together, Mary Alice discovered a lump in her breast, which was diagnosed as malignant. It had to be removed. After the first operation in Beverly Hills, her care was transferred to Seattle. Through our internist, she was fortunate to be put in the hands of Dr. Kaplan, the oncologist at Swedish Hospital. When we met him for the first time and talked about the prognosis of the disease, I asked him if we could hope to see our 25th wedding anniversary. He smiled and said he could not promise that, but he was sure that 15 years was within reach. Though not the news we were hoping for, it could have been a lot worse. It would be hard to imagine a more thoughtful and competent person to help her through this ordeal. During that time we did go to the Mayo Clinic, and to be on the safe side, she elected to have a full double mastectomy. After those first two years of treatments and the successful results, she was allowed to take a rest from the chemo and with the exception of regular checks began to live a normal life again. The initial course of treatment seemed to be successful and she remained in remission for over five years.

Our apartment was downtown within walking distance of most places we wanted to visit daily, so we found that we walked much more often. If there were further destinations, the bank arranged for a car and driver for me, making transportation to and from the airport and places like that convenient. It also became an enormous help when we attended various social events, as we were able to enjoy the entire evening without having to worry about who was going to drive home. People were kind to us and we both made many good friends. My business travel continued, but at a much less intense rate. I took Mary Alice with me whenever I could, and she was willing to go.

We worked hard at combining our 11 children into one group. The ages were staggered a year or two apart, and they seemed to get along. In those first four years we took everyone, grandchildren included, to Vail for Christmas and they became good friends. In smaller pairings there were also summer trips to places like Sun Valley or bike trips to France and Germany.

I found the work at Seafirst interesting and satisfying. The bank continued to recover, and it became a very rewarding investment for Bank of America. At Wells, being chief executive officer of the third-largest bank in California was challenging and rewarding, but when you are the biggest and oldest bank in your state, as was Seafirst, it is a slightly different situation. There is a greater opportunity to set the tone and be an influence in the community than when there is always a bigger, stronger competitor across the street. There is a chance to lead rather than just reacting to the competition. Being the biggest entity in any market gives one a chance to take a constructive leadership role in providing new services or ideas. There is an opening for greater creativity in the work one does for the whole area.

Although not as large as San Francisco, Seattle was no backwater Pacific port. It received a fair amount of attention, especially during national elections. President George H. W. Bush was one of those people who had a Phi Beta Kappa key from Yale. He was highly intelligent, and an excellent athlete. George and I played tennis together in our teens. While still in college, he married Barbara Pierce, who was the daughter of Marvin Pierce, my father's close friend and my first boss at McCall's. I was a year ahead of George at Yale, but we knew each other because of the family connections and growing up in the Greenwich – Rye area. During World War II and afterward we went in different directions. On the rare occasions when we ran into each other, Barbara and George were always friendly. There is the tie-in between George Bush and Miguel de la Madrid, the only two presidents of state I have really known. They both were kind enough to remember me out of long lines of presidential greeters.

When George was running for his second term as President, the campaign brought him to Seattle. As a modest donor, I was invited to meet him at the Westin Hotel, along with a multitude of others. In the back of the hotel, down the spine of the building, was a floor of meeting rooms that were connected by a service hallway. We were divided into appropriate groups, probably by size of contributions, which put me in the third or fourth room. The President went from room to room using the back hallway as he passed. In each room he gave a short version of his stump speech and answered a few questions. When he came to our room, I was in the back of the group and was not able to make eye contact with him. He was probably with us for 10 minutes or so before sliding out the door and on to the next room.

After he left, the group filtered out gradually, and I was standing in the middle of the room across from the door to the back hallway. Shortly, there were some cheers and hubbub and people moving back down the hallway in the opposite direction, signaling that the President's party was leaving. I looked up and there he was, glancing into the room, and our eyes met. He stopped cold, smiled, and came quickly through the door right to me. He stuck out his hand and said, "How are you, Dick? Great to see you here! How are your parents?" It was short but friendly. It had been more than six years since he had seen me. It was impressive that he picked me out so quickly in that short glance as he was rushing to his next appointment. Later that evening, my wife and I went to a larger reception to hear the full speech and had our picture taken with George and Barbara. He never forgot his friends.

From time to time in Seattle I would run across someone connected to my past like Peggy Vance. I found out that her father was Sheila's older brother Murray McDonnell. Murray had married Peter Flanigan's only sister, Peggy, and they had nine children together. One of them was Peggy Vance. She married Cyrus Vance Jr. and moved to Seattle sometime in the late 1980s. Mary Alice and I got to know them quite well, and while we were not in the same social group, we saw them fairly often. They had two children here, and Cy did an outstanding job with his Seattle law firm. He was a Democrat and interested in politics, which he might have inherited from his father, who was secretary of state under President Carter.

As the bank recovered, the board began to think in terms of management succession. They did not want to have my five-year contract mature and not know who was going to manage the bank. I began to think about a successor. Dick Rosenberg, an old associate from Wells Fargo, had gone to Crocker Bank as its number-two person when Carl Reichardt took over at Wells. After a time it was clear that Dick would not move up to become Crocker's chief executive. I knew that being head of a major bank was his goal. He had been a talented marketing guru for Wells, as he was very bright and ambitious. I thought he would be a good fit at Seafirst, so I went down to San Francisco to sound him out. He was thinking of moving and was considering an interesting offer from a bank back east. I was able to tell him about Seafirst and that if he came to Seattle, I would retire in a year and he could run the bank on his own. He was concerned about Bank of America's ownership, but the fact that Seafirst had kept its own name and board of directors was a plus. Needless to say, before talking to Dick I had cleared it with both the Seafirst board and the Bank of America management.

Dick thought it over, talked to some of our people, and decided to move to Seattle, which made a lot of people happy.

Not long after Dick, and his wife, Barbara, arrived in Seattle, Bank of America's loan problems were exposed and its management changed. Tom Clausen was brought back from retirement to head the bank. Bank of America had been going through some hard times with its international investments and loans. Its management bench needed strengthening, and some competent Wells bankers had moved across the street. Glenhall Taylor, who had done such an outstanding job pulling together Seafirst's portfolio, was taken down to San Francisco to do the same for Bank of America. It was a big challenge for him, as the B of A was so large and so diversified globally. Turning around a bank that size was not going to be easy or happen too quickly, but he was ultimately successful. He did it well.

I had been elected to the Bank of America board while Sam Armacost was running the bank. As the head of an important subsidiary, I was an inside director and not involved with the executive committee and all the actions that were going on. Still, I was able to see and understand the progress of the changes. With increasing Bank of America problems, the deposit line of the bank began to waiver. Its large California branch network was its biggest asset. Its board elected Tom Clausen to succeed Sam Armacost as the bank's chief executive, and Tom decided he needed a strong marketing head to turn it around. There was no one better than Dick Rosenberg for that job, and Tom came after him. Dick was happy in Seattle and doing well operating the Seafirst organization, and he was not too excited about going back to San Francisco in the marketing slot. He turned down the first two offers, and Tom was getting frustrated.

One night after a long and discouraging Bank of America board meeting in Los Angeles, Tom took me aside and asked me what he had to do to get Dick to come to San Francisco and take that job. Among other things, I told him that he should think about coming up to Seattle and taking Barbara and Dick out to dinner and making them an offer that could not be refused. That offer was a much bigger salary and the clear opportunity to have a chance to succeed him as the bank's chief executive. Having come back from retirement, Tom was not going to be around too long. I did not think Dick would go for any less than that.

They finally worked it out on the third try, and I was back in the succession business looking for my replacement. Dick went down to San Francisco as vice chairman. He came up with a new deposit and loan plan that was sold successfully through the branches. The deposit line of the bank stabilized, and the loan product turned the losses into profits. Dick saved Bank of America, though he never received the proper credit for it. He did get a more important recognition a few years later when the Bank of America board voted him chairman and chief executive officer and he succeeded Tom Clausen.

When Seafirst's board asked me about a successor initially, I told them I did not think anyone in senior management was ready, but there would be candidates in the future. Almost two years later, as we began our second search, I concentrated inside the bank. Of the top managers, Luke Helms seemed to be the best one for the job. He was smart, experienced, and well liked in town. Dick agreed and so did the Seafirst board. Luke succeeded me when I retired at the end of 1990. The board kept me on as a nonexecutive chairman of the executive committee. Luke ran the bank on his own and did well with it. I was given a small suite of offices on a lower floor and administrative help. I rarely went up to the executive floor except for scheduled meetings.

After 42 years as a banker, one acquires connections and relationships that do not die the day you retire. One continues to provide help to people and customers who need it. It is the nature of the business. But in Ernie Arbuckle's words, it was time for me to be repotted.

My Seattle-based community commitments included three years as president of the Seattle Symphony board. Here I'm shown with Chairman Emeritus Sam Stroum.

RETIRED PRODUCTIVELY

I had a friend named Walter Wriston, who ran Citibank for many years. When asked what retirement was like, he responded, "Retirement? It's like walking down a pier and falling off the end into the water."

There is no question in my mind that the day one gives up the office and the responsibility of leadership, one is faced with an enormous new challenge. Even though you may be receiving an outrageous settlement, as some definitely are, it is hard to prepare yourself for the gravity of the experience. It is the table at 21, or the box seats, or the jet and the personal car and driver. Suddenly all that stops, and it is hard to slam on the brakes. Everything you have worked for has been passed to the incumbent. The workforce feels like it has moved on with a new momentum and tide. Fresh policies are implemented. People are hired and fired. The media quotes the new guy instead of you. Retirement is a hard thing to do gracefully, but I have seen it done well.

One particularly good example of a graceful exit was Chuck Pigott's retirement from PACCAR. After 33 years as that company's CEO, he retired and no one was following his orders. It is a hard thing to get a handle on, but I think he managed to step down with dignity and let his son Mark run the company with tremendous success. Though he never admitted it to me, he saw that Mark was trained carefully for the job by experts. Transitioning to a new lifestyle, Chuck supervised the building of an impressive yacht and traveled the oceans with many of his friends. When he is not traveling, he shares himself with several community activities of importance. That is an A grade in retirement.

Unfortunately, many executives retire without sufficient thought about what life will look like in the future — should one reinvent oneself or decide to drop into a lower gear?

The transition was not as difficult for me as it might have been for someone who had no idea what to do.

Many chief executives who retire have not planned for anything besides more time to play golf and gin rummy.

They are too old to go out and raise hell, and they may not want to do that at 65 anyway. One has the old connections to the business world, but those relationships fall away, and one is left with a lot of unscheduled time.

For me it was different. When I retired the first time from Wells Fargo after 33 years, I was not really retiring but moving on to a new challenge that excited me. After eight years at Seafirst, my retirement at 68 was more conventional. I was alive, energetic, and looking for something to do. I had some ideas but not a clear plan.

When I retired from Seafirst at the end of 1990, Mary Alice suggested that it would be good to get out of town for a while. There were two reasons. She thought I needed the rest, and she also believed that Luke and his team would have a better chance of getting under way if I were not around to look over his shoulder. She was right on both counts. A change of scenery was the perfect solution. We settled on London and the U.K. In most of our European visits we had traveled through Heathrow, never spending more than a day or two before going to a new destination. We decided to dedicate the entire sabbatical to the British Isles.

Renting a flat for three or four months in London seemed like the best way to go about our plan. In mid December of 1990, we stayed a week in London at the Berkeley Hotel while looking around for a place to stay. There were many flats/apartments for lease, but they were hardly exciting. Finally on the last day, through a friend at United, we found a lovely flat in Chelsea, which we took even though it was a six-month lease.

We arrived at Tedworth Square in Chelsea in the middle of February. There was snow on the ground and a chill in the air, but we were lucky to have a new two-level flat that was warm and cozy. Getting settled took a couple of weeks. It was not like living in a hotel with all the conveniences already in place. Instead we had to find everything from scratch, and that took some know-how because the culture was different. For example, there were two TVs, but they would not work until I found the Chelsea Town Hall and purchased a TV permit. I had to buy a parking permit so we could park in front of our flat. There were all the usual necessities of daily life, the markets, the cleaners, the newspaper stands, the florist, the Church and Mass times, etc. In the first week, an IRA bomb blew up in Victoria Station about a mile away. The Thames was about four blocks from the square, so we shared many fun and interesting walks.

Our idea had been to experience all we could see and learn about England. With that being our intent, I purchased two British Rail passes and we made plans to see much of the countryside on the weekends. We also had a desire to experience the London theater. I would look through the *Times* and pick out several plays that were recommended and appealed to us. Getting tickets was not a problem. If I arrived at the theater in the morning and stood in line before noon, I was usually able to pick up reasonable seats for the most popular plays without difficulty or a big surcharge.

Since we expected to stay three or four months, we each wanted to have something of interest to do during the day. For Mary Alice this meant finding an art school where she could continue her painting education that she had been working on at Cornish College of the Arts in Seattle. As luck would have it, there was an arts college only 30 minutes from our flat. I was also fortunate to find the London School of Flying, about 17 miles west of our residence. Mary Alice rode a big red double-decker bus to within a block of her school, and I drove through the countryside and roundabouts out to the airfield three times a week. These were great experiences for both of us.

Through friends of friends we met people who were kind enough to offer assistance so we could learn the system and get things done. A tennis club called the Vanderbilt was suggested, and they offered a temporary membership. That was a great boon, and we tried to use their indoor courts regularly. The club's claim to fame was that Princess Diana played there occasionally, though we never saw her. It was not the weather for golf, but the wet and cold days lent themselves to brisk walks of exploration visiting marvelous museums and historical sites.

We stayed with our original plan to see as much as we could of England by whatever means. When Mary Alice's daughter Anne-Marie and her friend Stephanie were with us, we spent a night at Oxford and had a chance to visit that wonderful institution. Later we went out to see Cambridge, which though similar, seemed a little more friendly to me. One of our English friends strongly recommended a visit to Bath, and that turned out to be quite wonderful. Since we were driving to Bath, we routed our way back via Downside Abbey, a 500-year-old Benedictine school from which many of the Portsmouth monks had come. Mary Alice and I used British Rail for both shorter and longer trips. We traveled to Cambridge and Salisbury and took longer trips to the Lake Country, northern Wales, and of course, Glasgow and Edinburgh. It seemed like the most civilized form of travel, as we did not have to think about driving ourselves or mapping out our destinations. Six to eight hours on the train gave us the freedom to relax and enjoy the countryside.

All in all, the time passed quickly. Toward the end of our stay, Mary Alice developed pains in her side. She had passed her five-year stretch of remission from her tumor problems, so I was hoping it was nothing big. Though it was disturbing, she felt well enough to continue our trip. We were able to travel to Stuttgart, Budapest, Vienna, and Berlin. After these travels we dropped off her new Mercedes-Benz to be shipped home and flew back to Seattle on May 19. It was a time that I will long cherish. When we arrived, snow had covered Tedworth Square, and as we left, it was a garden of green and a profusion of flowering plants and trees. What a privilege those months in England and the short trip on the continent had been.

We were coming home with equal parts fear and excitement. In the early 1990s, Mary Alice and I started looking around Sun Valley for a vacation home, and we were able to find one that suited the family in 1992. We did not have enough beds for everyone in the family at once, but we were able to fit all those who wanted to ski sometime during the winter. Mary Alice loved to ski, and we would often spend a week or two on our own, taking advantage of all the great runs Mount Baldy presented. It was the right time for most of our young grandchildren, and we found that summer visits were just as desirable as those during the ski season, if not better.

———

Filling the void after retirement was not easy. After the initial transition period, I filled it by teaching. I taught college-level business school classes for 15 years. Ten years with the Masters in Business Administration (MBA) program and five years with the Executive Masters in Business Administration (EMBA) program at the University of Washington, and five years with the MBA program at Seattle University. It was a new challenge, as I had never felt particularly comfortable behind a podium, but it was exhilarating. Teaching gave me something to focus on and worry about, and it moved me into a different world of academia and campus life.

Beyond our family activities in those first post-Seafirst retirement years, there were two things that were interesting and took up considerable time. The first was our airplane and our flying. There was a lot to learn and a lot to practice. Mary Alice had earned her private license after I did, and I think she enjoyed it. We were taught by Phyllis Baer, a fine instructor with more than 10,000 hours under her belt. I was trying to learn enough to get my instrument rating. Mary Alice and I flew together often. There was the occasional longer trip to Sun Valley or San Francisco, but more often the $100 hamburger trip to Tacoma or Port Townsend on a weekend. Once we flew down to Tucson to see the Mullikins and from there across the country to Augusta, Georgia. On that trip we encountered inclement weather and had to spend an extra day in Waco, Texas, before getting out late in the afternoon and making it to Little Rock, Arkansas, where there was another weather delay before we could leave. I remember just barely being able to see the Mississippi River as we flew across it at twilight. From there on we were in the dark until we landed at Augusta around 10 o'clock. We took turns flying and navigating and it was fun.

The second interest was the Washington State Health Commission. Governor Booth Gardner had initiated a strong legislative effort to improve the health-care system in the state, and this was well before he was diagnosed with Parkinson's disease. Paul Redmond from Spokane was appointed the first chairman. He was busy as Washington Water Power's (now Avista) chief executive officer, and after a year of getting the commission started he wanted to be relieved of the responsibility. I was offered the opportunity to replace him and I accepted. I had never taken a job like that for the state, and thought I had the time and should do it. Randy Revelle was the chief staff person and was in charge of coordinating the program and getting the report done on time. There were many meetings in Olympia and other parts of the state, as well as a series of public hearings where the commissioners would listen to ideas and recommendations from all parts of the health-care-delivery system.

After getting as much information from the various parties as we could accommodate, we were to prepare a report and recommendations for the legislature and the governor that were to be the basis for legislative action. It was hard to accommodate all the specific interests of the many groups that made up the system. We came up with a compromise report that would have helped a lot of people, though all were far from satisfied. In the second year of the project there was an election in which control of the legislature went from Republican to Democratic shortly before the report was submitted. With the normal controversy surrounding the subject and the change in legislative control, it languished and failed to generate strong political interest on either side of the aisle. It may still be on the shelf today. It was clear that this was a subject on which it was very hard to please everyone. Still, it was a good experience and I learned an incredible amount about health care and how the state government worked.

While these two items took up a lot of time at the beginning, there was still the matter of teaching at the UW Business School on my mind. I had not been successful in working out an understanding with the school before we left for London. The department heads thought they could use me for spot appearances in various finance classes and as a "brown bag" lunch lecturer on an irregular basis. I wanted a regular class where I was officially part of the school. The program managers were friendly, but not receptive to the idea of making me a part of the faculty. I had taught relatively successfully in the special week's training program for the EMBAs during the spring quarter, and that was the group that appealed to me the most. Students in this program still had their regular jobs and their experience level was that of managers, who worked for senior management people, who had reported to me. They were more mature and interesting to be with. However, the professors and the chief staff person who ran the program were very tight and let me know that there was no room for me in the group.

I had hoped the university would welcome someone of my experience in the "real world," but that was not the case. The same story came out of the regular MBA finance department when I offered to teach bank management. My persistent visits were a problem for them, and they did not know what to do with me. Finally, Bud Saxberg, head of the management and organization department, asked me what I wanted to do. They questioned what I really thought I could teach. My answer was that I was going away on a sabbatical, and when I returned I would talk to them. In the bank my experience interviewing the MBA graduates had been disappointing, and I thought the University's School of Business needed to expose the students to the practical business world, but that was not high on the academic agenda. The fact that I was not an MBA and had no graduate degree was harmful in this academic environment.

While in London I spent considerable time thinking about teaching. I questioned my ability to teach something new and different from the standard curriculum. After all, what did I really know enough about to share with business students who were interested in successful careers? For the past 24 years I had been chairman and chief executive of two major NYSE-listed banks, so I thought that I could teach about the chief executive position with some authority. Along with that came my experience with boards, how a board worked and how it was to be handled. There was no one in the business school with that kind of experience. They offered no courses on these subjects. As I thought more about it, I decided it was an opportunity that would solve both the school's problem of what to do with me and my problem of figuring out how I could add value to the student experience. I began working out the details.

The job of handling me seemed to fall to Professor Bob Woodworth, who was kind and smart and became a true mentor to me. We talked through my ideas for a class, and he went over it with Bud Saxberg. They discussed it and decided to give me a try. Bud offered me a job as an adjunct lecturer teaching a course on "The Chief Executive Officer and the Board of Directors." The class was to meet once a week for three hours in the spring quarter. The pay was $3,000 and it was to be an elective in the regular MBA program. It was not what I had hoped for but it was a start, and I was grateful to Bud for the opportunity.

While in London I had spent some time thinking about my career and what had been important to the success of the jobs that I'd had. What I came up with were generalizations on business and ethical behavior. There was nothing outstandingly different or precedent-setting in these statements, but they represented an update of several of the old golden rules I learned from my father. Initially there were 30 statements of ideas that had worked for me. I thought about how to make these ideas into a basis for the class. They turned out to be what I called a "low tech" leadership presentation, which I felt would be useful to the students in their careers whether they aspired to be a chief executive or not. I combined the 30 generalizations into six viewgraphs, as follows:

I. *Where are you going?* What chief executives have to do — for instance: work hard; have a mission and corporate goals; devise a plan to reach those goals and a team to do it, which could mean letting the team members do big jobs and make decisions.

II. *Useful skills for leaders:* Listen more than you talk, but when you do talk, ask lots of good questions. Cut down on office politics, speak well and clearly, be fair but firm, and have no misfits in key jobs.

III. Always get along with others: Become a good people picker, and trust your people. Give regular feedback to those who work for you, and set a good example at all times in all things.

IV. Hints for personal behavior: Use common sense and good judgment. Make decisions and believe you are right. Have no fear of failure. Keep in mind that it is okay to make an honest mistake. Take no actions on assumptions, be physically and mentally strong, and have personal goals. Write them down. Verbalize them.

V. Ideas from your oldest mentor: Communicate clearly, frequently, and in all directions. Control your ego. Try to be humble. Be honest. Have strong ethics and don't take shortcuts. Always have a successor trained to fill your job.

VI. Looking ahead: Take intelligent risks. Do not be afraid of new ideas. Be imaginative. Stimulate creativity. Add value. Keep learning. Think ahead. Be lucky. Be confident. Be a winner.

My first experience in teaching the EMBAs had been when the then-acting dean of the University of Washington School of Business asked me to teach the morning classes of the inaugural "off campus" week. Since I had come to Seattle to take over Seafirst, the dean wanted me to go through the trauma and the actions it took to keep the oldest and biggest bank in the state alive and functioning. Several of the students worked for managers who had worked for me. Since the story was topical and very close to me, I was able to make it interesting and got through the week in good shape. The real-life experience and the students' ability to ask questions about it went over well. This took place while I was still working at the bank. The story of the Seafirst demise was not sufficient as a base for an entire class and neither were the six viewgraphs, but they provided me with

I began teaching MBA courses at the University of Washington's Foster School of Business in the spring of 1992, and I later taught MBA classes at Seattle University's Albers School of Business.

the idea of how to proceed. However, it did not come easily. When I came back from England and went to talk to the UW Business School, I had this idea about a class. In those days you could have an elective with only one class a week. I started with one class a week, teaching regular MBA students in the School of Business.

The class began in the spring quarter of 1992. Over the next 10 years it evolved gradually into a format that worked well for the students and satisfied me. During that time the academic requirements at the school changed, and two classes per week rather than one became the minimum. It was clear to me that I could not entertain, much less teach, for three hours straight, and even two was not productive or easy. I looked for a curriculum that would involve the students either as individuals or in teams throughout the time period. I decided that having outside speakers from the business community would be interesting and useful to the class. The curriculum had to be a series of subjects having to do with chief executives and their boards. While it varied a bit over the 10 years, following is a list of the basic subjects.

1. Audit Committee
2. Board Mechanics
3. Chief Executive Officer and Retail Operation – Customer First
4. Chief Executive Officer and the Community
5. The Chief Executive Officer, the Job: Gets It, Keeps It, Is Boss
6. How the Chief Executive Officer Relates to the Board
7. Corporate Ethics (team)
8. Corporate Governance and Sarbanes-Oxley Act (team)
9. Corporate Leadership
10. Corporate Strategy
11. Diversity: Women/Minorities on Boards (team)
12. Evaluations of the Chief Executive Officer and Board
13. Executive Pay (team)
14. Family Holding Companies

15. Mock Board Meeting (2 teams)
16. RISK (team)
17. Small Business Boards – Entrepreneur (team)
18. Succession Management (team)
19. Turnarounds (team)
20. What an Outside Director Expects from the
    Chief Executive Officer

———————

I cannot remember when I got the idea to bring in extra people to talk to the class. The format evolved, and it soon developed into a class of participation. The students had to be involved. They had to ask questions. While it was not that way in the first year or two, it evolved into splitting the classroom into teams and taking different business subjects and having each team prepare a presentation for the class on that subject. That was combined with bringing experienced chief executives and businesspeople who were currently active into the classroom to talk to the students about their experience and what they were interested in. Each year I tinkered with the format a little. Every year I tried to start over, making a conscious effort not to repeat anything but to bring something new to the students.

I decided I did not need a textbook. Instead I made my textbook from the media. It was going to be a class about business practice because after all, that was why I was there. I wanted the students to be prepared to understand the "real world." That meant I would read books and select a text from the ample business literature available, then read magazines, newspapers, periodicals, and essays. They were obvious and practical. Clearly, students would have to understand how the corporation worked and the mechanics of running a company, from the board of directors' level on down to the operating levels.

The class evolved gradually. I learned to ask questions. I learned that I had to have a lot of questions for the students and there had to be homework. When one is teaching a subject based on personal experience, it is not easy to find a class text to cover the topics most pertinent to class discussions. The media articles provided the necessary background reading. Doing that also underlined my thought of wanting to expose the potential MBAs to the way businesses truly functioned instead of textbook analogies. I would clip articles, for instance, from the *New York Times, Wall Street Journal, Fortune, BusinessWeek*, etc. Typical subjects were:

1. What kind of people are there in the company for future management?
2. How to handle a takeover.
3. How does a chief executive officer deal with his board?
4. What does an independent director expect from his board?
5. How do you develop the future strategy for the corporation?
6. Management succession.
7. Where do you go for product?

Each class was divided into teams of three or four. The items marked *team* in the previous list were team assignments. These groups were asked to research a topic, prepare a PowerPoint presentation, and present it to the class on a certain date. Some of the presentations were fabulous and the question periods intense and everyone learned a great deal about the subject. Some were average, but rarely did a team bomb. Usually the guest speaker went first, with the day's team following after the break. It was flexible enough so that I had time to comment and raise my own thoughts about the subjects.

The exciting thing was that you could get someone like Jim Sinegal or Mark Pigott to come in and talk about his company. Jim would always talk about Costco, and Mark would talk about Paccar. They usually had slides, and afterward students would be able to ask questions that would help them form a good overall understanding of what was going on in the company. Depending on who it was and how quickly questions were answered, we would get in about 25 to 30 questions, sometimes fewer if the answers were fuller. The point for the class was that they had a chance to ask someone who was currently doing a good job in a chief executive position to explain what it was like to work there and hold that position. The questions covered topics such as What do you have to do to get there? What kind of promotion can you expect? What kind of movement can you expect? For someone wanting to join the company, what do people in charge look for? and What is important in climbing the hierarchy ladder? There were lots of questions, including personal ones such as How do you manage all the travel with a family? and What do you do with your children? Many were topics that they would never have a chance to ask a high-level executive about in any other forum.

I also asked chief executives of privately owned companies to speak to the class. Mike Garvey explained the chief executive's role from the perspective of a serial entrepreneur. He was a founding partner of what became Chateau Ste. Michelle. He was the principal owner of Saltchuk Resources, a holding company for maritime interests including TOTE, Foss Maritime, and Sea Star.

So the class was split in half — the visiting speaker and the presentation by students. Gradually I got better at it. There would be times in between the speaker and the business presentation when I might review what I had heard and what the students should have learned from the speaker by asking a lot of questions. We would discuss the meat of what the visitor had to say about his company, as well as his presentation and some of his answers to student questions. That was very popular. Then there would be a chance to discuss the subject that the team presented. When the class was over, hopefully they had covered two subjects thoroughly. The speaker talked about something different than the team, and the students would get a chance to explore two different important business subjects.

The class was a discussion of key business ideas. There were certain subjects that did not lend themselves to speakers, so I would cover such topics as corporate governance or the community. Always I would give them a quiz. I liked quizzes because I wanted to know if they had done the reading. In the early days, I would have them write it out in class, but I found that the answers to the quiz were rarely legible. That was something I wanted to improve on, but there wasn't much I could do about their handwriting skills at this level. Finally, it evolved over the years that I would give them a question and they would take it home on their computers, type up their answer, and bring it back to the next class. They also had a paper to write on one of the subjects presented in class. I would give them five or so topics, and they could pick one to write about. In some cases the mark they received was a pass/fail, and for other courses I had to give them an absolute mark. The grade consisted of 25 percent for the quizzes, 25 percent for the team performance, 25 percent for the longer quarterly report, which was a four-page report, and then a subjective mark on their class participation. This last was the hardest thing to do because it was difficult to keep track of it all, but I was able to get a sense of how much certain people participated and whether they had something intelligent to contribute to the discussion or just sat on their hands and took it all in as entertainment. I had to speak to several of them on that latter subject more than once. I was not a hard grader. I would say I was fair, but I did expect them to do the work and contribute to the overall discussion. It was important that they collaborate with the other students and present ideas in a constructive way, the whole point being that it was an interactive class where they could learn from one another. They certainly learned from the speakers, who so openly shared their knowledge and expertise.

I taught this class at the School of Business for 10 years and then took a year's sabbatical because I thought I was getting out of touch. It was right about the time of the dot-com bust. That's when I found out that some of the things I was telling them were really important and were working. The new director of the EMBA program invited me to come back after that and teach in those classes, which were older students. This was exactly what I had wanted to do from the start. Initially I thought I would be best suited to teach the people who were a little higher up in their business. The regular MBA student runs agewise from 25 to 35, with much less experience in the business world. The EMBAs are usually people in middle management in their companies. In the past, their companies would send them, but as companies began to cut costs, these people had to send themselves. In 2009 at the University of Washington it cost about $30,000 a year to be in the EMBA program. When you combine everything else, it's closer to $75,000 to $80,000 a year for them. Although some are still paid by their companies, many have to borrow it. This is a change that I have seen over the past 15 years.

As I transitioned into the EMBA schedule, the same class format worked well. Over the entire 15 years, the speakers came and went as their schedules varied. Some taught for only one year, while others put in years of helping these students. A sampling of the quality of their different backgrounds is indicated by this partial list: Bill Ayer, chief executive of Alaska Air Group; Renée Behnke, chief executive of Sur La Table; Jeff Brotman, chairman of Costco; Phyllis Campbell, president and chief executive of the Seattle Foundation; Boh Dickey, president of Safeco; Joan Enticknap, president of the HomeStreet Bank; Dan Evans, former governor and senator from the state of Washington; Anne Farrell, founding chief executive of the Seattle Foundation; Mimi Gates, director of the Seattle Art Museum; Gerald Grinstein, chief executive officer of Delta Air Lines; Joanne Harrell, president of United Way of King County; Kerry Killinger, former chairman and chief executive officer of Washington Mutual; Harry Mullikin, retired chief executive of Westin Hotels; John Nordstrom, retired cochairman of

Nordstrom; Mark Pigott, chairman and chief executive of PACCAR Inc.; Judy Runstad, attorney and former chairman of the Federal Reserve Bank of San Francisco; Mal Stamper, retired president of Boeing; and Kathy Wilcox, chief executive officer of the Washington Software Alliance. To these and all the other wonderful people who shared their experiences, I say thank you for your time and generosity in giving EMBA/MBA students the exposure they had never had before and which they treasured.

The chance to be involved with these young businesspeople was rewarding beyond all measure to me. Aside from the class work and the presentations, all students had to write a four-page paper on an appropriate subject they had studied in the quarter instead of taking a final exam. "Why I want to be a chief executive officer" was a much-used topic, which produced many interesting papers. Then occasionally they would write about their experience in their own company, which often was fascinating and sometimes a little scary. All in all, teaching turned out to be a second career for me that was thoroughly satisfying and engaging. I was sorry when it came to an end.

All through my 15 years of teaching, I tinkered with the overall result. By the time I got through my last quarter in 2006, I was comfortable with the format of the class and the reviews. Some reviews went up and down. Some classes were easier to deal with than others. Regardless of the outcome, it was a pleasure to teach, and I truly enjoyed my second career.

I sort of fell into my position at Seattle University. While I was teaching at the University of Washington, Father Steve Sundborg, president of Seattle University, invited me to one of the breakfasts he was having for community leaders about what was happening at the school. He was looking for ideas and responses on how to make Seattle University better, and more relevant. After I went to that breakfast, which included three or four people outside his staff, I offered to try my course at

Seattle University's Albers School of Business. They did not have a program like the one I was teaching at the UW, and I thought it might be helpful for them. Eventually, I was turned over to the dean of the Business School, Joe Phillips, and then he turned me over to one of his department heads and they decided to give me a try, although there was not much excitement there or much interest. As it turned out, the Seattle U. students were slightly older than the UW students and it was a night-school class, running from 6 to 9, with the same format. We had the teams, visiting speakers, and all the rest. It took a while to get off the ground, but when it did it went like gangbusters. It was well regarded and the reviews were excellent.

As I came to my retirement in 2006, which was my last quarter at Seattle University, they decided to continue the program. My replacement, Annette Jacobs, has kept the same general curriculum and question-and-answer sessions with business leaders. The University of Washington Foster School of Business has continued the program with Bill Ayer, of Alaska Airlines. The classes are going forward, although I am sure the format has changed considerably. Over the period when I was teaching, I learned that getting good speakers comes from who you know and what you've done with them. As I get older, my friends are at least in their seventies and not as active in business anymore, and I know only a few current chief executives. Mark Pigott is a wonderful example of someone the class could relate to. He is in his mid-fifties and highly successful. I just didn't know enough people like him. You cannot keep going on the same old stories. A big story to me means nothing to one of these students. That is why it was important that I retired when I did.

MARY ALICE PLAYING TENNIS ON HER COURT IN BEVERLY HILLS
BEFORE MOVING TO SEATTLE IN 1983.

LOST, FOUND, AND REMEMBERED

After we returned from Europe, the first and most important necessity for Mary Alice and me was to visit Dr. Kaplan and find out about the pain in her side. The news was unexpectedly bad. Scans showed tumors in her ribs. After six years of remission, her cancer was back. She began another program of chemo and regular visits to Hank Kaplan's office. As time went on, the effects of this insidious disease became apparent. She gave up flying and lost her stamina to play tennis. She was more often tired now and had to pace herself. She may have had more pain than she let on, but she went on with her life almost normally, although her exercise was limited to easy walking. If one were not aware of her condition, I doubt that anyone would have noticed the change. She was warm and affectionate, reaching out to all those she encountered. During our time in Seattle she came to cherish people here.

The treatments and various kinds of chemo continued. In the latter part of the 1990s they became stronger and more difficult to sustain. It took a lot of courage to face those trips to the hospital for visits that were painful and all-around not easy. By 1999 the cancer was out of control and was affecting her daily life to the point where normalcy was no longer possible. We knew there was not much time left, but we did not talk about it as the end of a wonderful life and what to do about it. There were obvious things that we discussed, but mostly we talked about what we were doing to help her physically day by day. She became very close to Hank Kaplan and his assistant Jeanie.

They were both tremendously supportive, and Mary Alice felt truly blessed by their support and care.

On October 4, 1999, Mary Alice died at home in bed. Her daughters Karin and Susan were holding her hands when she took her last breath. Hank had come to see her that Saturday afternoon and told us it would probably happen within the next day or two, so we were trying to make her as comfortable as possible. She carried a lot of pain at the end. It was hard to believe that it had finally happened because even when it is expected, one is never prepared.

When Mary Alice died, I did not cope well. I was surprised at my reaction because I knew she was going to die and yet I could not put my arms around the fact that she was going away and I was losing her. It was a concept that we had discussed on many occasions, but rationale flew out the window with her passing. I loved her deeply and found that in the weeks and months after her death, I dwelt increasingly on the ache and hollowness and absence. I have learned about myself that if something awful happens, I try to absorb it. When my parents died, I knew they were going to die and I was prepared for that. I miss them more today than the day they died, but they were older and had lived long and productive lives. I marvel at what they taught me and how they loved me.

Mary Alice was my wife from 1983 until her death. While we did not live together before 1983, we saw a lot of each other, and it was an experience not to be equaled. When I pray for Mary Alice, I pray that she will be full of love and close to God in heaven. She was an extraordinary mom and a wonderful wife. She contributed to everyone she ever met in her life, and she will always have a prominent place on my prayer list.

One of the things that I look back on with pride is my affiliation with Woodside Priory School, a Benedictine boarding school. The Benedictine monks at Portsmouth Priory gave me such a tremendous education and spiritual backbone that I am grateful they are able to continue their mission on the West Coast.

Woodside Priory was founded some 50 years ago after eight Hungarians escaped from behind the Iron Curtain in the late 1940s. They made their way to Canada and eventually settled in the San Francisco area. I was living in San Francisco at the time, and one of the monks put in charge of securing a site for the school contacted me for help. A location was found in Woodside, in the hills behind Stanford University, and the Priory was opened in 1957. Father Egon was one of the school's founders, and I came to know him well during my years in San Francisco.

The Priory remains a high-level coeducational college-preparatory school for more than 300 students, including boarders from South America and Asia. People from this deep peninsula area have welcomed and supported the school with incredible influence and generosity.

Fr. Egon Javor died recently at age 91, the last of the original monks. My oldest son, Pierce, and I went to his funeral. He was laid out in the school's chapel and he was beautiful. His face looked rested and as though he was at peace. I think about him a lot and I will always miss him. I am glad he was my friend.

This death was real and sad, but it did not have the impact of Mary Alice's passing. I tried to cope with my sorrow in a rational way, but it got worse. For the first time I was unable to find a place to tuck my grief. Absorbing this one did not happen. After Mary Alice died, my thoughts and dreams became extremely upsetting. I had to take sleeping pills for a couple of months just to get through the fretful nights. I was living in a space that we had shared, and memories overtook me. She had been such a wonderful friend and partner to me. But her death did not come as a shock. The momentum had been building and building until the last second. I did not know the exact date and time it would happen, but it was a reality we both accepted. At one point in the final stages of life, those left behind are faced with the physical demands of those who are dying. We are asked to facilitate the body's demise and the soul's departure. At that time, one becomes so involved in the present that there is no time to think about the future. Then in an instant, I had to cope with her passing and that was enormously difficult.

———

I never expected to get married again. Although this may sound rather callous, I had no interest in trying to find someone to duplicate the kind of relationship I shared with Mary Alice. We had built something unique to us, and I wanted to savor and preserve it. For a while I was almost "anti-casserole." It was not a time when I wanted anyone to come by the house with food or be nice to me. I wanted to be alone in my pain, even though below the surface I understood that all attempts to help were offered by people with huge hearts, who only wished to do whatever they could to honor Mary Alice and lessen my sorrow. I may have seemed ungracious and selfish, for which I am sorry, but I desperately needed to grieve.

When Mary Alice made the decision to move to the Northwest, it solidified our life together. We came to Seattle unmarried, with many questions as to whether it would suit us well. We soon realized that Seattle was a city where each of us could pursue interests and thrive. It became apparent that the move would create a marriage of love, friendships, new beginnings, and experiences. We enjoyed our newly formed life together among great people who genuinely wanted us to embrace the city and its citizens. I loved sharing the experience with her and making those friendships. Rightly or wrongly, when Mary Alice died, a part of me left those connections behind. There are people who draw comfort from familiar settings, but for whatever reasons I drifted away. I had built a life with Mary Alice that I treasured. It seemed that any effort to diminish that memory would take away from my love for her. In case anyone may have felt slighted by my disappearance after her death,

I wish to assure you that it was no reflection on your kindness or friendship. It was strictly my absence of coping skills.

Sometime after Mary Alice's death, a friend told me that it takes three years to recover from the loss of a loved one. Although I am sure there is validity in his statement, I had no desire to find a replacement for my loss. It is not that I felt my life was over, but I did not think I would find anyone to share it with. And I was not looking for anything but peace.

———————

I suppose this is the perfect time to admit that along the way I found many opportunities to make mistakes, or as my tolerant family may attest, blunders that set me back in their eyes. I was confused, unsettled, and had little idea of where I was to go. Time passed . . .

I paid slight attention when an attractive young woman came up to me one day in the middle of what had become my daily workout at the Seattle Tennis Club.

"Hi, you don't know me. I'm Bridget McIntyre. Someone told me you flew a P-38 in the war."

I did not know how to react, or how to reply. It was a true statement, of course, but it rattled me a bit and I did not say anything for a moment. It didn't matter because she continued to question me: "What is a P-38? Do you fly now?"

It turned out that Bridget was a pilot herself and was working on getting her instrument rating. I told her that I was flying now, but not in a P-38. Then I gave her a brief description of the plane and what it did in World War II. Bridget seemed curious about all things flying. As she turned to go, she told me that she wanted to hear more stories about the P-38. I let it go and went back to my book and my 30 minutes on the bike, but I began to wonder about this woman who had interrupted my exercise program and wanted to hear war stories about my favorite airplane.

Seven months went by, and at times we would pass each other in the hallway heading to or from a workout. Other than smiles, nothing was exchanged. Then one day I saw her coming toward me. I was expecting another smile when she blurted out something about wanting to hear my stories about the P-38. Again I didn't know how to respond, so I said, "Your face is red." She explained that she had just come out of the sauna. I invited her to lunch, but she turned me down. She said, "I don't take lunch breaks." So I asked her to dinner, only to be turned down again.

As my personal mending continued, I thought more frequently about Bridget. She started it with her quizzing me about a P-38, and there were her smiles. But she turned me down when I asked her to lunch, and again when I asked her out to dinner. She became a puzzle and a bit of a challenge. After several weeks, and with my damaged ego under control, I called her. I was only able to leave a brief message on her answering machine. Finally, after several efforts, we made dinner plans for a Saturday night in May. A Saturday night dinner seemed more like a date than I had intended, but I was determined to get beyond my fear of any involvement following Mary Alice's passing.

I stood at her door with no expectations, and knocked. The door opened and there stood a young woman I had never really seen before. Her hair was short and very blond. Her smile was the only thing I recognized. At the club she had been wearing a baseball hat and sweats. For a moment I thought I had made a mistake because the reality was so different from what my mind's eye was expecting. We went to a nearby restaurant on Capitol Hill that I liked. Bridget ordered water and I went straight for a martini, and entered a conversation that went on from there as we began to find out about each other. Small talk included family and kids. She had been single for about six years and lived alone in the Edgewater Apartments, about a mile from my house. She had worked for Piper Jaffray for 18 years and was a broker's assistant. She lived frugally and managed to support herself with considerable effort. She rowed competitively at the national level, swam beautifully and competitively (she was a joy to watch in the pool doing 100 or 200 laps), ran marathons, and skied fast and furiously on the double-black trails at Sun Valley. She was a natural athlete honed by an addiction to speed and competition. Her principal interest was to develop her flying skills. At one point I asked what her goals were for the next five years, to which she answered, "My goal is to get my instrument rating, my commercial rating, my certified flight instructor rating, do volunteer work, and then get married, in that order."

She did get around to my family, starting with my wife. When she asked about Mary Alice, I wondered what she was thinking. I assumed she had heard that Mary Alice had died the previous October. That was a bad assumption, as she knew nothing about me except the listing in the Tennis Club roster and the fact that I had flown a P-38. I was not as strong as I thought I was, and unannounced, the tears quietly started rolling down my cheeks. Bridget was somewhat startled. We talked about Mary Alice and what our life had been like in Seattle. She found out about my job, and my 11 children. I drove her home after dinner, said my good nights, and went home confused and stimulated by a pleasant evening that had turned out to be so different than I expected.

By the next afternoon I was more curious and excited, and I called her and invited myself to her apartment for a drink. Since Bridget did not imbibe, I brought the vodka, the cheese, and the crackers. She had some glasses and a nice sitting room where we could spread out and begin the exciting business of learning about each other. We discovered that we were both Catholic, and for us both this was important. It was the start of an adventure that continues today.

In the spring of 2003, as our relationship deepened, we planned a trip to Europe. It would be a tour of major cities, with heavier emphasis on Italy and the foundations of our Church.

Over three weeks we traveled to London, Rome, Florence, and Paris. Bridget had not been in Europe for more than a decade and she found traveling there stressful. She was not crazy about Rome, but she fell in love with Florence. That trip did not lead to the succession of travel abroad that I had hoped for. In fact the next big trip we took was entirely within the borders of the United States.

I inquired about the airplane I had purchased with Mary Alice and had sold. It seemed that the woman who bought it had little time to use it and was willing to let me buy it back. It was a fast four-place, single-engine Beechcraft Bonanza. With the help of Phyllis Baer I began flying again, and it was again fun. Phyllis had taught me everything I knew about one-armed flying and helped me repurchase the aircraft. She has been with me for many of the 1,000 hours I have recorded in my pilot logbook. She is a good friend who in her 10,000 hours of flying has learned more than most pilots I know.

Bridget and I flew across the middle of our country through Nebraska, Iowa, Illinois, as far east as Providence, Rhode Island. We returned by a more northerly route. At the time neither of us had our instrument rating, so we were ducking July thunderstorms all the way. Bridget completed her training and earned her instrument rating after we returned to our home base. She went on to receive her commercial license, multi-engine rating, and has since become a certified flight instructor.

We were married in July 2003. The best way to summarize our adventures is to say that through it all, our relationship has kept growing and maturing in an incredible way that I had never hoped for in my wildest dreams.

AMONG MANY OTHER COMMON INTERESTS,
BRIDGET AND I SHARE A LOVE OF FLYING.

A LATE-IN-LIFE HIGHLIGHT OCCURRED IN 2007, WHEN I WAS ONE OF
FIVE RECIPIENTS OF THE GEORGE H. W. BUSH LIFETIME OF
LEADERSHIP AWARD AT YALE. HERE I AM PRESENTED WITH A
COMMEMORATIVE VASE BY RICHARD C. LEVIN, PRESIDENT OF YALE (CENTER),
AND THOMAS A. BECKETT, DIRECTOR OF ATHLETICS.

RETURN TO YALE

I can see with some clarity that I began everything in my life too early. I was always feeling the need to catch up. Things turned out well, but with less haste, the contributions I made and experiences I had could have been more meaningful. However, there is an order to my life, a bell-curve-like course, from my Rye, New York, childhood to my wonderful life in Seattle.

My bell curve has been influenced by both joy and tragedy. Being accepted at Yale at age 16 was exciting and challenging, but at that point I was not far up the curve. While there I played varsity football as well as other sports, but I was still ascending my bell curve. The crash of my P-38 during World War II could have abruptly ended my climb, but arguably it altered but did not extinguish my life. Who knows when I went over the top of the curve? I still experience moments of bliss, like when I received the George H. W. Bush Lifetime of Leadership Award in 2007.

———————

When the Yale Athletic Department commemorated the University's 2001 Tercentennial, it created the means for recognizing Yale's rich athletic heritage as an important component of the undergraduate educational experience. The development of a competitive temperament to ignite the trained intellect may explain many of the contributions that Yale has made to our planet's insatiable appetite for leadership during the last 300 years. The Yale Athletic Department established the George H. W. Bush Lifetime of Leadership Award to recognize and honor alumni athletes who in their lives after Yale made significant contributions in their worlds of governance, commerce, science, technology, education, public service, media, and the arts. The award was named in recognition of George Herbert Walker Bush, Yale class of 1948, who as an undergraduate played varsity baseball and served as team captain in his senior year, then went on to become the 41st president of the United States. He represents the epitome of one who has successfully and selflessly committed a lifetime to addressing the diverse global leadership demands of his generation.

Alumni athletes nominated to receive the award are selected by a large and broadly representative alumni honors committee. The committee's selections are based on the candidates' participation as undergraduates in intercollegiate athletic competition and, more important, their lifetime contributions in their respective fields. President Bush gave his name to this award because there did not seem to be any recognition for Yale people that was nonacademic. The honorees are selected every two years and the awards are presented during the Yale/Harvard football game weekend in New Haven. The 2007 awards were made at the Blue Leadership Ball, the fourth recognition dinner since the award's creation.

Every other year, five people are selected by the honors committee for the award. The head of the selection committee had called me in 2005 and asked if I would participate, and I told him no. At the time, life for Bridget and me was very complex, and it was not possible to make the journey to New Haven. I told him I was very sorry and that I knew I might be passing up something I would later regret. I also acknowledged that probably not too many people would say no.

I didn't say no twice. I felt humbled to be asked again. When I inquired about the award selection process, I was told there was a committee of 47 people.

I said, "What? How can you ever get anything done?"

"The selection committee," explained the committee person, "has to be that large because it has to make certain that all parties have their input and are represented." If you look at the five people who were selected for the 2007 awards, there was a very accomplished businesswoman; an African-American, a lawyer and former mayor of Baltimore who had become dean of Howard School of Law; The Boeing Company's chief executive; and the man who controlled Franklin Templeton Investments. What the committee head said was that they have to consider all kinds of things. It was not going to be a group of five WASPs. Yale considers itself a national university and it may be becoming a global university, so it has to look at the selection in terms of many varying factors.

Former President George H. W. Bush wrote a letter announcing those to be honored at the 2007 Blue Leadership Ball. It read in part:

I have often said that any definition of a successful life must include service to others. We can all look to Richard Cooley, Charles Johnson, Anne Keating, James McNerney, and Kurt Schmoke as marvelous examples of selfless giving. They have made important contributions to their communities, their professions and, indeed, their country; and this tribute is fitting recognition of their efforts.

Richard P. Cooley, '44, fashioned an inspiring business career on the West Coast. A letter-winning varsity competitor in football, squash, and tennis, he left Yale in 1943 for military service during World War II. A plane crash cost him his right arm and all further Yale athletic competition, but did not prevent him from becoming a national squash champion — left-handed — in the mid-1950s.

Cooley joined the San Francisco-based Wells Fargo Bank in 1949. He rose to president and chief executive of the firm in 1966, becoming chairman and chief executive officer in 1978, and retired from Wells Fargo after 33 years in 1982. Almost immediately he was elected president, chairman, and chief executive of Seafirst Bank in Seattle, positions he held until his retirement in 1990.

In addition to his banking career, Cooley held directorships in such firms as United Airlines, Pacific Gas and Electric, and Egghead Software. In both San Francisco and Seattle he chaired the United Way; he has served on boards for opera and symphony orchestra organizations, museums, and hospitals. He also assisted educational institutions as an instructor, director, trustee, or member of the board of governors.

Charles B. Johnson, '54, has applied his economics studies at Yale to the investment and securities business. A varsity football player, Johnson spent three years in the U.S. Army before joining Franklin Distributors, Inc., as president and chief executive officer in 1957. Johnson helped spearhead the efforts of his class to restore the Yale Bowl as that landmark approached its centennial.

Anne F. Keating, '77, excels as a senior-level executive recruiter in the financial services and consumer sectors at the New York office of Korn/Ferry International. A three-sport athlete, and captain of field hockey, Keating earned nine varsity letters in field hockey, basketball, and lacrosse, and was on the U.S. lacrosse and field hockey teams. Keating was the first recipient of the Nellie P. Elliot Award, given to the top Yale senior female athlete. In 1999, she was named to the Ivy League Field Hockey Silver Anniversary Honor Roll. Keating earned an M.B.A. in marketing from the Wharton School, University of Pennsylvania. Keating is a founding member of Yale's WISER (Women's Intercollegiate Sports Endowment and Resource) Endowment, and serves on the board of the U.S. Lacrosse Foundation. She is a trustee of Helen Keller International.

W. James McNerney, '71, has served several of the world's largest corporations at the highest levels of management. A baseball and ice hockey player at Yale, he earned his M.B.A.

from Harvard in 1975. He is the current chairman, president, and chief executive officer of the Boeing Company. He has worked at 3M, General Electric, and Procter & Gamble, where he is still a director. He is chair of the U.S.-China Business Council and The Business Council.

Kurt L. Schmoke, '71, distinguishes himself in the field of law, politics, and education. A lacrosse and football star while a history major at Yale, he attended Oxford University as a Rhodes Scholar before receiving his law degree from Harvard in 1976. After serving as assistant director of President Carter's White House domestic policy staff, Schmoke returned to his native Baltimore as Assistant United States Attorney, and was thereafter elected State's Attorney. In 1987 he was elected mayor of Baltimore. For 12 years he achieved outstanding success in programs to improve public housing and to enhance community economics development that won widespread praise. For his efforts in promoting adult literacy, President H. W. Bush, '48, awarded Schmoke the National Literacy Award in 1992. After retiring as mayor, Schmoke returned to the private practice of law with an international firm. In 2002 he was appointed dean of the Howard University School of Law.

Bridget was ill and could not fly, but my daughter Sheila and her husband, Mark, joined me. Their son just happened to have an interview that day in New Haven, so he joined us as well. We had three of my five children, and two of my sisters — one of the twins and my youngest sister. It was wonderful to have them all there at such a pleasant family gathering. Just seeing a lot of people and places that I had known as a young man brought back many memories that I had put behind me.

The event took place on November 16 in the Payne Whitney Gymnasium, which was newly renovated. It is one of the largest and most complete indoor facilities in the world. The building was given to the university by the Whitney family in honor of their

STANDING BEHIND MY SISTERS IN SUN VALLEY.
SHOWN FROM LEFT ARE KAY, ANN, AND HELEN.

son Payne Whitney, class of 1898. The structure stands nine and
a half stories tall, with a sports medicine center, training areas for
each sport, and the Kiphuth Trophy Room, which displays all
sorts of Yale memorabilia dating back to 1842. It is an enormous
athletic complex that seemingly has been there forever.

The squash courts that I had played on had been dismantled,
and in their place are 15 international-size squash courts and
three exhibition courts, one of which is the only four-wall glass
court in the country. You can have three or four hundred people
watching the squash games now. It is very nice. I was really glad
to see it. They went from 21 courts to 15 courts because the
new courts are bigger. The new facility was a gift from my old
teammate Nick Brady.

The selection committee asked the honorees to come early in
the day so they could have time with some of the current team
members, and I was asked to go to a luncheon with the squash
and tennis teams. The squash coach arranged the event. The
women's and men's squash teams and the women's and men's
tennis teams were present. There were probably 30 or 40 people
there for lunch in Timothy Dwight, my old residential college,
but aside from the dining area, the rest of the building was all
locked up, so I could not see my old room. The dining hall had
been renovated. We used to have waitresses come out and serve
us, but now it is buffet-style, which is much more practical, and
the food looked good. Next to the dining room was a meeting
room with a long thin table, and there I sat down next to a
squash player from Hong Kong. We talked while the rest of the
teams filtered in. Dave Talbott, the coach, got up at the end of the
lunch and gave my bio. He talked about my athletic career and
then asked if I would say a few words.

Since he had already covered my sports history, I had to
come up with some thoughts that could offer something of

interest and maybe of use to these bright young athletes. I told them how I had returned from the war earlier than my peers because of a war injury and rushed through my final semester, only to graduate in uniform before going back to the hospital to finish the final work on my arm and learn to use the prosthesis. In a way, I told them, "I missed my senior year with my classmates because of my sense of urgency." Most of my class had not rushed to finish up, but I had been in a hurry to graduate and get on with my life. The people I went to school with that summer were younger and had not been in the war. I was one of the first to return, and the university gave returning servicemen a semester of credit for what we had learned in the Army or Navy. I was able to graduate in 1945. I told the young athletes that I considered business school, which my father had offered to me, but I wanted to get started on my life, so I took a long ski weekend in Vermont and began my first real job in early February.

Although circumstances are different today, I asked them not to do the same, not to move so fast that they miss the moment. "You get more out of life if you address it with patience. Here I am at this point of my life, a man who attended Yale a long time ago, and I would like nothing better than to go back and study for four years. Do not rush through this place. Learn what you can and be glad for every moment you have the privilege to study here. It's a big part of your life, so take your time and breathe it all in. In a way it is a little like playing squash or tennis. You have to be patient. You have rallies that go on forever, and you have to be able to wait it out in order to play your opponent the right way. Do not try to put the ball away immediately. Do not always try to go for the ace, because you may not make it and your opponent may have figured that out and it will cost you the point. Be patient with the point, with the game, and with life."

After lunch I had an hour to kill before Yale's women's squash team was to play Stanford. The brother of the Yale coach had gone out to coach a new team at Stanford. The team had been in place for only three years. There is not a lot of squash on the West Coast in comparison to the East Coast. It was the first game of the season for both Yale and Stanford.

With my free time I went looking for what we used to call the Yale Co-op. It does not exist anymore. There was now what is called the Yale Bookshop, which is run by Barnes & Noble. It is a much bigger place, right around the corner from where the Co-op used to be. It is big and beautiful, with two sides to the structure, one for textbooks and school supplies, and the other for clothes. It had very little similarity to the old place. It was bigger and better, but it did not seem to have the same charm that I remembered.

I found that I recognized spots even though they were different in some ways and not so much in others, but buildings do not change. Buildings outlast people. In my time there were 10 residential colleges that were dormitories where we ate, slept, and maybe studied. Timothy Dwight was the place where I did all of that for maybe two years, and when I came back from the war I lived there again for my final semester at Yale. There were two new residential colleges that had been built closer to the gym, which was a little farther away from the heart of the campus. I found Yale's new underground library. The old campus was still there, and that's where freshmen live before they go into a residential college. My freshman class was just over 1,000 students, but today's entering freshman class is about 1,300 students, so as things go it has not grown that much. I am sure there are many more graduate students now than there were when I attended school at Yale. It was sort of bringing everything back, like I had been transported in time to my old neighborhood from the 1930s and '40s.

When I returned to the squash courts, there was a little
ceremony before the match where I was introduced again as a
former tennis and squash player. During the ceremony they gave
me a picture of my 1942 team. You would never be able to pick
me out if I showed you the photo. I was a totally callow youth.
It was terrifying to see, and later when I showed it to Bridget,
she did not recognize me.

At the match I saw the number-two woman play her match.
It was terrific. The Yale woman was superior. In fact, she was so
good I could hardly believe it. They hit the ball so hard. It did not
look like women's squash to me, but more like men's squash. It
was very professional. That is when I learned that it is hard to be
a three-letter person at Yale today because one gets onto a team
and there is training all year round. There is a fall season and a
spring season. Football always had spring training, but I never
went to it because I had squash and tennis. Today the physical
training and the practice dominate what you do. It would be very
hard to play more than one sport, two being the max.

When I was at Yale you could do anything you liked. When I
finally got on the varsity football team as a junior, I was playing
on the left side of the line with two sophomores, Cottie Davison,
who was a guard, and tackle Bolt Elwell, who in 1942 was elected
best athlete of the year. I was number two. He played football,
basketball, and baseball. I did not attend spring practice, but
instead played other sports, like tennis. Today you could not do
that. Each team would want you to spend more time working
with them, and the coaches want to win, which means they want
you to practice more. It is a full-time job. That's something I did
not know about, and it surprised me. It just goes to show how
things have changed over the years. Even though the Ivy League
schools are not considered to have first-class athletics, they
still have their rules and compete feverishly with each other.
They will never be in the same category as the Pac-10, as big as

Washington or California, or even Stanford, but I am honored to have played for Yale.

––––––––––––

After the squash match I went back to my room and put on my black tie for dinner. The reception was held in the Kiphuth Trophy Room, on the second floor of the gymnasium. There was a party there for all the awardees, the previous awardees, the generous donors, and many of the athletic department staff. One of the older men from the selection committee came up to me and said, "Well, I wanted to meet you. You turned us down last time." I told him it just did not work out for me, and he commented, "Glad you could make it this year." Basically it is a "Queen for a Day" situation, he said, and it is a nice thing to have happen in terms of how you can help other people. I think the idea is good, but I knew it would be upsetting for me, and it was in a way. Just seeing a lot of people and places that I had known as a young man brought back many memories that I had put away in the past.

On the first floor they had everyone who had paid to come to the dinner, which was about 600 people. There were over 800 in all at the event. There was a photographer who took many pictures. We went down to dinner, which was held on the basketball floor. There were two cocktail parties that were held from 6 until 7:30, and then the dinner program was supposed to start at 7:30. A little after 7 they started moving everyone from upstairs down to the basketball court. Initially we were in a holding area with a big screen next to it where we would be eating. There we had another cocktail area to keep the tone of it instead of losing the momentum. It was a great feeling, with everyone doing things to make the night a success. Then they opened the curtain and we went in to find our table. We had a nice table up front.

We had an excellent dinner and then the program began. The five awardees were seated on the left side of the podium, and on the right side sat the president of the university, the director of athletics, the master of ceremonies (Patrick Ruwe), the dinner chair, and the university chaplain. As we congregated, someone asked what order we should go in and it was determined that it should probably be alphabetically. I was the first in the alphabetical lineup and I was also the senior in the group. I sat next to my friend Charlie Johnson, who was the only one I knew. He had his yellow pad with his written speech, and he had been over it and practiced. I said, "Geez, Charlie, I'm just going to wing it." He said, "Good for you, but I didn't have time to do that." In a sense winging it for some people takes longer and is often riskier.

There were several short welcoming talks and a very warm greeting from President Richard C. Levin, who welcomed the group, acknowledging the university's athletic philosophy, which emphasizes the enduring lessons that commitment to competitive athletics offers to its students. "Learning how to strive to win, to compete with pride and honor, to make sacrifices, to persevere when all seems lost, and to develop a sense of obligation and responsibility for others are among the important lessons athletics teaches," he said. Yale offers 35 varsity sports, as well as a variety of club, intramural, and recreational competition, which, President Levin observed, "provide camaraderie that often endures beyond the recollection of game statistics."

President Levin's speech recognized the quality of Yale alumni leadership in the world. Perhaps it's my bias, but I think that Yale has more chief executives and top business execs than any other school, many more than either Harvard or Princeton, as far as I know. That is a statistic that I cannot prove, but the fact is that Yale teaches one balance. Yale recognizes its alumni who become leaders, and naturally likes leaders who stay closely connected to the school. I felt I was a disappointment to Yale because I have not maintained close ties. This was the first time I had been there in many years.

Thomas A. Beckett, director of athletics, was given a special award for all he had done for Yale in the previous 13 years.

It was a total surprise to him and was enormously popular with everyone at the dinner. In effect he was our gracious host and clearly deserved the warm acknowledgment.

Then it was time for me to speak.

Good evening. I am really honored to have this award tonight. It means a tremendous amount to me. As someone who went through Yale as a gentleman's C type person but as an athlete, it is wonderful to see athletes get this kind of recognition. I have three things I want to tell you tonight, or tell you about. One is my experience in the Yale/Harvard game in 1942, when I was playing on the Yale team and I started at left end. It was fortunate because that year we beat Harvard. We beat them 7 to 3, so you are getting the end of the story first.

There was one incident in that game that I will never forget. Game day was a gray, dark afternoon and the field was muddy. We were leading them by four points toward the end of the game, but Harvard was driving down on us hard and we were having a tough time stopping them. They got close to the goal line and all of a sudden there was a play that fooled us. The Harvard quarterback dropped back to pass to a wide-open receiver running across the field against the flow of the play. I could not get to him. Nobody could get to him. The ball sailed through the air for what seemed like an eternity, slightly behind the receiver hitting him in his midsection on his hip. I thought to myself, there goes the game. We did not have time to score and come back, but as it turned out, we did not need to. He dropped the ball, and we ended up beating Harvard 7-3. It was so wonderful! I can still remember that awful sinking feeling when that man ran across the goal line and bobbled the ball. I don't know who he was, but it does not matter. The point is, we won the game and ended up beating Princeton as well, so Yale finished with a 5 and 3 season.

We were not terrific, but we beat Princeton and we beat Harvard and that made it a great success. This little gold football

I received has both those game scores on it, and it is a treasure that I will have for my whole life. To be starting in both those games was a big thing for me. It was the biggest thing that happened to me at Yale as far as I can remember. A lot of wonderful things happened, but that was certainly the tops. That is the first thing I want to mention just to have you know as we play the Harvard game again tomorrow. Let's hope we win again. Looks like we have a good chance.

Secondly, I want to tell you about my arm. I was in the Army Air Corps and I lost my arm on a test flight. I was over in the 9th Air Force flying into Germany, and one day I had a test flight. I was flying over Northern France when something went wrong and the plane went in. I was lucky to get out of it, but without my arm. I did not come to until two or three days after the crash. I did not know I did not have my right arm because I still had those phantom feelings. I was in that hospital for a while and then another hospital for a while. It was the time of the Battle of the Bulge, and I ended up in a hospital just before Christmas in mid France someplace, halfway between Paris and Le Havre. I do not know what caused it, but all of a sudden I knew I had lost my arm and it hit me. As I started to think about it, I realized that I was going to live and I was going to get home, but no matter what happened I would never be able to play football my senior year on the Yale football team. That was devastating. In fact, I get teary-eyed thinking about it right now because that was when I cried. I cried and cried and cried because I could not have that one more year of playing football at Yale. And that is a true story.

Third thing I wanted to mention is what a great man we had here for many years, for over 40 years . . . a man named Johnny Skillman, who coached squash and tennis. I played for him all my time here. He was wonderful and I used to play well, but I could never beat him. I was always close to the top of the team on both squash and tennis with my right arm, and I came back

and Johnny was still here, and he helped me and I started play-
ing squash left-handed. Tennis not so much, because squash was
easier and I got to play more. I was not as good because I had
been a big hitter with my right arm and I did not have the
strength or dexterity in my left arm to play the way I used to.
Hopefully, with good coaching, the brains and the legs and the
desire, I ran and got myself into the top level of squash. In 1953 I
was very lucky. I had moved to San Francisco by then and with
much help from a lot of people, starting with Johnny Skillman,
I had learned to play the game again. I became a member of the
Pacific Coast Squash team in 1953 that went to the Squash
Nationals in Pittsburgh and won the national team champi-
onship. I have a picture of all of us who came out of the West to
win this East Coast championship. It started at Yale with Johnny
Skillman, and the wonderful Yale squash courts, which have
been upgraded to the magnificent squash facility it is today by
Nick Brady's generousness and imagination.

It is great to be a part of this celebration. I am so grateful
and so touched that the committee would think it was worth
inviting me here tonight. What a privilege! I just cannot thank
you enough. If I had to do it again, I would.

That was it, but it went over well, seemingly. My kids are
prejudiced. They said, "You were the best, Dad!"

During the program the awardees received biographies
written for the occasion, and commissioned oil paintings of each
of us were unveiled that were to be hung in the trophy room.
The committee also presented awardees with a recognition gift, a
heavy crystal vase, so heavy in fact that I could not hold it up,
so when I was being presented with it, I asked President Levin to
hold it for me.

The next morning, Charlie Johnson and his class of 1954, who
had done a tremendous fund-raising job to rehabilitate the whole

Yale Bowl, were honored. Charlie rededicated the Yale Bowl. They did that in the Coxe "Cage," which is a big enclosed building where the track team works out in the winter. It has been there forever. They put on a brunch that started around 9:30, and about 10:45 they had a program that was basically to thank everyone for giving the money to rebuild the Bowl. The Yale Bowl is old. It was the first big college bowl ever built, because football began at Yale. Even though we are not in the category of Ohio State or USC, it is still an important thing. Over time we have won more than 850 games and we've lost not quite that many. Overall, we are still a winner.

We could never say that we are the best athletes in the world, particularly today when college teams are run professionally. It is a different thing at Yale. We do not offer anything to athletes other than the opportunity to receive a very good education. They have to be able to be people like lawyers or doctors. What Yale wants to put out there is a balanced person, one who is intellectually capable but also knows what teamwork is. Teamwork is making businesses run these days. It is the emphasis in the business schools right now that you have to be on a team because no person can do it alone. Life has become too complicated and businesses are too complex, so you have to construct a team that will get the job done. You get the right people on your executive team and you can do a lot of incredible things. Having received the leadership award, I was able to say that to the crowd. Everyone loved that in the sense that "we are okay." I did not feel bad about saying it because it was true. My dad told me that Yale was a good place for me. He went to UC-Berkeley, but he worked in New York with all these Ivy League types. And the impression he got from his conversations with others was that Yale was a school where students can learn something. They do plenty of cutting-edge research, too, but they also have professors whose objective is to teach the students.

I have to make a comment about the entire weekend because it made an impression on me. The dinner on Friday night was for 800 people. It was delicious. What struck me was that for that amount of people on a basketball court, which was not exactly set up for such events, they did an incredible job. The brunch the next day was another impressive meal. They had made such an effort. The place was decorated with an enormous picture on each side of this big building of the renovated Bowl. They had tables, good silver, thousands of servers . . . it was done really well. Then when it was over we were all trundled off to the game. It was supposed to start at noon. At the halftime they got us all out on the field with Charlie Johnson. The five honorees stood in front. I was standing next to the Yale President Levin as Yale songs were sung.

We were each introduced and given a brief acknowledgment. The exciting thing for me was that it was the first time I had been on the Yale football field in 65 years. The last time had been when I played in that game where the Harvard player dropped the pass. Sixty-five years ago! It is still the same place. It is real grass and pretty soggy. People were falling down and slip-ping in the mud because it had rained. It brought back a lot of things that I had not thought about in a very long time. It was sad that Bridget was not able to attend because I wanted her to see it. She felt horrible that she could not be there, but she was ill and it was very cold that weekend. I had my two sisters and my kids to take care of. It was my job to make sure they enjoyed themselves because I had brought them into something they had never participated in. It was their first chance to see it, and I felt responsible for them.

One thing that hit me was walking on that turf again and realizing it had been 65 years since I had had that experience. What a lucky person I am! How many people get to experience something full circle again? The fact that I could walk on a field that had meant so much to me as a teenager and experience it again this many decades later was great. It was truly satisfying. It reminds me again how lucky I am.

How God has kept me going. I think about all the people who have kept me going in my life and it makes me thankful for my time here. When He decides it is over, well, that will be it, but in the meantime I am thankful for all the people who have helped me keep going, and that includes the people at Yale.

The weekend brought back a lot of emotions for me. As I told you, I like to look forward and not go back. When I look back, it gets me riled up. I am not saying that it is bad, but I tend to escape when I walk away. It is what this book is doing to me. Going over things that I have not gone over in a long time makes me look at what was good and what was not so good, what was satisfying and what I could have done better. Some things make me sad, and there are other things I wish I had not done. The event at Yale was a little bit like that in the way that I recognized things and it was almost as if I had never been away. I felt so glad and privileged that Yale had been a part of my life.

The only awful thing was that Harvard creamed us. At the dinner on Friday night everyone was saying, "Go Yale! We will be the next Ivy League champions!" It just blew up in our face! We were supposed to beat Harvard, but when I left we were behind 37 to 0. I think Yale got a touchdown after we left in the last minutes, but it was too little too late. Harvard looked like a well-coached team.

After the game, my sister and my son and I went to church. Later the five of us who were left went to dinner in the hotel. It was a nice close to a great weekend. The next day we got up early, caught all our connections, and after a full day of travel returned home. It was a long day, and I realized that I was really tired. It was a drain on my psyche. I was glad I went, but when I returned, it was like a window in my life had opened for a while and brought me back to my early days. It was warming and nostalgic and reminded me again of how lucky my life has been. I had a wonderful time, but now it is time to remember that life has moved on and there is still much to be done here. I had to plug back into the routine of things. I am comfortable and happy with that, but it is just a strange feeling.

———————

The closer I come to the end of my bell curve, the more aware I become of my dependence on other people. Ailments meet me each morning. My fingers do not work the way they once did, and my bones are sore. One appears to lose control over bodily functions as well. As the years stockpile, I have learned to accept help from others and be grateful for it.

Bridget and I have become closer and closer, and she worries about keeping me alive and vital. It is understandable as there is more than 30 years' difference in our ages. It may be a hard time for her when I go, but I tell her that it will be okay. I've lost loved ones. I know God will take care of her, I tell her, as He has taken care of me. Besides, you can never tell what might happen in 16 years. I cannot handle this for her, much as I would like to, but my faith is strong, and I know God will look after her.

The other day I told her about the bell curve and that she had better be nice to me because she may have 16 more years to worry about me. My mother reached 98 and my dad died at 93, so maybe I will reach 100. It might not be a pretty sight, but on the other hand my warm heart will be there to keep her happy. We have longevity in our family and try not to worry about it, but it is in the genes. My sisters do not want to live that long. My twin sisters will celebrate their 83rd birthday this year, and my youngest sister will be 78. If I can just keep going and keep Bridget going the way she is, that will be fine.

It's a documented fact that people are living longer. Younger people do not understand that changes come over your body, but not over your mind. Your mind tells you that you can do almost anything, but the body wonders "how?" When people get older, their problems change. It is not about retirement anymore. If you are 65 and retired, you are not going to be able to play golf for more than another decade, or certainly not as well as you once did. One gets stiff and loses muscle tone. People cannot hit the ball as far. In golf, that starts happening when one gets to be around 60.

My memory is not the same as it used to be. I forget things, like my wallet in the car. I have to worry about my watch, my wallet, and my glasses. Those are things I have to remember when I leave the house every day. You cannot rely on your memory. I can go down to the kitchen for something and forget what I went down there for. It adds to my day, so it is nice when you can avoid some of those trips. I do not think people are planning for those things or about developing systems for aging. We are all getting older, lasting longer. We all have memory problems. Everything is not as tight as it used to be. But it is okay. It is perfectly normal, but how do we help people deal with it? There is no point in getting mad or frustrated by the process of life, because it is normal.

As you get older you need to develop systems so you can live the same way you have always lived, and that is easier if you find ways to ease the aging process. Sometimes people try to commiserate and say that they forget things too, and although they are trying to be nice, it does not help the people who are forgetful. For instance, I write on my calendar the things I need to do each day, and during the day I check them off. That is probably one of the reasons people retire — so there is more time to deal with this kind of thing! Because we are living longer, it is important to be positive about it and try to help with ideas that lessen the burden of aging.

I've had a lot of operations. It started when I had a torn cartilage in my knee at age 16. That was my first operation. I fell on a rock skiing in Vermont. That year there was not enough snow and it was easy to hit something. The knee operation is most likely the reason I did not get into the Navy Air Corps during WWII. They said my knees would not hold up, but I played football for two years and those knees held up fine.

The army was not as particular and it took me, bad knee and all. I had the cartilage repaired on the other knee after the war in 1953. I had fallen on a tennis court. An arm weighs about six pounds, and the loss of it changed my balance. Many of the operations I have had in my life had something to do with the P-38 accident. There were many skin grafts. As I get older I have had melanoma and prostate cancer surgery, then I have had nerve operations for different things, not to mention the knee and hip replacements. When I go to a medical office and they ask me to fill out the form stating all of my operations, I write, "Too numerous to mention." I cannot remember all that stuff. It is strange because I know I have probably had lots of operations in comparison to most people, but they have all been good. After all, if I had not had them, I probably would not be here.

One of the things I want anyone who reads this book to take away is that I feel good about myself and the course my life has taken. I appreciate what I have been given. I have no complaints, and I feel good about where I am right now. There are no burning desires that need to be filled.

STANDING WITH FATHER RYAN,
PASTOR OF ST. JAMES CATHEDRAL PARISH.

FAITH AND MY CATHOLIC FIBER

I am always praying for more faith. I cannot explain it to anyone. I hope my belief in God never goes away. It is a gift to believe, but it is not logical. It does not fit inside your mind easily in a secular society. God has let me choose and let me go my own way. God witnesses terrible things, but He still loves everyone. There is no understanding of the awful things people do to each other, but that is because the outside self becomes more important than the inside self. The outside self is what we show to others — worldly stuff, desire, power, and authority — and it becomes more important than the inside self where God resides in you, in your soul.

When I die, I hope that God will decide the day and that it will not be unpleasant. I just hope that it will not be today, but that God will decide the right time and I can die happily with the hope that I will be going to heaven. There are temptations that stand in the way of faith. Faith is a gift. You cannot buy or sell it. There is no book that can tell you how to find it. Some people do not have it, which is sad. I feel very fortunate to have faith. I have not seen anything that has shaken my faith in the church. I can distinguish between what I consider to be some of the poor behavior of the hierarchy and the good behavior of so many more. Going to Mass is the same in the general sense of the word no matter where you pray in the world. Christ is with you everywhere.

My faith is strong enough that I do not have doubts. That is where I am now anyway. When you get to the end of your life, which is where I certainly am, you begin to think, When I die what is going to happen? Where will I go? Who am I going to see? What is heaven? What are the joys of heaven? So what do you have at the end of your life? You have your mind, your heart, and your soul. And you have the ability to love people and the ability to help people. I do not want to be without love for all of eternity. I would like to be with love, and I think that is where heaven is. Whether there is a time in between that is truly a purgatory, a time to be purified before you can enter the place of love, no one knows. It is clearly a mystery, a big one, but I have faith in my final destination.

During my remaining years I want to help people. That gives me something to look forward to every day.

I am not sure how it works, but through the Church I can trust. I can feel that if I stick with the Ten Commandments and the rules of the Church that are God inspired, then I will be okay. I will do what He wants because no one can do it all on their own. It is a big philosophical thing. I have been able to feel that way all during my lifetime. At times when I get busy and involved in the daily pressure of living, it is harder to remember. Right now I do not want anything badly: I have gotten past wanting things. I do not want to be rich. I do not want to own a Picasso. I would like to have enough money to live easily, which so far I have. I enjoy mentoring some of my MBA students. Having one or two of them each quarter gives me a chance to keep up with what the current generation is doing and to participate modestly in their activities. Sometimes I am amazed at how they approach opportunity, and sometimes my advice, though old-fashioned, helps them get ahead.

Age tends to make a person more thoughtful and possibly more mature, hopefully less selfish and self-centered. We all fight that. We all take care of ourselves first. I have learned in life that you have to have the ability to change and adapt. When you give money away to those in need, you will not go broke. It is that little extra boost that may help someone who is having a hard time. In the last couple of decades I have tried to tithe, but I could have given away much more and not perished. How much more? It is difficult to say because at what point are you really showing your love for your fellow man? How far should you go? Spiritually, that is a big moral and ethical question, and it is a question that each one of us must answer on our own. I think about it a lot because to me, the needs always appear to be greater than my gifts.

Every single person helping would make a difference, even if the difference is inside you, because you have overcome your own selfishness. I walk by homeless men and women on the street every day. I always try to give something and not make judgments. It is not fair to judge others because how do we ever really know their plight? They want something, so I give them something because if that were Christ, I would not want to walk by Him because He died for me and helped me get along in life so I could overcome my sinfulness. He has given me direction and someplace to go, so I feel that I need to help those people somehow. We all have just as much right to be here. It is really hard because as far as I'm concerned, God loves all of us and we would not be alive without His love. What is hard to imagine is that God loves the homeless just as much as anyone else, but He does, and maybe even more. He is not making a choice, so if that is the case, then it is our job to help them and not make any choices ourselves.

God loves everybody, so the two big commandments that I try to follow in my life are love thy God and love thy neighbor. The homeless are our neighbors, and we have to love them and do what we can for them. There is always the thought that there is nothing you can do to change their lives and maybe you can never give enough, but I don't believe that is true, so I give what I can when I can.

In the olden days when there were many priests, there were several large churches in New York every 10 or 15 blocks. Confessions were given every day in the morning around Mass, and sometimes in the afternoon. If you had been naughty, you could rush down and confess right away. The idea with confession is that you promise not to do it again. In other words, you say, "I promise God that I've done this sin and I won't do it again." But everyone does it again. Even Jesus said that in the Scriptures when Peter said to him, "Lord, how often should I forgive my brother when he does something wrong? Seven times?" And Jesus said, "No, 70 times 7 times." In other words, Christ knew that we are human and that we would make the same mistakes again, even if we did not want to.

Our humanity would come up and we would forget our promise. So you could go to confession, and in the old days there was confession all the time. If I was seeing someone and being a little more promiscuous than the Church thought I should be, I was running to confession all the time. It sounds silly, but it was true. Today we rarely have a confession. I hardly ever go. I want to go once in a while because early in my life it became a ritual. Today there is a scheduled time on a Saturday afternoon for a half hour at an inconvenient moment, or you can make an appointment. There are not enough priests to sit around waiting for penitents, and it does not seem to be the practice in the Catholic Church any longer.

Penance seems to have gone away, but it is still a sacrament of the Catholic Church. No one said it is not real, and no one said that God will not forgive you for your sins. The point is that somehow, like a lot of things in the Church, even though they did not change the rules, the practice shifted a bit. They have gone on to other ways of observing Christ's laws. It is not the same as it was. I think the current pope is trying to bring back the penance thing a little bit. You have to say your own act of contrition, and you have to excuse yourself to God. Say you tell Him you are really sorry and that you will not do it again. The last part of the act of contrition that everyone says is "I promise to confess my sins, to do penance, and to amend my life. Amen." So I confess to myself and to God, but I should confess to some authorized priest, do the penance, and try to do better in my life. The basic thing is "Amend my life." In other words, do not make a habit of committing the same sin over and over again. I'm older now. The nature of my sins has changed, as has their frequency, but I still feel the need to amend my life.

It is hard for some people to understand, but the church that I grew up in dominated its people by fear. You were afraid to go to hell and you wanted to go to heaven.

Many of the old-world Irish priests who populated the churches in America would talk fire and brimstone. They would get up in the pulpit and say, "You can't do this! You will go to hell!" There is lots of truth in that, but the way it is presented makes a difference. If you are trying to bludgeon the faithful into good behavior, then that is not good. I think it colored a lot of the things I used to do. You should do the right things because you love God and want to please Him, not because you feel the threat of eternal damnation.

————

Making the varsity football team at Yale was a personal victory for me over my fears. It was a physical fear — not being seen as cowardly, not standing up for myself. I never thought I was good enough to be a martyr. On the other hand, if you point a gun at me and say, "Christ is not good and if you believe in him I will shoot you," then I hope I would say I believe in Christ, so shoot me. Then I am a martyr. That kind of bravery comes with great faith, and you have to believe in whatever you are doing.

Whatever you believe in, you must believe strongly enough to take a stand, or determine how much you will listen to someone else tell you this or that, and you sort of compromise. What you are doing is making a compromise about your beliefs with those around you or those who are trying to influence you. If you do believe in a life of eternity, it is not a very good bargain. You have to ask yourself if you are strong enough. What I pray for all the time is faith. I hope I have this faith and it will never desert me. It is not this little thing we do when we go to Church. It is very different, and it's deep inside you. My mother thought I had a remarkable faith. She had faith, but was not confident that she believed enough and was worried about her position before God at the end of her life. She was afraid to die, yet watching her struggle at the end, I could never think of any time she had ever displeased her God.

So faith remains a gift from God, and those who have it are truly fortunate. There are Buddhists, the Jews, and all the other religions who believe in what they do. They have their faith just as much as the Christians, and for them it is just as vital.

So I guess what I am trying to say is that in the long run, I have this desire to do good. I want to do good, and in that exists a concern about things I have not done that I could have done because I was afraid to make a mistake or that I would look different from my contemporaries. I am not talking at all about my strengths or my weaknesses. I am not concerned about that. I care, but I have to be honest, I am who I am. That is what this memoir is about.

Church is humbling. Going to church makes me think about doing the right thing. It is a big basis for my existence. It cushions everything in a way. The idea of going to church every day is not to suggest that I am a "holy roller," and not that I am tremendously spiritual or mystical; it is not that at all. It is that I need to go every day because I need that sort of structure. I need the reminder of who I am. I need to know that there is someone up there running the show and not me. I need to understand that

I am just one of six billion people and God is keeping track of all of us. He loves you and He loves me. This is where the humility comes in. The biggest things in life are humility and love.

———————

One of the things I learned when I went to Portsmouth Priory was that the Benedictines were about work and love. You love God and you work. Benedictines work and pray and try to stay in the background. I do not like to be in the front. I can be in the front and am happy to do that when necessary, but I prefer to be behind the scenes and work hard to be sure that whatever the project, it will work out the best it can for everyone.

Religion keeps me in balance.

I used to be afraid that if I did not go to church every day, I would get out of the habit of going, and then I might never go again. Now I go every day that I can because I love God. It is an act of devotion that helps me love everyone else the right way. We can all stand that reminder every day. The point is that it holds me together. It is a big part of my life and of my DNA, so to speak. I am third on my prayer list. I pray that I will be humble and full of love. I pray that I will be gentle and kind, that I will be patient and understanding, and that I will be wise, even though these goals may seem to be almost unreachable. I hope that I will overcome my selfishness and pride and that I will do God's will each day.

This desire to do good certainly came out of my accident. There is a need to thank God for keeping me going and helping me as He has my whole life. Mostly, I am appreciative of what I have been given. I want to thank the hundreds of incredible people who have helped me along the way. I have had a good life and I am comfortable, and as I have said before, I have been very lucky. Although there are some things I have failed to do, I have been able to do some positive things along the way.

Trying to become a better person is an endless task.

My first meeting with my grandson Bruce Tickner.

A PARTIAL LIST
OF SPECIAL PEOPLE

I am not sure I understand it myself, but when I look back on life I think about the people who have been wonderful to me, the people I care about, those who have been instrumental in so many important incidents that have happened to me that I want you to know many of them. There are also those who have made a fantastic impression, or prompted a result or consequence. It may have been one time only, but the effect on my life was huge. I found it impossible to add each one to the prayer list because there are so many to whom I owe a debt of gratitude.

Over the course of my 86 years, my prayer list has become an integral part of my life. Each day I pray in bits and pieces, often while I am in the car. Lately it is becoming increasingly hard to recite them, not because I have any less affection for those who have made my life rich, but because the list is long and covers so many years. Along with the regular list, there are others I pray for spontaneously on special occasions. I usually know if I miss someone. I do not want to miss anyone, but each day I ask God to please cover the ones I may have missed.

The thing about the prayer list is that I am always adding to it because I meet someone I want to pray for, or someone asks me to pray for them or someone they know who is in need. I don't know why they ask me to pray. Maybe it's just because they know that I pray.

I suppose it is a little like giving alms. Do not blow a trumpet so that everyone knows your good deeds. Do it quietly and your heavenly father will see it and reward you later on. You should be humble and full of love. I have always been sort of a secret Catholic. I have never promoted it or paraded my faith around and have generally lived in a non-Catholic social world. I think some people who know me might expect a higher standard of responsibility. If I do something off-color, it might disappoint those for whom I may have been a force for good. Everyone is affected by what you do, so you have a responsibility to do the right thing. You never know how many people are depending on you. There is good in everyone. Sometimes you have to dig a little deeper to find it, but it is there.

PRAYER LIST:

BRIDGET MCINTYRE COOLEY
We were married in July 2003

When I tell you about the prayer list, I am going to start at the top with Bridget, but it does not mean that it is going to be totally chronological all the way through. If you look at these names and you see why each person is on the prayer list, you will get another viewpoint about the things that have happened to me in these first 86 years of life. I want to start with Bridget because she is my wife, my love, and the person who is so incredibly entwined in what I am doing each day. Back in the end of Chapter Ten there is a description of what she has done athletically, but it does not include her warmth and intelligence, or her sensitivity. She is funny and entertaining and a marvelous hostess. She handles people well and reaches out to everyone around her. Her friends are legion and she never forgets a one.

The only thing I want to add is to say that Bridget is important to me and important in my whole life, whether in this world or the next. I will be forever grateful. I have learned so much from her that it would take another book to describe all the things and ways in which our relationship has prospered and been fully rewarding. It continues to grow.

MY UNNAMED SAVIOR
The man who saved my life after my P-38 crash in 1944

I pray for this man and I hope that his kindness has been repaid many times over. I just wish I had been able to thank him in person.

RICHARD P. COOLEY
Husband, father, bank chief executive officer

I pray that I will be humble and full of love. I pray that I will be gentle and kind. That I will be patient and understanding, and that I will be wise. I hope that I will overcome my selfishness and my pride. I pray that I will do God's will each day.

SHEILA MCDONNELL COLLINS
My first wife, and mother of my children

We enjoyed travel and golf. After we parted company, she went on to be the first woman granted membership at Cypress Point. On that course she made two holes in one, and they were both on the same hole, number 15. She was a very good athlete.

After 20 years of marriage, Sheila and I went in different directions. I became head of the Wells Fargo Bank and was busy with that. In the matter of expectations, there was a lot left to be desired, both at home and at work. The combination of the two things was very difficult. When it got to be too much, or when I thought it was too much, I decided to leave. It was not a good decision for any of us. Sheila died in 2008. I never had the opportunity to tell her how in retrospect I felt about our marriage, and that for all those intervening years she has been a part of my prayers. I pray for Sheila every day, hoping that she has found peace in heaven.

OUR CHILDREN
I pray for all our children, who include my children and Mary Alice's children. Mary Alice's children have lost their fathers, and

with her passing, they have lost their mother. While I am not able to see them all the time, I consider them to be my children. I want to be the best stepfather I can be. Three of them live in Los Angeles, one in San Francisco, and two in Seattle.

LESLIE COOLEY
My oldest daughter, college professor

Leslie thrived. She was born with a quick wit and has become quite successful. She began college at Scripps, and later graduated from Stanford with a degree in psychology, after which she became a counselor for the Davis School District. She continued her education, and a decade later she received her Ph.D. Along the way she married her college boyfriend, but the union failed. Her education and life experience led her to an unconventional relationship, and she announced that her choice as a life partner would be Kristine Jensen. Kristine fit well into our family. Leslie joined the faculty of Sacramento State University and earned tenure before she turned 45.

MILES COOLEY
My grandson and Leslie's son, an attorney

While in Davis, California, Leslie in her work met a young African-American boy whom she cared for a great deal. She became deeply involved in his troubled life, and when he turned 18 she adopted him. He is my oldest grandchild and is an outstanding young man who is now a litigation partner in a Los Angeles law firm.

KRISTINE JENSEN
Leslie Cooley's life partner, an experienced psychologist who specializes in difficult, complicated cases

RICHARD PIERCE COOLEY JR.
My first-born son, who is a natural athlete and who also has incredible mechanical skills

His first marriage was to an attractive woman, Laurie, from Woodland, California. They had two children, Richard Pierce Cooley II and Ann Cooley. They had some hard times, and after 10 years they divorced. In time they found other partners and remarried. Through it all Pierce and Laurie remained good friends and took loving care of their children.

He is now married to Christie Lane. She is smart and quiet, easygoing, and she really loves him. He now has a new job with an international construction firm and hopes to grow with them.

LAURIE TENHUNFELD COOLEY
Pierce's first wife, and mother of Pierce II and Ann

RICHARD PIERCE COOLEY II
My grandson, and Pierce and Laurie's son

ANN COOLEY
My granddaughter, and Pierce and Laurie's daughter

CHRISTIE LANE COOLEY
Pierce's wife

SHEILA COOLEY
My second daughter, family law attorney

She is capable and thoughtful, and she has made something of herself, and done it all on her own. Her legal practice includes wills, family law, guardianships, and such, and she does a large amount of pro-bono work. She is concerned with money, but only in the sense that she wants to take care of her family obligations and make sure things are well covered.

Her husband, Mark Fagan, is a researcher, teacher, and administrator at Brown University Medical School. Sheila has a full life with her family and her law practice. Before their 20th wedding anniversary, Sheila paid off the mortgage on their home. My father would say to me, "That Sheila, she's a great piece of work." She loves her husband and her three fine children, Kate, Dylan, and Charlotte, and that is what it is all about for her.

MARK FAGAN
Sheila's husband, Brown Medical School
researcher/instructor/administrator

SEAN COOLEY
Fourth child for Sheila and me, works in commercial real estate

People like him, they trust him, and he is smart. His first marriage did not work out, but they did have two children, Bridget and Sean Jr. Sometime later, Sean met Jean Kayser, and they were married in Sun Valley nine years ago. Jean graduated from the Wharton Business School, but decided that she wanted to be a doctor rather than a businesswoman. She went back to school and eight years later became an obstetrician/gynecologist, and she went to work at the Kaiser Foundation in Oakland, California.

As a couple they like to travel, play golf, and ski. They also are totally attentive to Sean's children, spending much time with them.

BRENDA PAYNE COOLEY
Mother of my grandchildren Bridget and Sean Jr.

BRIDGET COOLEY
My granddaughter, and Sean's daughter

SEAN COOLEY JR.
My grandson, and Sean's first-born son

JEAN KAYSER
Sean's second wife, obstetrician/gynecologist, Kaiser Foundation

MARK COOLEY
My youngest son, and the family entrepreneur

He has become the family entrepreneur. Undeterred after a
failed attempt to start a smoothie business, he and two friends
bought an organic foods company in South San Francisco.
He learned a lot in his first business venture, but learned again
that you have to have sufficient capital to sustain a business.
Mark and his partners have built the business to a small profit
and are hoping for further increases. Whatever Mark does he
does well, and with no children so far, he has turned into an
exceptional caregiver.

JOAN D'AMBROSIO
Mark's wife, attorney

Mark married Joan D'Ambrosio, a smart, attractive woman
he had known since high school. While he was slugging it out
in the food business, she went through law school, joined a
San Francisco law firm, and became a full partner there before
she was 40. They have good common sense. They work hard
and travel extensively.

MARY ALICE CLARK COOLEY
We were married from 1983 until her death in 1999

While we did not live together before she moved to Seattle in
1983, we saw a lot of each other, and it was an experience not to
be equaled. When I pray for Mary Alice, I pray that she will be
full of love and close to God in heaven. She was an extraordinary

mom and a wonderful wife. She contributed to everyone she ever met in her life.

Mary Alice was widowed three times. Four of her six children (Karin, Susan, Michael, and Jim) were the product of her first marriage. Anne-Marie and Bruce were the children of her second. The older three were out of the house and gone before I came onto the scene. I pray for each of them every day.

KARIN BURNAP
Mary Alice's oldest daughter, animal lover, sales management worker.

Karin, Mary Alice's oldest child, was married to a Hollywood stuntman and was in the midst of a divorce when I met her. She was working in the movie business as the personal assistant to the well-known director John Carpenter. She worked for eight years for Weight Watchers and managed the Southern California sales district for three years. She loves dogs, horses, and people. She is fun and interesting, and everyone likes her a lot. She has a boyfriend, but getting married does not seem to be in the program for now.

SUSAN BURNAP
Mary Alice's second-oldest daughter, travel agent

Susan was married to John Janneck, an accountant and investor. They lived in Hollywood Hills a few miles away from Mary Alice. She worked as a travel agent at a company in Brentwood. I am always amazed and inspired that she has stuck with it and done so well in such a vast and changing industry. Her marriage to John did not last, but she has a nice home in the San Fernando Valley and an incredible young son, Nick, who is beginning to work for Morgan Stanley. He is handsome and smart, a tremendous golfer, and someone she can be enormously proud of.

MICHAEL BURNAP

Mary Alice's oldest son, banker

Michael was through college and working on an oil rig in Southeast Asia. He had gone to Taiwan during his third year of college and had married a Taiwanese woman. After a year working out of Singapore, he came back to California and graduated from the business school at the University of Southern California. For a time he worked for Seafirst, but left the bank when it was sold. He now works for a smaller bank that is owned and operated by people in Los Angeles. He is smart, great fun, and a person you can count on. I guess I see him the most of all the children because we live in the same city, but regardless of proximity, I enjoy his company immensely. He has two fine children, Calvin and Brian.

JIM BURNAP

Mary Alice's middle son, commercial real estate

Jim was living with Mary Alice in Beverly Hills, and as she prepared to move to Seattle, he moved out to a local apartment. He was seeing a friend from the University of the Pacific in Stockton, and two years later they were married. Jim works in the commercial real estate business.

Jimmy is married to Sarah, a smart, capable woman who is in media sales. They have two sons, Clark and Alec, who are growing up to be creditable young gentlemen and people with good futures ahead of them.

ANNE-MARIE CORDINGLY

Mary Alice's youngest daughter, teacher

With her second husband, Bruce Cordingly, Mary Alice had two children, Anne-Marie and Bruce. Anne-Marie lives in San Francisco. She had some terribly difficult years with her first marriage, which ended in divorce. Recently she seems to have beaten back the attacks on her children, Tres, Quincy, and Bruce, and now has full custody of them. She is a teacher at the Town School for Boys. For a time she taught Latin to fourth and sixth graders, and now is teaching the second grade. She is a gifted athlete. How she gets everything done that she does amazes me. When you see pictures of her, she is the mirror image of her mother at the same age. She is a delight and someone who is cherished and respected by all.

BRUCE CORDINGLY
Mary Alice's youngest son, writer and documentary film producer

Bruce was going into the 10th grade when we married, and at the last minute was accepted at Lakeside, which turned out to be fortuitous. Since we had no close relatives or friends in the area, we became a small nuclear family for a time. Through our business connections, Mary Alice and I began to get acquainted around the town, but it was harder for Bruce. School started in September and he did not know one person at Lakeside. His first personal phone call to do something outside school came the following March. He turned out for Lakeside's football team and he played racquetball. However slow the start, more than 20 years later the closest friends he has are those he met at Lakeside, and they keep in constant touch.

Bruce is Mary Alice's sixth child. He writes and produces television documentaries. But he has been through a lot of school and done many things. He does publicity work for a Japanese trading company, and through his many business dealings has still managed to keep in touch with the whole family, particularly my daughter Sheila. He has found a wonderful young woman, Anne Marie, who wanted to move back to Seattle, where her family lives. They were married in 2009 and had their first child, Elliot.

HENRY CLARK
A self-made man, GM executive, and Mary Alice's father

I pray for Henry and Helen Clark. Henry was a self-made man. I never met Helen, but I did know Henry, who was Mary Alice's father. He had to go to work when he was 14 or 15 and support his family, which he was able to do. He had a long career at General Motors and ended up running their big Los Angeles plant. For a long time he worked in Detroit as the assistant to the chairman. He was a remarkable man. He did not get a lot of schooling, but he taught himself through reading and hard work. He was conservative. He was not a born Catholic, but converted. Henry became well known to the Cardinal in Los Angeles. He was a knight of Malta and an erudite, bright man. Henry loved Mary Alice. She was his little girl, and he took great care of her.

HELEN CLARK
Wife of Henry, and Mary Alice's mother

HENRY FORD II
Sheila's brother-in-law

He was a good man, tremendously pressured, and sometimes criticized for his lifestyle, but I always thought he was terrific and appreciated his giving ways, spirit, and kindness to all of us. Praying for him every day is the biggest thank-you I can give him, and I will never stop. Also, I always buy Ford cars, and that is something I will always do.

JUDY CHASE LUDWIG COOLEY
My second wife, and mother of Jessica and Coco

Judy's first husband had worked for Saks, and through him Judy was well acquainted with all the names in the fashion industry. She was interested in colors and decorations and knew clearly the kind of home she wished to have. Her daughters, Jessica and Coco, were attractive young ladies and as a family group we seemed to get along fine. There was not the friction that there was in my first marriage. I feel bad about Judy because she tried hard and was a good person and a good wife. The problems were in my head. Even though our marriage did not last, I pray daily for the two girls as well as Judy.

DICK COLLINS
Sheila's second husband, and an equestrian

My two youngest boys went with Sheila to Pebble Beach and lived there with Dick as their stepfather. He taught them about horses, polo, and work. In fact, they both became accomplished polo players. Sean became the captain of the University of California-Davis polo team that won the national championship four years in a row. Mark also played on the team but not as long as Sean.

JAMES MCDONNELL
Sheila's father, stockbroker

MRS. MURRAY MCDONNELL
Sheila's mother, and family organizer

CHARLOTTE MCDONNELL
Sheila's older sister, the fourth of the McDonnell children

BASIL HARRIS
Father of Basil Jr. and Dick

MARY HARRIS
Mother of Basil Jr. and Dick, and my unofficial godmother

BASIL HARRIS JR.
Childhood friend in Rye, New York

DICK HARRIS
Basil's brother, and later Sheila's brother-in-law

PETER FLANIGAN
Portsmouth Priory classmate, and lifelong friend

THEA FLANIGAN
Peter's second wife

JOHN FLANIGAN
Peter's brother

NANCY FLANIGAN
John's wife

HORACE FLANIGAN
Peter's father, and a New York City banker

MRS. HORACE FLANIGAN
Mother of Peter and John, and my mother's close friend
and godchild

PEGGY FLANIGAN MCDONNELL
Peter's sister and Sheila's sister-in-law, and mother of
nine children

BRIDGID FLANIGAN
Peter's first wife, who passed away more than four years ago

GEORGE COOLEY
My uncle, and my father's youngest brother

HELEN COOLEY
Uncle George Cooley's wife

HAROLD PIERCE
My mother's younger brother

HELEN PIERCE
Harold Cooley's wife

Aunt Helen Cooley is my uncle George's wife, and Helen Pierce is the wife of my uncle Harold. I pray for the two of them for no particular reason other than I like them and I think someone should be praying for them.

JIM PIERCE
My oldest cousin from my mother's side of the family

Jim was my oldest first cousin, the son of my mother's oldest brother. He was a good man who took care of everyone, particularly my mother. I pray for Jim as sort of a catchall because I have so many family and friends who have deceased over the years. There are so many gone that I cannot name them all, so I have this category in which I pray for cousin Jim and all close family and friends who have died.

JIM COOLEY
Uncle George Cooley's only son

Uncle George Cooley was my father's youngest brother. Jim is his only son. I pray for them daily. Jim is one of my two first cousins who are still living. I see him occasionally and we correspond. He keeps in touch with my sisters and is a good man. He did not go into business like his father but worked in the post office his whole life. He is comfortable, and he travels a great deal.

HELEN PIERCE COOLEY
My mother

VICTOR E. COOLEY
My father

RANSOM COOK
My boss, mentor, and predecessor at Wells Fargo Bank

STEPHEN CHASE
Chairman of Wells Fargo Bank

MARY CHASE
Stephen's wife

ERNIE ARBUCKLE
My friend, adviser, and also chairman of Wells Fargo Bank

KITTY ARBUCKLE
Ernie's wife

JERRY DWYER
Tennis partner at Portsmouth Priory, and lifelong friend
   Jerry was a bachelor most of his life and finally started going out with a woman, Jane, who was 20 years younger. She told him when he was in his late fifties that if they were not married before he turned 60, it was over. They did get married. I think he was 59. They have had a wonderful marriage and still have a good life together.

JANE DWYER
Jerry's wife

CARL LIVINGSTON
Lifelong intimate friend
   I pray for Carl and Jean Livingston. They were friends from San Francisco, one of the first couples Sheila and I met. We had

the notable experience of sharing the same baby nurse when we were having our children. Carl's family had a dry goods store in downtown San Francisco that his father ran, and then when he died, Carl ran it. They are close, intimate friends.

JEAN LIVINGSTON
Carl's wife, and close friend

GORDON MCSHANE
Classmate with Peter, Jerry, and me at Portsmouth

CAL KNUDSEN
Seattle entrepreneur, Seattle Art Museum board member, and friend

JULIA LEE KNUDSEN
Friend to Mary Alice when we first moved to Seattle

Julia Lee was the wife of Cal Knudsen, whom we met through Peter Flanigan, my friend in NY. Cal and Julia Lee were down on the Oregon shore on a weekend and she suddenly died in her rocking chair. It was a shock. No one could have seen that coming, and I have been praying for her ever since.

JACK LAMEY
Seattle doctor, husband of Diane, and golfing friend for me

DIANE LAMEY
Friend to Mary Alice and me, and wife of Jack Lamey

As with Julia Lee Knudsen, Diane suddenly came down with a brain tumor. We went to see her in Swedish Hospital, but she did not survive for long. It was a terrible shock. She had been one of Mary Alice's earliest friends in Seattle and we missed her. I pray for these two ladies because they were kind, good women who died too early and so unexpectedly.

HERMAN PHLEGER
My father's best friend through life

ATHERTON PHLEGER
Herman Phleger's son, and good friend

MURRAY MCDONNELL
Sheila's older brother, stockbroker, and father of Peggy Vance

Murray McDonnell was Sheila McDonnell Collins's older brother. Murray was fifth in line of the 14 McDonnells. Murray was the one who took over the family brokerage, had trouble with it, and eventually lost it. He married Peter Flanigan's only sister, Peggy, and they had nine children together.

PEGGY FLANIGAN VANCE
Peter's niece, and wife of Cyrus Vance Jr.

One day I was talking to Peggy at a social function. We got talking about the family and somehow the subject of her father came up. It was after he died and the business had gone south. She defended him, and defended him well, I might add. She said that a lot of people criticized him inside and outside the family about the way he ran the business and the fact that it was not successful, but she told me that he was a good father. "He would call us all at least once a week. He always kept in touch, and we always knew he was there for us," she said. After that talk with Peggy, even though I had not felt close to Murray, I thought that I should pray for him, so I put him on the list and he's been there ever since.

CYRUS VANCE JR.
Former Seattle attorney, and son of President Carter's secretary of state

Peggy and Cy have two children, and Cy did an outstanding job with his Seattle law firm. He is a Democrat and interested in politics, which he must have inherited from his father. He was elected New York District Attorney in 2009.

SALLY MAILLIARD
Daughter of my mother's best friend, Miriam Van Sicklin

Sally was a second cousin of mine. She was the daughter of my mother's best friend, Aunt Miriam Van Sicklin, who was my godmother. I had always known Sally even though she was somewhat younger than I. When we moved to San Francisco I got to know her better. We moved in the same circles as Sally and her husband, Jim. Sally was a strong lady. She had five children, which she appeared to have with great ease. Jimmy died of cancer and Sally died almost a year later of the same thing. In each case it was unexpected and much too early in their lifespan. I like thinking about them and I like to pray for them every day.

JIMMY MAILLIARD
My domino partner at the Pacific-Union Club

Jim was from an old San Francisco family. We used to do one thing a year together — we partnered in the Pacific-Union Club Domino Tournament. It is a big tournament that happens once a year and takes nearly an entire year to complete. Jimmy was a good domino player and played a lot, whereas I was an average player and did not play that much. Jim felt it was one way that we would make sure we saw each other, so he always signed us up to play together.

TOMMY SULLIVAN
San Francisco friend, real estate broker

Tommy and Amy-Ann Sullivan were social friends of Sheila and mine. We saw them a lot at parties in San Francisco and

Burlingame. Tommy was in the real estate business and died young. Amy-Ann lasted longer. She remarried, not totally successfully, but she died within four or five years of Tommy and was also considered to be a young death. I wasn't that close to either one of them, but for some reason I started to pray for them and I just decided to keep doing it. There is no reason in the world to quit. They were nice to us in many ways when we lived in San Francisco and I hope that they are doing well in heaven.

AMY-ANN SULLIVAN
Friend to Sheila and me

ROBERT WATT MILLER
Director of Wells Fargo Bank, and head of San Francisco Opera

Bob ran the San Francisco Opera for many years and was known as a very distinguished gentleman in the Bay Area. His father had been chairman of the American Trust Company. Bob was an influential member of the bank's board. What sticks in my mind about him was that for all his aura and dignity and elevated standing, when you talked with him one-on-one he was not formidable and frightening. Bob had four children. I knew them all, liked them all, but I was particularly close with his youngest son, Dick Miller.

DICK MILLER
Bob's son, and my close friend in San Francisco

ANN MILLER
Dick's wife, mother of his children, and later a Carmelite nun

MY GODCHILDREN
My record of keeping close to my godchildren is not great. First comes my niece Priscilla Buckley, then Gregory Kilduff, David Miller, Peter Phleger, Shelly Samson, and Allison

Willoughby. (The names of the female godchildren are their maiden ones.) You became a godfather because a lot of people we knew were Catholics but did not move in Catholic circles. There were not that many people they could ask to be a Catholic godfather for their children. I think that is one reason why I became involved with some families as a godfather even though we were not that close. I understand the situation. We had the same problem when looking around with some of ours. If they weren't Catholic, they couldn't become a godparent, so that made it difficult sometimes to come up with the right people. I pray for them as a group each day. I pray that they know God and love God and that God gives them the gift of faith and blesses them in their lives.

BEVAN BRADBURY
Australian friend with a wonderful singing voice

Bevan Bradbury was a friend I met on business trips to Australia. The first time we went there, he said, "Dick, come back. Come back at Christmas time. It's a lovely time of year." We had been there in the summertime, which was their winter. I could not believe anyone would like visitors to come at holiday time. We had planned a three-week trip to New Zealand and Australia, and of course we went through Sydney in the process. I wrote to Bevan and told him we were coming with our youngest son, Bruce, and his friend. I wrote that letter three weeks before Christmas and I never heard from him. We were fine with that as it was a busy time, but when I got to Sydney I decided to call him. Bevan answered the phone and said how happy he was that we had arrived. He said that he would come down and pick us up the next day for lunch, which was Christmas Day. That was a pretty big offer. I felt guilty about it, but I couldn't say no because I really wanted to do it. Bevan came to the hotel and he said, "Dick, your letter just arrived. It's a J.I.T. (Just in Time). We got your letter yesterday." So he had one day's notice that we were coming for Christmas. He stepped up and was as kind as he always was.

We went to his house for a wonderful Christmas luncheon. It was tremendous. They had all their children and grandchildren, and everyone sat around one table. It was the kind of thing that you would hope to have happen in another country because you'd like to see how others celebrate. One of the remarkable things Bevan did was to sing a long song at the end of the lunch. It was a dirge about Australia's beginnings. It described all those early years when all the convicts were sent to Australia and how they got started and made the country what it is today. It was mournful but wonderful. It was a tradition each year. Clarisse was his wife and she had presents for all of us. What an outpouring of friendship and love. Just what you would hope for. Bevan died a few years later. Even though we saw very little of him, he is number one on my special list of five gentlemen that I pray for.

SHERM SIBLEY
Friend, and chief executive of Pacific Gas and Electric

WILLIE CANNON
Hawaiian friend, and Bank of Hawaii's chief executive officer

Willie Cannon was Hawaiian. I met him through the Bank of Hawaii in Honolulu. One of Willie's children was in school with one of mine. Willie smoked too much and got lung cancer. I was in Hawaii when he was dying. I flew to Honolulu and went by the hospital to see him. He was wheezing, but sedated. There was no one there, so I stayed with him and prayed. I will always remember him in that bed, hours before he died, breathing out his life. It didn't seem right that he was alone at that time. Leslie, my daughter, who was a friend of his son in school, came with me to the funeral. Willie was a nice man. Everybody loved him.

EDWARD GILLETTE
California born, insurance man, and Bohemian Club member

My old friend Ed Gillette was from San Francisco and in the insurance business. My connection with him was the Bohemian Club. We entered the club about the same time and stayed in the open camp for new members. Two years later we joined the Mandalay Camp together. For the first 10 years at Mandalay we roomed together. Those were the years when I was going up three weekends in a row during the month of July. We would act in the plays or do whatever they asked you to do. Ed was a character. He was a golfer, and we played some together. He'd been through the Naval Academy in the war and grew up in Santa Monica. Our time together was mostly at the Grove, and there we saw a lot of each other. He died many years after Sherm Sibley, but he died in a similar fishing accident, drowning in a river. Always a friend, he was upbeat and willing to help you any way he could.

DICK ALDEN
Prominent Los Angeles attorney, husband of Margie

Dick Alden was a newer friend. He was married to one of Mary Alice's closest friends. When we lived in Los Angeles we saw a lot of them. There was a group of eight or ten that we seemed to join, and they were a part of that group. Dick was a lawyer and he did very well. He got out of the law firm to work with Hughes Medical. He became a businessman and made himself a small fortune. He also worked for the Irvine Estate, where he was the lawyer for Don Bren, the owner. Dick and Margie were a wonderful couple. They lived well and traveled a lot. Dick died after a long bout with cancer. It was somewhat similar to what happened to Mary Alice's third husband. It went on for a year or so. It was very hard on him and also on Margie. Both of them had been married before and had children by other partners. They had a house in Sun Valley where they would put us up until we bought our own house. They thought the world of Mary Alice, and I guess they accepted me as we went along.

MARGIE ALDEN
Dick's wife, and close Los Angeles friend of Mary Alice

Margie is the next name on my list. I pray for her because she is a survivor. She has four children of her own. I am sure they are taking care of her. She also has many good friends in the Los Angeles area, some of them being the same friends we would spend time with when we lived there. Since moving to Seattle and Dick's death, I have not had much contact with Margie. In fact, the move to Seattle, followed by Mary Alice's death and marrying Bridget, has taken me away from that group. I am sure if I saw them again it would be friendly, but we are just not in the same group anymore.

STEPHANIE CHASE MCCALL
Judy's younger sister

Stephanie is the younger sister of Judy Chase Ludwig, my second wife. She is a fine lady and has two children. Her husband used to work in the bank. He's from Rhode Island and is independently wealthy. They live in San Francisco. She was someone I could talk to when Judy and I were breaking up. She was upset by it, but she could talk to me about it. I always want to remember her favorably in my prayers and her two children. I haven't seen much of them since leaving San Francisco, but they are on my list. They are the only living family in that Chase group — everyone else has died. It is important to pray for them because I'm not sure who else is alive to do it.

ANN COOLEY BUCKLEY
One of my twin sisters, and wife of Jim Buckley

Annie is married to my old roommate at Yale, Jim Buckley. They live in Sharon, Connecticut. Each day I pray for my family,

and that includes my three sisters, but especially right now
for Annie and Jim, because they have so much to do, with
Annie's automobile accident resulting in her paraplegic existence.
Their whole world was turned upside down. Annie has endured
her situation with incredible courage and grace, setting a fine
example of how one accepts God's will. Jim has handled it like a
star and a saint. They seem to be getting along as well as anyone
could under those circumstances. They are dear to my heart.

JIM BUCKLEY
My first Yale roommate, and my brother-in-law

KAY COOLEY
My sister

My sister Kay lives in New Jersey. She is single and lives in a
Quaker residence home. She has her own apartment and is very
much involved in the activities that go on at that center. The place
is called Medford Leas. She started something that she calls the
Medford Leas University where she invites different speakers to
talk to the residents from the various colleges in the area. It has
been successful and she has done it all on her own. She is constantly planning and trying to figure out who she can get to come
speak and how to make people interested. She holds the position
of secretary to the board of directors who run the place. She has a
full life although at times she can be lonesome, but she has managed to keep herself active, which is wonderful when you consider
that she spent many years in quite a different life as a nun.

HELEN COOLEY REILLY
My youngest sister, and wife of Miles

Helen Reilly is my youngest sister. Her husband, Miles, was a
wonderful man and died several years ago. She told me not too
long ago that she is coming out of the grieving period. I told her
to allow herself at least three years, and she's just about there.

She seems to be taking hold well. She has women friends and I think they have been a big support to her. She just came back from a trip to Peru to see the sights of Machu Picchu, and she is beginning to do a lot of things she did before. She was overwhelmed by the situation for a long time. It's nice to see her coming back and getting on her feet again. She is an active woman, a contributor to the community in many ways, and she has a full and meaningful life. The fact that her next-to-youngest daughter, Megan, lives relatively close in North Carolina is a boon to her. She has two grandchildren, and I think Helen makes that a big part of her life. Megan and her husband, Steve, have been very helpful to her, enormously caring and supportive. Her youngest daughter, Sheila, lives and works in Alaska, hopefully fighting successfully to survive her recent bout with breast cancer.

MEGAN BUSER
Helen's daughter, and my niece

STEVE BUSER
Megan's husband, and Helen's son-in-law

LUKE HELMS
Seafirst chief executive following my retirement
Luke Helms was at Seafirst when I came to Seattle in 1983. He was one of the top managers, running all the national business. He is an attractive, smart man. I tried to hire him once at Wells Fargo in Beverly Hills, but it did not work out for him or us. However, when I came to Seattle, he was a friend and someone I could respect. Luke is very creative. When I retired from Seafirst, he was the one who took over as chairman and CEO. I was chairman of the executive committee for a few years after that, but he did a good job of running the bank. In fact, he did such a good job that Dick Rosenberg took him down to

San Francisco to do media and marketing for Bank of America Corporation. It turned out not to be a good fit. He was not as successful as he had been in Seattle. After a year or two he resigned and went out on his own. In Seattle, Luke was well regarded and known by all in the Seafirst Corporation and in the community. I've never been able to find out what he did after his retirement from Bank of America. He built a place in Scottsdale, Arizona, which is the state he originally came from, so in a sense he went home. I always thought he would come back to Seattle, but he has not. He has three boys; at least one lives in Seattle. Luke has invested in lots of things, moves around a great deal, and has recently built a home in Montana. He is a managing director of an investment firm called Sonata, which handles people's money. He is one of a kind. Luke is into new ideas and thoughts and keeps things relatively close to his vest, so it's hard to know exactly what he is doing. I pray for Luke and his family — his wife, Gail, and their three boys — who were close to us and important to my time in Seattle.

GAIL HELMS
Luke Helms's wife

SEAFIRST BANK
There are three banks I pray for. Seafirst is the first, and then next on my list is the Bank of America Corporation and the people I worked with there — Dick Rosenberg, Sam Armacost, and all the people who took us over when Seafirst was going broke in 1983. Bank of America bought the stock of Seafirst and saved us from bankruptcy and gave us time and the capital to get back on our feet, which we did. We became an outstanding investment for the Bank of America Corporation, one that was important to their survival when they had their difficulties in the mid to late 1980s. The third bank I pray for is Wells Fargo.

BANK OF AMERICA

Sam Armacost was in charge of Bank of America Corporation when they bought Seafirst. When they had their troubles, Sam lost his job and the directors brought back Tom Clausen. He stayed there for five years. He had already retired from the World Bank when he made the decision to return to run Bank of America. In the meantime, I hired Dick Rosenberg to come up and take my place when he'd been working for the Crocker Bank in San Francisco as the number-two person. He wanted to run his own bank and I told him that if he came to Seattle he could run Seafirst, but he did not stay long enough to do that. He was in Seattle for about a year and a half. He was so impressive that Tom Clausen could not leave him in Seattle. He went to San Francisco to take over the top second or third job at Bank of America and then succeeded Clausen when he retired for the second time.

DICK ROSENBERG

Chairman and chief executive officer of Bank of America

SAM ARMACOST

Bank of America chairman who in 1983 agreed to purchase Seafirst

TOM CLAUSEN

Bank of America chief following Sam Armacost

CARL REICHARDT

Wells Fargo chief following my retirement in 1982

As well as Carl Reichardt, this includes all the Wells Fargo people whom I worked with from 1949 through 1982. That was my primary career. Ernie Arbuckle and I hired Carl from the Union Bank in Los Angeles. We brought him to Wells Fargo to run one of our holding company subsidiaries. He did such a good job, there was no question that he was the person to take over for me when I retired. He brought in some very good people and he brought a wonderful sense of making money with him. He was an outstanding banker and an excellent credit man and someone who was bound to be successful. We were lucky to have him.

WELLS FARGO BANK
Guided by values and strengthened by its people

I always thought of myself as a Wells Fargo person. That has changed now because I have been in Seattle almost as long as I was in San Francisco. Wells has been sold to a company in Minneapolis. When that sale occurred, the Minneapolis people, as part of the arrangement, moved their headquarters to San Francisco and took over the management of the bank while retaining the name Wells Fargo. It has been a great success.

FRANK MELCHER
United Way chief of staff in Seattle

MICHAEL MELCHER
Frank Melcher's physically challenged son

After Wells Fargo, on my list I have the United Way people and a young man named Michael Melcher. I spent five years working with the United Way in San Francisco. When I came to Seattle they asked me to get re-involved with the United Way, which I did. In every campaign there is always a chief staff person who runs it and does all the work and manages the volunteers. When I became chairman of the campaign in 1986, there was a man named Frank Melcher who was the chief United Way person. He was the person I depended on the most when I was running that campaign. He was a nice man and knowledgeable and experienced in the organization. He was married and they had a child, Michael, who was born deaf and blind. It was such a sad thing for them, but they embraced their child and they were as proud as any parents could be. When I pray for the United Way people, I always pray for Michael Melcher. I don't know what happened to him because that was more than 20 years ago and he may no longer be with us. His father, Frank, is still active in United Way but in different cities.

EVA GARZA LAGÜERA
Wife of Eugenio Garza Lagüera, who lives in Monterrey, Mexico

Eva Garza Lagüera and her family. She is the wife of Eugenio Garza Lagüera, a business friend from Monterrey, Mexico, whom I knew from Wells Fargo. I used to go to Mexico at least once a year because we had lots of business going back and forth and hoped to get more. Eugenio was one of the movers-and-shakers in the town of Monterrey, which is sort of like a Chicago, a big manufacturing area. We became social friends as well as business acquaintances. One day we must have been talking about religion or at least a subject that could make an easy transition because Eva said to me, "Will you pray for me?" I said, "Sure, I'll pray for you and your family. I'd be happy to do that." She asked me more than 20 years ago and I am still praying for her every day. Eva was a bright star. She was a good mother, attractive, and smart. Eugenio has passed on, but I hope all is well with them and I pray that they are safe.

MIGUEL DE LA MADRID
Former president of Mexico

Miguel de la Madrid was the president of Mexico for six years, and I mentioned him earlier in the book. I got to know him through Wells Fargo when he was head of the Credit Department of the Mexican national bank. I liked him and we got along well. After he was president I didn't see him very often, but he was someone I wanted to pray for.

UAL

For the strength of its people

Harry and Judy Mullikin and Eddie Carlson and the United Airlines people I worked with. When I went on the board of United Airlines in the early 1970s, there was a fracture in the management and the existing CEO was asked to resign. Eddie Carlson was running Western International Hotels at the time and was asked to come in and take over the chairman and CEO position of UAL Inc. and United Airlines. UAL Inc. was the holding company, and it had purchased Western International Hotels the previous year.

Eddie Carlson and Lynn Himmelman were chairman and president of Western International Hotels, and they were put on the United board. There was no search and it was just decided that Eddie would be a good replacement for the departing chief executive. That began a 24-year relationship for me with United Airlines. It was the most important and interesting business relationship outside the banks that I had.

When Eddie went to Chicago to take over United, Lynn Himmelman stepped up to be chairman and chief executive of Western Hotels. He kept the job until he retired and then was replaced by Harry Mullikin, who was also put on the UAL and United boards. Eddie was my sponsor when I first came to Seattle, and Lynn Himmelman helped a great deal as well, but I was closer to Eddie. I began praying for him and then I combined it with Harry and Judy because they were a big part of my life when I moved to Seattle. Harry Mullikin was the head of the search committee for Seafirst in 1982 and was the person I negotiated with to get the job of running Seafirst in 1983.

HARRY MULLIKIN

Board member at UAL and Seafirst

JUDY MULLIKIN
Harry's wife, and close friend to Mary Alice

EDDIE CARLSON
UAL chairman, and friend

LYNN HIMMELMAN
UAL director, and chairman of Westin

CALTECH
Its vision, research, and leadership
    I pray for the Caltech people I worked with. I've been on that board for over 30 years.

KAISER FAMILY FOUNDATION
Its purpose and contributions to humanity

RAND CORPORATION
Its work for America and its leaders

DON RICE
Chief executive officer of RAND for 17 years

JIM THOMSON
Chief executive officer of RAND following Don Rice

FATHER EGON
Woodside Priory founder

SEATTLE SYMPHONY ORCHESTRA
For its contribution to my city
    On my prayer list is the Seattle Symphony Orchestra and the various problems that presented themselves. When I came to Seattle after leaving Los Angeles in 1983, I was president of the

Los Angeles Philharmonic board. After I was in Seattle for a while I was asked to join the SSO board, which I was happy to do, but I did not want to be active in the management or take on any large fund-raising job. I had to get the bank under control and get through the United Way campaign. After that I did spend more time with the symphony and ultimately became president. I joined it with a man named Sam Stroum, who was one of my big supporters and directors at the bank. He was chairman and I was president of the symphony for two or three years. He got slightly ill and tired of it, so I became chairman of the symphony board. I did that for a couple more years, until it got to be too much and I found a replacement, which turned out to be an unhappy choice. I left under terms that were not absolutely wonderful, but the symphony has been doing much better lately. They almost went under once or twice, but mostly through Sam's efforts it came together. We have a new hall thanks to Jack Benaroya, who was never on the board, but he gave a really large contribution to the symphony's hall, which now bears his name and that of his wife, Becky. Seattle is proud of its musical heritage. That was one of my boards.

SAM STROUM
Seafirst board member, and Seattle Symphony Orchestra chairman

SEATTLE ART MUSEUM
A cultural gift to Seattle

Almost at the same time I can talk about the Seattle Art Museum. They came to me early on in my time in Seattle, in the mid 1980s. I told them I did not want to be on the board. I had been on the Los Angeles County Museum board, and I did not want to take that on in Seattle because I did not think I would have enough time. However, a friend of mine and some people I had to listen to said that the museum did not have much business participation and they wanted me to join it. Along with three other business contemporaries in town, I joined. I went to the meetings and although I did not participate as much, they put me on an operations committee and shortly after had me run the committee. From then on, it was not too long before they asked me to be chairman of the board of the museum, which I did for a couple of years.

I was chairman of the board when Mary Alice died, and if I had not had that organization to worry about and deal with, life would have been much harder. It gave me something to do when my life was bereft and empty. I have maintained my connection with them ever since in sort of a senior advisory capacity. In my opinion, it is the best board in Seattle. It is active and has just completed an enormous fund-raising campaign. Museums always require new money, this one in particular. In addition to the downtown museum, there is an Asian Art Museum. Part of the recent expansion was to build a sculpture park near Elliott Bay, which has proved to be an enormous boon to the city. It is a nine-acre plot of land that could have been more condos. It was acquired by the Art Museum, and the board committed to raising the money to build the Sculpture Park. Over a million people went through it the first year and it is growing in popularity. The Art Museum is an enormous factor in town culturally. The people you meet on that board are well positioned as leaders in the community. They command a lot of respect and envy.

ARCHBISHOP'S OFFICE
For their guidance and sacrifice

Next on my list is the archbishop's office. I put it that way because in raising money or being involved in some of the efforts that the archbishop wants to see happen in the community, you do not always deal with the archbishop personally but often with someone who has been appointed to get some job done. In my case, he has supported the Fulcrum Foundation, which is the next name on my list. Through the time I have been here, I have been able to know three archbishops.

The Seattle Archdiocese went through a lot of problems with Archbishop Hunthausen, who had strong ideas about government and what was the right moral thing to do in certain situations. He was rather liberal, and there were many conservative Catholics in town who objected to his views on life. He was more accepting of the gay population, and he had his own ideas. He did not like nuclear arms, and he did not like the fact that nuclear bombs were in this state and that the Trident submarines were 30 miles away from downtown Seattle. One year I think he refused to pay half his taxes in protest against the nuclear effort here. In any event, the church hierarchy in Rome and in Washington, D.C., got after him and tried to make him resign. His chancellor, Father Michael Ryan, was able to defend him well enough so he was not forced to resign until he was 75 years old, when all bishops must retire.

While that was going on, they sent an auxiliary bishop out to be his backup, and apparently the Vatican people in Rome told him one thing and did not tell the archbishop in Seattle what the powers of the new bishop were to be. There was a political brouhaha in the church, and the first backup was sent away to Pittsburgh. He was Archbishop Wuerl and he has done well since he left Seattle. He was put in a difficult position and was not able to sustain it. It was poorly handled by the church, which is not surprising because they often do not show good organizational abilities or understanding of how things work in big organizations.

After that there was another bishop sent out from Montana, Archbishop Murphy. He stayed and when Archbishop Hunthausen retired, Archbishop Murphy took over. Archbishop Murphy was popular, but unfortunately he became ill and died in office after he had been in the job for a few years. He was replaced by Archbishop Brunett, the current archbishop, who also came here from Montana. Archbishop Brunett is 75 and had to submit his resignation. The Vatican does not have to accept it, but he had to make it. Whether we have a change coming up in the near future, I do not know, but it is amazing to me that I have known three archbishops here in the short 27 years that I have been in town.

Over the years I have worked with the archbishop's office on many occasions. I have contributed to the level of my ability, which is not tremendous. A lot of the people who work around the archbishop have become fine friends, and I have felt fortunate to have the opportunity to meet them.

The biggest thing that came out of the archbishop's office is the Fulcrum Foundation as far as I am concerned. It is an organization set up to provide scholarships and help for the parochial school system. The church school systems all over the country are in dire need of funding and support, just as the public school programs are. It turns out that many of the Catholic schools cannot make it. There are probably 70 of them in this archdiocese, and 10 of them are facing bankruptcy much of the time. They do not have the income from their parish and cannot charge the students enough to keep the schools running.

The archbishop needed to have an organization devoted to raising money and keeping the school system going. That is what the Fulcrum Foundation has done. It has only been going for eight years, but its first drive was for $40 million. They did more than make their goal and have raised more money for this group of Seattle schools than has ever been raised before. They have one fund for giving scholarships. They are not big scholarships. It used to be $500 per person, but now we have it up to $650 a person. It is just a partial scholarship, because it costs $2,300 on up to go to a parochial school these days. If you compare it to other private schools in the area, they charge upward of $15,000 a year. It is a solid education, not only for the moral and religious values of the Catholic schoolchildren, but also for the community.

They are an asset. Keeping them going is probably one of the
most important things that a Catholic can do in any part of
the United States. Father Rowan was the chairman, the initiator
appointed by the archbishop to do this job. He was succeeded
by Father Ryan when Father Rowan moved to Portland to be
dean of humanities at the University of Portland. I am the vice
chairman and there are three or four other founding directors on
the board. The board has been expanded to 20 people or so,
and it is an organization that in its short eight years has gained
considerable respect.

All over the country Catholic dioceses are having the same
problem with schools. Everyone is looking for a solution. There is
not one solution, but they can learn from each other, and I think
our success in Seattle has been an inspiration to many other
dioceses that are trying to solve the problem of funding a good
education for the children.

FULCRUM FOUNDATION
Care and keeping of our community and Catholic education

ARCHBISHOP HUNTHAUSEN
A humble man of God with strongly held opinions that were not
always popular

FATHER MICHAEL RYAN
Pastor of St. James Cathedral Parish, and chairman of the
Fulcrum Foundation

ARCHBISHOP BRUNETT
The current head of the Church in the Pacific Northwest

FATHER ROWAN
Founding chairman of the Fulcrum Foundation

SEATTLE PREP
The oldest private school in the city of Seattle

I pray for the people at Seattle Prep, which is the oldest private school in the city of Seattle and run by the Jesuits. I was on that board for four years, during which time they got into trouble. They were running a campaign and had a disaster with the president, who had to be relieved and replaced. They had a board of 12 to 15 people. It was interesting but at the same time it was frustrating. It was impossible to get anything done without lengthy discussions including all sectors of the community, with many of them represented on the board. It was a debating society. Meetings would go on for four hours without fail, covering matters that on other boards could have been dealt with in an hour or less. There was a lot of discussion, and everyone had a chance to say what they thought. Needless to say, it was interesting and I learned a lot. After four years of bickering, I got off it and had myself replaced because Mary Alice was getting worse and I could not spend all the time that the board required to function.

The school has done well. Gradually they got through the weak spots. They had a successful fund-raising drive early on when I was on the board. Since I have been off, they have had another successful fund drive. The faculty of about 70 members have been there longer than anybody, and it is hard to move them around. I was able to help them a little bit with their finances. More parents and capable people have come on the board since, which has caused a rejuvenation in the last 5 to 10 years. They have a new president this year, who was president at one of the biggest high schools in the diocese, Blanchet. There is a good intellectual quality there and they are tied in to Seattle University, also run by the Jesuits.

UNIVERSITY OF WASHINGTON
My EMBA students

SEATTLE UNIVERSITY
My MBA students

When I retired from the MBA program at the University of Washington after 10 years, my class was one of the most popular classes at the school. I think we were able to get the message out to the students about the "real world" experience. We have covered the teaching subjects at UW and SU earlier. It is important to pray for each of them.

ST. JAMES PARISH
An attentive Seattle Catholic institution

St. James Cathedral Parish and the Immaculate Conception Parish are different but they are both parishes, which I lump together. St. James is the one I go to almost exclusively. I occasionally go to Mass at other places, but my principal support goes to St. James, where Father Michael Ryan has been the rector for over 20 years. He is an outstanding person, loved by everyone, and has done an enormously productive job for the community, not only for the Catholics but for everyone else as well.

IMMACULATE CONCEPTION
A parish of color and commitment to its community

The Immaculate Conception Parish is a parish of color. It is the oldest parish church in Seattle. Their church was supposed to be the cathedral 100 years ago, but it turned out that the bishop wanted to move the cathedral farther downtown, so the Immaculate Conception Parish is on 18th Avenue and St. James is on 9th Avenue, closer to downtown. I support them both. At Immaculate I am not active, but I have helped them with some of their drives and things they have needed.

MARK PIGOTT
Paccar chairman and CEO, contributor to both my MBA and EMBA classes

My educational bent after I retired from the bank was supported by Mark Pigott and PACCAR Inc. I was on the board at PACCAR for a while. When Charles Pigott retired, Mark was made chairman and CEO. The board has 10 members, mostly outside members, and Mark has run the company for more than 10 years. His record has been extraordinary. The stock has done better than most tech stocks or almost any other stock around. They have done a super job of creating high-quality truck transportation for this country and around the world. They bought a company in The Netherlands (DAF) that was in financial difficulty, developed it, and now they are going gangbusters in Europe. They leverage one company against another, with almost no debt, and it works well. Mark has handled that and he has taken technology to the highest level ever in a trucking company. He calls PACCAR a technology company. Their earnings have been fabulous, their dividends have been incredible, and the price of their stock has gone up and up. It has decreased with the slowdown in the economy, but it is still enormously successful. In the United States, the company holds about 25 percent of the market for heavy trucks.

Mark has taught at my classes at both Seattle University and the University of Washington. He has been a fabulous teacher and a tremendous supporter of the program. Mark is good on his feet. He comes in with slides and videos and trucker's hats for the class, and they love it. He is firm and strong and there is no doubt about what he thinks and where he is going. No one has pushed him around in my sight yet.

When I retired from teaching last spring, the schools were able to find successors in both programs at Seattle U and the University of Washington. Mark insisted that he be maintained as a guest speaker in both programs. He remains committed to teaching students and enjoys fielding the questions. He has sponsored it financially through the company and personally to a great extent.

THE PIGOTT FAMILY
For their contributions to education and our Church

The Pigott family has generously supported education and the needs of the Catholic Church since William and Ada Pigott established their family in Seattle in 1895.

THE LEE FAMILY
For their support of Catholic education and our Church

The Lee family generosity supports Catholic education and the Church. They are an extraordinary and well-liked family.

THE STAMPER FAMILY
For its support of elementary education and ethical training

The Stampers' specific support for the elementary grades in reading and training in the ethical values of life through books has been successful countrywide.

POPE BENEDICT XVI
For the strength he must possess to lead the Church

Then I pray for the Pope and Archbishops Brunett and Hunthausen and all the bishops of the Catholic Church that they may be humble and full of love. That they may run the Church the way Christ intended. That Catholics and all other Christians may be recognized by the love they have for each other.

THE MEDICAL COMMUNITY
For their efforts over my life that have helped me

I pray for the doctors and nurses and all the others who have helped me survive thus far. There are so many of these extraordinary people that I am not going to list them separately, even though my gratitude and debt to each one is huge. Without that lifelong support system, my time would have been entirely different and probably would have ended many years ago.

When this memoir started, it was not totally clear to me why we were doing it. Bridget wanted me to write about many of the happenings and events that had taken place in my life because she thought the thread of my faith followed me clearly in almost everything that I have done or that happened to me over the years. That fact was important to her in deciding to marry me. She also thought the story would be interesting to many people.

A few months ago Father Ryan preached a fine homily on what Saint Paul said about average Catholics and Christians. Saint Paul said that all the faithful should be missionaries, not just highly motivated saints and heroic people in difficult parts of the world. Every one of us has the duty to share the good news of Christ's life and teaching and can become a true missionary in our own backyard without having to travel to the deepest part of Africa or Asia. As I thought about that homily, it began to dawn on me that this memoir might give me an opportunity to share some of my beliefs about my faith that could help some people understand what Christianity is about, and by example how it has affected my life. If I did that, maybe Saint Paul might think I was doing my part, however small it might be.

If you have come this far with me, I hope that you think this is true and that you have enjoyed the ride. I also hope that some of the lessons I have learned will be helpful to you as you pursue your own future. As we have gone along, that hope has been one of the main drivers to complete the project. Another driver has been my need to tell you about my faith and what it means to me. As a matter of principle, it is important to stand up for what you believe and share it with your family and friends. If it helps your life in even the smallest way, then the effort and time were more than worth the price. Thank you for sharing my life experiences with me. The opportunity to think about them and put them down on paper has been interesting and personally rewarding.

As I said at the beginning of this appendix, and I want to say it again, I am grateful to all the people who have been my friends, taken care of me, taught me, and protected me along life's path. While there is not room to name you all, I want you to know that I am truly appreciative of all that you have given and shared with me. It has been generous beyond words.

INDEX

Jet Propulsion Laboratory, 147
Johnson, Belton K., 121
Johnson, Charles B., 206, 214, 217-218
Johnson O'Connor Research Foundation, 66-67
Juan Carlos, King, 112-113
Juffali, Ahmed, 121
Juffali Group, 121

Kadoorie, Lord Lawrence, 121
Kaiser Family Foundation, 148-149
Kaplan, Hank, Dr., 166, 193, 194
Kayser, Jean, 238, 239
Keating, Anne F., 206
Kemper, Robert L., 150
Kennedy, Michael, 145
Killefer, Tom, 87-88
Killinger, Kerry, 189
Kiphuth Trophy Room, 209, 213
Kirk, Harris, 79-80, 82-83
Kirk, Vandy, 64
Knudsen, Cal, 248
Knudsen, Julia Lee, 248
Kracht, Adolf, 121

Lamey, Diane, 248
Lamey, Jack, 248
Lapham, Roger, Jr., 121
Lee family, 272
Levin, Richard C., 202, 214, 219
Littlefield, Ed, 100-101, 126, 151-152
Livingston, Carl, 247-248
Livingston, Jean, 248
Lockheed P-38 Lightning, 39
Ludwig, Judy, 163, 243-244

Mailliard, Jimmy, 250
Mailliard, Sally, 250
Maines, Bruce, 160
Mandalay Camp, 26, 75, 254

Manufacturers Hanover, 72
MasterCard, 115
Matson branch, 83-84
McCall, Stephanie Chase, 255
McCall's, 67-68, 71
McDonnell, Ann, 81
McDonnell, Charlotte, 70, 244
McDonnell, James, 244
McDonnell, Mrs. Murray, 71, 244
McDonnell, Murray, 169, 249
McDonnell, Peggy Flanigan, 169, 245
McDonnell, Sheila, 69-70
McIntyre, Bridget, 197-201
McNerney, W. James, 206
McShane, Gordon, 25, 26, 248
Melcher, Frank, 260
Melcher, Michael, 260-261
Miller, Ann, 91-92, 251
Miller, Arjay, 103, 126
Miller, Dick, 91, 92, 251
Miller, Robert Watt, 91, 251
Mullikin, Harry, 152-153, 154, 156, 164, 189, 262
Mullikin, Judy, 262, 263
Murphy, Archbishop, 266

Neu, Richard, 144
New York Bell Telephone Company, 15
9th Air Force, 39
Nordstrom, John, 189

Overholt, Bill, 146

P-38, 39-40, 43, 45, 46, 47-49, 197
P-51 Mustang, 46
PACCAR, Inc., 271
Pacific Gas and Electric, 132-135
Payne Whitney Gymnasium, 207, 209
Peltz, Eric, 145